# LUNAR RETURNS

Ciro Discepolo

## LUNAR RETURNS
The many things you should know
about this fantastic tool of forecasting

Ricerca '90 Publisher

Translation and editing: Luciano Drusetta and Ram Ramakrishnan
Graphic design: Pino Valente

Copyright © 2010 Edizioni Ricerca '90
Viale Gramsci, 16
80122 Napoli - ITALY
info@cirodiscepolo.it

www.solarreturns.com
www.cirodiscepolo.it

ISBN  978-88-964-4705-5
Printed in Italy

*In the very moment of our birth our entire destiny is written in our birth chart down to the smallest detail – but we can change the screenplay.*
**Ciro Discepolo**


*Gli astri non sparano mai a salve.*
**Ciro Discepolo**

The birth data of the people mentioned in this book proceed mainly from Lois M. Rodden's database and from Ciro Discepolo's archives. Other birth data are taken from web-based databases.

Astral maps and calculations are produced by the exceptionally precise astrological software **Astral** and **Aladino** (also referred to as *Module for the Automatized Research of the Aimed Solar Returns 'RSMA'*).

## Preface to the English second edition

This book is dedicated to all my English readers. It is not only the result of a separation of certain pages from my book *Lunar Returns and Earth Returns*, Ricerca '90 Publishing – an operation that has left in this volume only the pages related to the Lunar Returns. No, it is not. I think that it is something more; something quite important for those wishing to study the subject on which focuses my present work.

I wanted to do different things together, namely:

1) I removed the section on Earth Returns, for not all the Readers showed a real interest in it; and I've published this new edition of the text, lowering the cost of the book.

2) I've tried to explain further and better what the Lunar Returns are and how they work.

3) I've tried to clarify what are the different applications of the Lunar Returns.

4) In relation to one of those applications – the dating of the events within a Solar Return year – I've added something that I think will appeal to Readers: the complete discussion of the terrible saga of death in the Gandhi family, widely illustrated with many charts of birth skies (104 new charts and 88 new pages), Solar Returns and Lunar Returns, and further clarified by tables of transits – precisely to explain how you can use the LRs (Lunar Returns) for dating events within a year covered by a specific Solar Return.

I hope my Readers will reward this work of mine, purchasing it and suggesting it to other colleagues. Let me take leave from you by wishing you new amazing, deep dives into the wonderful world of Astrology.

Ciro Discepolo
Naples, the 1st of June 2010

# Preface to the English edition

In almost forty years of passionate studies, many of my books have been read and studied by dozens of thousands of readers all over the world.

One of my luckier volumes (*Transits and Solar Returns* is its title in English) has been published once in English, in German, and in Spanish; and twice in Italian and French. It may be claimed that, especially thanks to that wonderful virtual shop called Amazon, this book is now being read all over the world including Mongolia, the Philippines, Australia, Canada, etc.

Other volumes of mine on Solar Returns or on Lunar Returns are presently studied in Slovenia, in Hungary, in Russia...

Soon further versions of my books will be available in other minor languages.

What you are browsing is my most recent book, since it was first sold in Italian bookshops in September, 2008. This is its second English edition, containing slight but significant amendments.

Since they are usually particularly attentive to this kind of technical astrology, I trust that my English-speaking readers will appreciate this new 'Northwest Passage' of astrological research, which may lead you to heuristic paths of great interest – as it is the case of Earth Returns, a subject that I consider to be extremely interesting.

Other subjects of mine are presently widely applied here in Italy: I trust that one day they might become useful also to my American or anyway English-speaking colleagues. I am referring to different astrological threads, such as the protocol for a rectification of the time of birth of an individual; the method for the dating of events within a year; my rules of medical astrology; my concept of the exorcism of symbols; and many other subjects.

Nice reading to you all.

Ciro Discepolo
Naples, the 2nd of January 2009

# Preface

Predictive astrology is the most fascinating branch of our discipline. Within predictive astrology, the study of the Solar Returns and of the Lunar Returns represents the milestone of all the theoretical and practical scaffolding for the benefit of those moved by the ambition of casting fairly exact forecasts.

This book analyzes some of the most critical subjects for this kind of study: those chapters that – in my opinion – rightfully legitimizes the consideration of the segment called 'Solar and Lunar Returns' as the ultimate course in the study of astrology.

We'll come back to this point. First, let me develop a few theoretical digressions apparently farther off from this point which, I believe, may be of a great interest within the work that you have just started reading now.

And so I begin with discussing two wonderful masterpieces of literature – *One Thousand and One Nights* and the *Odyssey* – and then will draw a parallel with the movie *The Devil's Advocate* (USA 1997, with Keanu Reeves and Charlize Theron, directed by Taylor Hackford) to eventually come back to what was mentioned in the first lines of this preface.

For the sake of those who have never read the *One Thousand and One Nights*[1], let me explain in brief what it is about. It is undoubtedly one of the most precious masterpieces of the literature of all the times: a collection of tales that is in no way inferior to William Shakespeare's, Dante Alighieri's or Giovanni Boccaccio's *opera omnia*.

In a way, the tale of Shahrazad is the core of the *One Thousand and One Nights*. The following passage is made up of fragments taken from *The Book of The Thousand Nights and a Night*, translated by Richard F. Burton.

In the Name of Allah, the Compassionating, the Compassionate!
PRAISE BE TO ALLAH * THE BENEFICENT KING * THE

CREATOR OF THE UNIVERSE * [...] AND GRACE, AND PRAYER-BLESSING BE UPON OUR LORD MOHAMMED * LORD OF APOSTOLIC MEN * AND UPON HIS FAMILY AND COMPANION TRAIN * PRAYER AND BLESSINGS ENDURING AND GRACE WHICH UNTO THE DAY OF DOOM SHALL REMAIN * AMEN!

Verily the works and words of those gone before us have become instances and examples to men of our modern day, that folk may view what admonishing chances befel other folk and may therefrom take warning; and that they may peruse the annals of antique peoples and all that hath betided them, and be thereby ruled and restrained [...]. Now of such instances are the tales called *'A Thousand Nights and a Night'*, together with their far famed legends and wonders.

Therein it is related (but Allah is All knowing of His hidden things and All ruling and All honoured and All giving and All gracious and All merciful) that, in tide of yore and in time long gone before, there was a King of the Kings of the Banu Sásán in the Islands of India and China, a Lord of armies and guards and servants and dependents. He left only two sons, one in the prime of manhood and the other yet a youth, while both were Knights and Braves, albeit the elder was a doughtier horseman than the younger. So he succeeded to the empire; when he ruled the land and lorded it over his lieges with justice so exemplary that he was beloved by all the peoples of his capital and of his kingdom. His name was King Shahryár, and he made his younger brother, Shah Zamán hight, King of Samarcand in Barbarian land.

These two ceased not to abide in their several realms and the law was ever carried out in their dominions; and each ruled his own kingdom, with equity and fair dealing to his subjects, in extreme solace and enjoyment; and this condition continually endured for a score of years.

But at the end of the twentieth twelvemonth the elder King yearned for a sight of his younger brother and felt that he must look upon him once more. So he took counsel with his Wazír about visiting him, [...] «Harkening and obedience!» quoth the Minister, who fell to making ready without stay and packed up his loads and prepared all his requisites without delay. When he entered the city he proceeded straightway to the palace, where he presented himself in the royal presence; and, after kissing ground and praying for the King's health and happiness and for victory over all his enemies, he informed him that his brother was yearning to see him, and prayed for the pleasure of a visit. [...] when the King had fully comprehended its import, he said, «I hear and I obey the commands of the beloved brother!» He [...] stablished his chief Wazir viceroy of the land during his absence. Then he caused his tents and camels and mules to be brought forth and encamped, with their bales and loads, attendants and guards, within sight of the city, in readiness to set out next morning for his brother's capital.

But when the night was half spent he bethought him that he had forgotten in his palace somewhat which he should have brought with him, so he returned privily and entered his apartments, where he found the Queen, his wife, asleep on his own carpet bed, embracing with both arms a black cook of loathsome aspect and foul with kitchen grease and grime. When he saw this the world waxed black before his sight and he said, «If such case happen while I am yet within sight of the city what will be the doings of this damned whore during my long absence at my brother's court?» So he drew his scymitar and, cutting the two in four pieces with a single blow, left them on the carpet and returned presently to his camp without letting anyone know of what had happened.

Then he gave orders for immediate departure and set out at once and began his travel; [...] Now when Shah Zaman drew near the capital of his brother he despatched vaunt couriers and messengers of glad tidings to announce his arrival, and Shahryar came forth to meet him with his Wazirs and Emirs and Lords and Grandees of his realm; and saluted him and joyed with exceeding joy and caused the city to be decorated in his honour. When, however, the brothers met, the elder could not but see the change of complexion in the younger and questioned him of his case whereto he replied, «'Tis caused by the travails of wayfare and my case needs care, for I have suffered from the change of water and air! [...]» So he let him wend his own ways and asked no questions of him till one day when he again said, «O my brother, I see thou art grown weaker of body and yellower of colour.» «O my brother,» replied Shah Zaman «I have an internal wound.» still he would not tell him what he had witnessed in his wife. One day his elder brother said to him, «I am going forth to hunt and course and to take my pleasure and pastime; maybe this would lighten thy heart.»

Shah Zaman, however, refused, [...]

So King Shah Zaman passed his night in the palace and, next morning, when his brother had fared forth, he removed from his room and sat him down at one of the lattice windows overlooking the pleasure grounds; [...] Thereupon Shah Zaman drew back from the window, but he kept the bevy in sight espying them from a place whence he could not be espied. They walked under the very lattice and advanced a little way into the garden till they came to a jetting fountain amiddlemost a great basin of water; then they stripped off their clothes and behold, ten of them were women, concubines of the King, and the other ten were white slaves. Then they all paired off, each with each: but the Queen, who was left alone, presently cried out in a loud voice, «Here to me, O my lord Saeed!» and then sprang with a drop leap from one of the trees a big slobbering blackamoor with rolling eyes which showed the whites, a truly hideous sight. He walked boldly up to her and threw his arms round her neck while she embraced him as warmly; then he bussed her and winding his legs round hers, as a button loop clasps a button, he threw her and enjoyed her. On like wise did the other slaves with the girls till all had satisfied their passions, and they ceased not from kissing and clipping, coupling and carousing till day began to wane; [...]

Now, when Shah Zaman saw this conduct of his sister in law he said in himself, «By Allah, my calamity is lighter than this!» So he put away his melancholy and despondency, regret and repine, and allayed his sorrow by constantly repeating those words, adding, «'Tis my conviction that no man in this world is safe from their malice!» [...] Next day he broke his fast heartily and began to recover health and strength, and presently regained excellent condition.

His brother came back from the chase ten days after, when he rode out to meet him and they saluted each other; and when King Shahryar looked at King Shah Zaman he saw how the hue of health had returned to him, how his face had waxed ruddy and how he ate with an appetite after his late scanty diet. He wondered much and said, «[...] I was desirous to carry thee with me to the chase but I saw thee changed in hue, pale and wan to view, and in sore trouble of mind too. But now Alham-dolillah—glory be to God!—I see thy natural colour hath returned to thy face and that thou art again in the best of case. [...] So speak out and hide naught!» When Shah Zaman heard this he bowed groundwards awhile his head, then raised it and said, «I will tell thee what caused my complaint and my loss of colour; but excuse my acquainting thee with the cause of its return to me and the reason of my complete recovery: indeed I pray thee not to press me for a reply.»» Said Shahryar, who was much surprised by these words, «Let me hear first what produced thy pallor and thy poor condition.» «Know, then, O my brother,» rejoined Shah Zaman, «that when thou sentest thy Wazir with the invitation to place myself between thy hands, I made ready and marched out of my city; but presently I minded me having left behind me in the palace a string of jewels intended as a gift to thee. I returned for it alone and found my wife on my carpet bed and in the arms of a hideous black cook. So I slew the twain and came to thee, yet my thoughts brooded over this business and I lost my bloom and became weak.

But excuse me if I still refuse to tell thee what was the reason of my complexion returning.» Shahryar shook his head, marvelling with extreme marvel, [...] «That were but a better reason,» quoth Shahryar, «for telling me the whole history, and I conjure thee by Allah not to keep back aught from me.» Thereupon Shah Zaman told him all he had seen, from commencement to con elusion, [...] When King Shahryar heard this he waxed wroth with exceeding wrath, and rage was like to strangle him; but presently he recovered himself and said, «O my brother, I would not give thee the lie in this matter, but I cannot credit it till I see it with mine own eyes.» «And thou wouldst look upon thy calamity,» quoth Shah Zaman, «rise at once and make ready again for hunting and coursing, and then hide thyself with me, so shalt thou witness it and shine eyes shall verify it.»

«True,» quoth the King; whereupon he let make proclamation of his in tent to travel, and the troops and tents fared forth without the city, camping within sight, and Shahryar sallied out with them and took seat amidmost his host, bidding the slaves admit no man to him. When night came on [...] the brothers disguised themselves and returned by night with all secrecy to the palace, where they passed the dark hours: and at dawn they seated themselves at the lattice overlooking the pleasure grounds, when presently the Queen and her handmaids came out as before, and passing under the windows made for the fountain. Here they stripped, ten of them being men to ten women, and the King's wife cried out, «Where art thou, O Saeed?» [...]

When King Shahryar saw this infamy of his wife and concubines he became as one distraught and he cried out, «Only in utter solitude can man be safe from the doings of this vile world! [...] Let us up as we are and depart forthright hence, for we have no concern with Kingship, and let us overwander Allah's earth, worshipping the Almighty till we find some one to whom the like calamity hath happened; and if we find none then will death be more welcome to us than life.» So the two brothers issued from a second private postern of the palace; and they never stinted wayfaring by day and by night, until they reached a tree a middle of a meadow hard by a spring of sweet water on the shore of the salt sea. Both drank of it and sat down to take their rest; and when an hour of the day had gone by: lo! they heard a mighty roar and uproar in the middle of the main as though the heavens were falling upon the earth; and the sea brake with waves before them, and from it towered a black pillar, which grew and grew till it rose skywards and began making for that meadow.

Seeing it, they waxed fearful exceedingly and climbed to the top of the tree, which was a lofty; whence they gazed to see what might be the matter. And behold, it was a Jinni, huge of height and burly of breast and bulk, broad of brow and black of blee, bearing on his head a coffer of crystal. He strode to land, wading through the deep, and coming to the tree whereupon were the two Kings, seated himself beneath it. He then set down the coffer on its bottom and out it drew a casket, [...] which he unlocked [...] and out of it a young lady to come was seen, white-skinned and of winsomest mien, of stature fine and thin, and bright as though a moon of the fourteenth night she had been, or the sun raining lively sheen. The Jinni seated her under the tree by his side and looking at her said, «O choicest love of this heart of mine! O dame of noblest line, whom I snatched away on thy bride night [...]: O my sweetheart! I would fief sleep a little while.» He then laid his head upon the lady's thighs; and, stretching out his legs which extended down to the sea, slept and snored and sparked like the roll of thunder. Presently she raised her head towards the tree top and saw the two Kings perched near the summit; then she softly lifted off her lap the Jinni's pate which she was tired of supporting and placed it upon the ground; then standing upright under the tree signed to the Kings, «Come ye down, ye two, and fear naught from this Ifrit.» They were in a terrible fright when they found that she had seen them and answered her in the same manner, «Allah upon thee and by thy modesty, O lady, excuse us from coming down!» But she rejoined by saying, «Allah upon you both, that ye come down forthright, and if ye come not, I will rouse upon you my husband, this Ifrit, and he shall do you to die by the illest of deaths.» So, being afraid, they came down to her and she rose be fore them and said, «Stroke me a strong stroke, without stay or delay, otherwise will I arouse and set upon you this Ifrit who shall slay you straightway.» [...] Whereupon out of fear King Shahryar said to King Shah Zaman, «O my brother, do thou what she biddeth thee do;» but he replied, «I will not do it till thou do it before I do.» And they began disputing about futtering her. Then quoth she to the twain, «How is it I see you disputing and demurring; if ye do not come forward like men and do the deed of kind ye two, I will arouse upon you the Ifrit.» At this, by reason of their sore dread of the Jinni, both did by her what she bade them do; and, when they had dismounted from her, she said, «Well done!» She then took from her pocket a purse and drew out a knotted string, whereon were strung five hundred and seventy seal rings, and asked, «Know ye what be these?» They answered her saying, «We know not!» Then quoth she; «These be the signets of five hundred and seventy men who have all futtered me upon the horns of this foul, this foolish, this filthy Ifrit; so give me also your two seal rings, ye pair of brothers.» When they had drawn their two rings from their hands and given them to her, she said to them, «Of a truth this If rit bore me off on my bride night, and put me into a casket and set the casket in a coffer and to the coffer he affixed seven strong padlocks of steel and deposited me on the deep bottom of the sea that raves, dashing and clashing with waves; [...] But [...] this wretched Jinni wotteth not that Des tiny may not be averted nor hindered by aught, and that whatso woman willeth the same she fulfilleth however man nilleth.» [...] Hearing these words they marvelled with exceeding marvel, and she went from them to the Ifrit and, taking up his head on her thigh as before, said to them softly, «Now wend your ways and bear yourselves beyond the bounds of his malice.» [...] Thereupon they rode back to the tents of King Shahryar, which they reached on the morning of the third day; [...]

There he sat him upon his throne [...] he carried her [wife] to the place of execution and did her die. [...] He also sware himself by a binding oath that whatever wife he married he would abate her maidenhead at night and slay her next morning to make sure of his honour; [...] On this wise he continued for the space of three years; marrying a maiden every night and killing her the next morning, till folk raised an outcry against him and cursed him, praying Allah utterly to destroy him and his rule; and women made an uproar and mothers wept and parents fled with their daughters till there remained not in the city a young person fit for carnal copulation. Presently the King ordered his Chief Wazir [...] to bring him a virgin as was his wont; and the Minister went forth and searched and found none; so he returned home in sorrow and anxiety fearing for his life from the King.

Now he had two daughters, Shahrazad and Dunyazad hight, of whom the elder had perused the books, annals and legends of preceding Kings, and the stories, examples and instances of by gone men and things; [...] and she was pleasant and polite, wise and witty, well read and well bred. Now on that day she said to her father, «Why do I see thee thus changed and laden with cark and care? Concerning this matter quoth one of the poets.— Tell whoso hath sorrow * Grief never shall last [...]» When the Wazir heard from his daughter these words he related to her, from first to last, all that had happened between him and the King. Thereupon said she, «By Allah, O my father [...] I wish thou wouldst give me in marriage to this King Shahryar; either I shall live or I shall be a ransom for the virgin daughters of Moslems and the cause of their deliverance from his hands and thine.» «Allah upon thee!» cried he in wrath exceeding that lacked no feeding, «O scanty of wit, expose not thy life to such peril!» [...] and she answered, «O my father it must be, come of it what will!» [...] Hereupon the Wazir being weary of lamenting and contending, persuading and dissuading her, all to no purpose, went up to King Shahryar and [...] told him all about his dispute with his daughter from first to last and how he designed to bring her to him that night. [...] But Shahrazed rejoiced with exceeding joy and get ready all she required and said to her younger sister, Dunyazad, «Note well what directions I entrust to thee! When I have gone in to the King I will send for thee and when thou comest to me and seest that he hath had his carnal will of me, do thou say to me:—O my sister, an thou be not sleepy, relate to me some new story, delectable and delightsome, the better to speed our waking hours;— and I will tell thee a tale which shall be our deliverance, if so Allah please, and which shall turn the King from his blood thirsty custom.»

[...] So when it was night their father the Wazir carried Shahrazad to the King who was gladdened at the sight and asked,

«Hast thou brought me my need?» and he answered, «I have.»

But when the King took her to his bed and fell to toying with her and wished to go in to her she wept; [...] «O King of the age, I have a younger sister and fief would I take leave of her this night before I see the dawn.

« So he sent at once for Dunyazad and she came and kissed the ground between his hands, when he permitted her to take her seat near the foot of the couch. Then the King arose and did away with his bride's maidenhead and [...] when it was midnight Shahrazad awoke and signalled to her sister Dunyazad who sat up and said, «Allah upon thee, O my sister, recite to us some new story, delightsome and delectable, wherewith to while away the waking hours of our latter night.» «With joy and goodly gree,» answered Shahrazad, «if this pious and auspicious King permit me.» «Tell on,» quoth the King who chanced to be sleepless and restless and therefore was pleased with the prospect of hearing her story. So Shahrazad rejoiced; and thus, on the first night of the Thousand Nights and a Night, she began... [2]

The undercurrent that the reader can perceive throughout the book – and also while watching its fantastic film version by Pier Paolo Pasolini[3] – is the sense of Fate, the theme of this work being the notion of an already written and immutable destiny which man fulfils from his very birth. Every single action had been already announced; the presence of good and evil genies – resembling the angels and the devils of the Catholic religion – represents a sort of bureaucratic administration regulating a traffic of destinies crossing each other like the clogging of many cogwheels.

The same can be told of Homer's masterpiece[4], in which virile and battling men such as the incomparable Ulysses bow to the will of the gods and to what had already been written at the moment of their own birth. The king of Ithaca struggles against Polyphemus and against the enchantress Circe and against the Sirens, and against the thousands of traps set for him by Poseidon. But he knows his doom already: coming back to Ithaca after an odyssey of twenty years just to briefly enjoy the coveted embrace with Penelope and their son Telemachus, and eventually leaving again for the final sea journey in which he faces death – a death forecast even by his protectress, Athena.

Do not fear – I don't have the presumption of racking my brain over the world's most ancient riddle: the chance that a human being stands to escape from a destiny that, as it is also projected by the two mentioned works of literature, seems to be based on a timeless willing that not only has already decided everything for us, but has also timed them[5].

Now let's add some consideration about the film *The Devil's Advocate*, starring a superb Al Pacino. The protagonist of this film is a young, unknown small-town-attorney who sets the whole country's tongues wagging because of his good track record of having never lost a case.

He's made an offer to work in New York City joining the largest law firm in the Big Apple, by one of its founders, John Milton. This latter character, starred by Al Pacino, is actually an allusion to the Devil. The young attorney may in fact be considered as the son of Satan: John Milton is planning to have him coupled with another of his daughters – an attorney herself – to eventually rule the world.

Among other things, I find it interesting to see the obsessive demonization of the role of attorneys in the fiction filmed in the States.

Eventually the young attorney realizes what's going on. In an attempt to escape from this hellish plot he attempts suicide shooting himself – but the Devil had foreseen that too, so...

As you can easily understand, this is actually like an *uroboro* eating its own tail; i.e. it is a self-reproducing process without any escape; a general intrigue which represents the synthesis of a written, unmodifiable destiny.

Of course I do not personally agree with it, neither am I trying to convince you. Those who firmly believe that they are already crucified since their birth, are free to genuflect and live in a hopeless Middle Age. Those who think otherwise will try to do like those gazelles in the savannah – maybe they are conscious of the fact that their destiny is to become food for predators, yet they attempt to escape anyway – and many of them do survive.

Also the strongest lions in Africa and the terrible tigers probably are automatically aware of being obliged to winning and predating forever, without any chance of living a different destiny. Nonetheless many of them become prey themselves: killed by other predators or by a mistaken movement, or victims of the predator *par excellence* – man.

So then, perhaps there's a small degree of freedom within the frame of destinies that are apparently fully prefabricated and unalterable. I happen to remember the considerations that my friend and astrological researcher Enzo Barillà[6] wrote once when he was asked to express his opinion about the chance of changing our destiny by means of the Aimed Solar Returns. In that occasion he proposed – cleverly, I dare say – a parallel with the answers given by the Swiss Jungian psychologist Marie-Louise von Franz when she was once asked about the chance of eluding destiny. More or less she answered, «If we the depth-psychologists didn't believe so, why should we apply depth psychology to our patients?»

Now, with these simple words the problem is solved – at least it is solved for a good portion of Humankind – barring the narrow domain of philosophical conjectures without solution and joining the even less vast realm of a universe in which our will represents a real value – not a chimera, as in the imaginary world of *Matrix* or in Gabriele Salvatores' *Nirvana*.

Within the several books that I have written, you can find many examples of biological or astrological twins in which – on the day of their Solar Return – one of them chose to leave for an Aimed SR while the other one chose to spend that day at home. As a result, the following twelve months for each of them was completely different. All the rest is philosophy.

As I mentioned earlier, in my opinion the subject 'Solar and Lunar Returns' represents, in a way, the University of Astrology. I know that many colleagues do not agree, and I don't mean to argue in any way. The Reader – free from any sort of conditioning – will read/taste a little of everything and eventually – and being under no pressure – will choose his own author and his own school.

**Notes**

1) Many decades ago, I had the pleasure of reading many editions of this book – which is, without any doubt, one of my favourites. The last that I read it was in the winter of 2007, in the excellent edition of publisher Einaudi, supervised by Mirella Cassarono, including an essay by Abdelfattah Kilito.

2) In fact, the bearing frame of *One Thousand and One Nights* is based on the expediency of the beautiful and cultured woman giving her 'literary drogue' to the king, night after night, in order to save thousands of other maids from certain death.

3) *Arabian Nights*, an Italian-French film directed by Pier Paolo Pasolini in 1974, starring Ninetto Davoli and Franco Citti.

4) The RAI edition of this DVD is really splendid! You will be amazed by watching it in *Full Definition* (1900 x 1080 pixels) – wonderful pictures and a wonderful definition.

5) Nonetheless I cannot but remark that even in such a religious (the term being used in the context of the notion of 'destiny') work like the *One Thousand and One Nights* the charming Shahrazad seems to have found the way to fool destiny: with the narration of tales for her king, telling a different story every night in order to delay her own execution.

6) See A *Few Facts on Aimed Birthdays*, Blue Diamond Publisher: it can be downloaded free from website www.cirodiscepolo.it.

**Naples, the 5th of October 2007**

# 1.
# Some short considerations

In a book of this kind I feel I am required to try to explain, first of anything else, what Lunar Returns are and how they work.

To do so, first I'll try to explain what the Solar Returns are and how they work.

Let us start from the horoscope (i.e. the natal sky, or birth chart or radix). Astrology theorizes that each of us, coming into the world, takes the distinctive features of the place and of the moment in which he/she was born – just like a good vintage wine. For everybody knows that a *Chianti* bottled in 1969 is completely different from a *Pinot* bottled in 1975. We astrologers claim that the very same thing happens with human beings in their relationship with the 'stars'. Those who do not believe so do not believe in astrology either – and the matter can be considered closed for them. But for those who believe in this reality it will not be hard to believe also in Solar Returns.

Let me also tress that the theory of the Solar Returns is extremely ancient: we can already find traces of it in texts dating back to several centuries ago. However, the author who first revived them in modern times is the French astrologer Alexander Volguine, more or less in the middle of the last century. My personal research took inspiration mainly from him. Nonetheless it soon took a different path, since personally and almost immediately (in 1970) I started to deal not only with plain *Solar Returns*, but also with what I call the *Aimed Solar Returns*.

Coming back to our initial conversation, let me remind that we the astrologers might swear on our own sons about the reality of astrology, but we would never be able to say how astrology works. The reader would find the discussion of the latter issue, especially from an epistemological/scientific point of view, in my book *Lunar Returns and*

*Earth Returns*, Ricerca '90 Publisher. The section in which this matter is discussed can be freely accessed at www.lunarreturns.com.

The most basic and classic 'explanation' that can be given in relation to this, is that, being born and breathing for the first time with our lungs, we 'fix' that astral *imprinting* featuring exactly a precise cosmic moment in a determined place. We also claim that that astral *imprinting*, that is to say: that horoscope or that natal chart (birth chart or radix) is nothing but a detailed map of our whole personality, of our medical history, of our destiny in general and in particular – this means in connection with our love affairs, our feelings, our professional life, our money, and so on.

Needless to say that if we believe in this, we should also believe that once we came to the world, not only the astral *imprinting* that we received with our first whimper would 'influence' our life but also many other occasions of imprinting, relentlessly.

Now it seems to me that both for the astrologer and for the layman it should be extremely clear that if we believe in other occasions of astral *imprinting*, we must not think to such occurrence of imprinting as a sequel of *random* events (i.e. fortuitous, occurring without a fixed timeline), but as a wave of events that cyclically repeat themselves according to a precise law. Now – what are the cycles that govern the universe, or at least, life on Earth? I would certainly say those that also regulate the movements of celestial bodies in our solar system.

Roughly fifty years ago a new discipline was established called chronobiology: the science that deals with biological rhythms or biorhythms. Before that time, doctors prescribed drug delivery either in the morning or in the evening indifferently. But when the scientists realized the importance of biorhythms in humans, they also understood that a molecule ends up being better activated or weakened down, simply depending on the time of day in which it is administered to the patient.

It is obvious to everyone, or at least I think so, that the cycles are related to the movements of celestial bodies in our solar system. Let us make only three examples of this. The beautiful book of Lyall Watson *Supernature*, published in Italy by Rizzoli, Milan in 1974 informs that it has been determined that, *in primis*, a circadian rhythm exist in humans – i.e. a rhythm that lasts about a day, just like the Earth's rotation around its own axis. There is plenty of evidence of this fact. Consider, for example, the curve showing how the function of urination or how the blood pressure varies within the twenty–four hours of a mean day. Or you can also consider the fact that every day in the animal 'man' there is a peak in the production of melatonin half–hour after the sunset (melatonin is a naturally occurring compound found in animals which favours sleep; it is in fact a fully natural, light antidepressant). Some specific laboratory test, such as the Takata test, show that certain chemical values in our blood are quite different at sunrise and sunset; and to make a long story short we have better not to go on and on.

The second example is the sight before everybody's eyes. It is relevant to the twenty–nine days during which our natural satellite, the Moon, takes a complete lap around the Earth: just think of the female menstrual cycle, if you have doubts about it. Of course the most important cycle of all is certainly the annual, 365–day long cycle, ticked by the revolution of Earth around the Sun. Evidence of this rhythm or cycle is numerous and very evident in nature: animals hibernate every year in the same period and do the same for migration and for the season of love. Even the trees bear fruit in the same period of the year. For example, around the 15th of May, be the weather good or bad, at our latitudes cherry trees give us cherries: this is a kind of birthday for the plant.

And the same happens for man: starting from the moment of birth begins a cycle of approximately 365 days, which is repeated *n* times until the death of the individual. The day of the (true) birthday, that is when the Sun, seen from Earth, returns exactly in degrees, minutes and seconds at the same point of the ecliptic that it occupied at the moment of an individual's birth, a cycle of 365 days ends and another one begins, just like in a sine wave, as shown in the following figure.

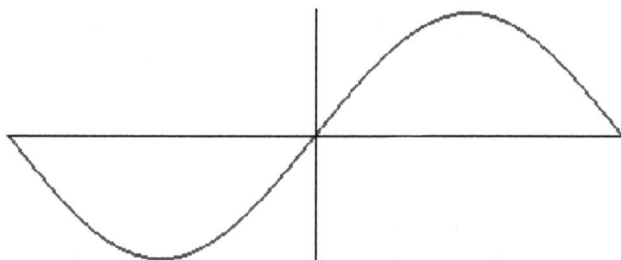

This is a point of extreme importance for us: the imprinting that we receive at this very moment is essential and it should not be confused with other occasions of random imprinting. In other words, the horoscope that we can draw upon our yearly solar return, which is beaten exactly by the time and is relevant to the exact place where we are in that moment, that horoscope would 'condition' us strongly for the following 365 days.

Now, if you believe in what I have just explained, you will also understand that if we study, for example on a computer monitor, how the sky of our next birthday looks like in different places on the Earth (we have – theoretically – 360 different possibilities of seeing the sky from the Earth), we can also determine in which town of the planet we may receive the best *imprinting* of all, according to the laws of astrology. So if the day of your birthday you are under the sky of your home place, say in Milan or Paris or New York, the astral *imprinting* is of a certain type; while if you choose a different sky, for example a very harmonic sky with certain features that you wish to 'activate', it would obviously be something quite different. However it should be noted immediately that a sky of Solar Return, contrary to what many people believe, can not and should not be read by the same rules of a birth or natal chart.

The above described is the starting point for the study of Solar Returns and of Aimed Solar Returns. Let me add that we define a *Base Solar Return* (BSR) the sky of the birthday that we 'take' if we stay at home on the day of our astrological birthday.

If you understand what is written above, you also understand that the same principle applies in the case of the Lunar Returns in relation to the biorhythm linked to the lunar cycle: about 28 days and a half.

But a question arises immediately at this point. You can calculate your Lunar Returns monthly, drawing a chart of the moment in which the Moon comes back to its very location occupied when you were born. Other fellow astrologers prefer to use another return which I would define a 'symbolic' one: they consider the moment in which the Sun returns to the position of one's natal Moon.

Which one is right? Each of the two, depending on the type of astrology practiced by each astrologer.

I would remind you that the great psychoanalyst Carl Gustav Jung was releasing a series of radio interviews to the BBC shortly before his death. In one of them he explained that he would die soon and that almost certainly he would leave life without being able to answer the following question: Does Astrology work on the principle of Jungian synchronicity or does it follow a classic law of cause and effect? In the latter case we should not talk of symbols; we should rather look for the physical forces (electromagnetic waves, magnetic fields, and the law of gravity or other) that may explain how Astrology works. He also had worked together with Austrian scientist Wolfgang Pauli, a Nobel laureate in physics, but they were unable to remove this doubt.

On the other hand, none of them knew the results of the huge statistical works of French pair Michel and Françoise Gauquelin, who before anything else had been able to show evidence of the so called 'Mars effect': the presence of Mars **after** the rise and **after** the culmination in the birth sky of thousands of champion athletes.

If the topic is of your interest, you can find my explanations and considerations also about this subject in the aforementioned text *Lunar Returns and Earth Returns*.

It is a fact of absolute importance for the scope of what I am trying to tell you. In fact, the Gauquelins showed a 'transitive effect' of the Red planet: only after passing the hot spots of one's sky, did Mars show an effect that could be converted into an astrological law. With a comparison that may be more easily comprehensible to everyone, I would draw your attention to another fact of nature that repeats itself cyclically. We all know that the summer solstice roughly takes place around the 21$^{st}$ of June in the Northern Hemisphere, when the Sun 'offers itself' for the greatest number of hours during the day compared to all other days of the year. Well, following a fairly logical reasoning we could say that on the day of the summer solstice we also have the maximum air temperature in a certain place, because that place has been exposed to the heating of the sun for the highest number of hours (AN, this time the name of the star that gives us life is written fully in small letters because here it is considered as an astronomical, not as an astrological body). Well, it is not so. In fact, usually around mid–August, after months of heat accumulation, in the Northern Hemisphere the Earth reaches its highest summer temperatures.

Similarly, if as a result of the conclusive researches of the Gauquelins we claim that a celestial body is much stronger **after** it passed the Midheaven of an astral map, rather than before (i.e. when it is in the ninth House and not in the tenth House for us, the astrologers!), then I believe that we cannot keep on talking about symbols: we must start talking of physical forces instead. Therefore the return we are interested in is the return of the transit Moon over the natal Moon – not the return of the transit Sun over the natal Moon!

Of course others may take the opposite view: the Readers, who are the chief judges, may use both systems and decide for themselves which of the two works.

Having cleared this point, we can define the following:

1) The Lunar Return is an astrological chart that you cast every month for a given subject, considering the moment when the Moon, passing over our heads, returns to the same longitude of birth (degrees, minutes and seconds of longitude in the Zodiac). You take good note of that moment and always make reference to GMT; then you convert it into the time in force on the place where the subject is at the very moment of the return. Thus you can cast and draw a map which is similar to a natal chart, while possessing the following possibilities and potentialities:

A) The chart of Lunar Return is a powerful tool of astrological analysis that allows you to know, even years in advance, the precise (precise in all its details) trend of a given month (about 28.5 days) of any individual. The rules of the correct reading a Lunar Return are the same with which you can read a Solar Return; they are listed in my book *Transits and Solar Returns*, Ricerca '90 Publishing (see this url: http://www.amazon.com/Ciro-Discepolo/e/B003DC8JOQ/ref=sr_tc_2_0?qid=1275403766&sr=1-2-ent). Being a volume of about 600 pages it would be nonsense to double also in this volume all those various pages of explanation. However, what you should know is that according to my personal experience (over 40 years of practice on SRs and LRs, over 20,000 aimed birthdays studied as for 2007, nearly three years of my own LRs studied almost every single month, plus the numerous Aimed LRs of my dear ones who let me study them) there are certain rules (approximately 30 rules) that should guide you to the reading the Solar Returns and there are certain rules (approximately 20 rules) that should guide you to the reading of Lunar Returns. The 20 rules relevant to the LRs are all listed in the already mentioned book *Lunar*

*Return and Earth Returns*, but you'll find them also in the following pages of this very volume.

B) The chart of Lunar Return can help you to improve your quality of life, just like the Solar Returns. When considering *aiming*, i.e. relocating a LR, I suggest you to consider it as an *investment* rather than an *expense*. It may seem a trivial difference, but it's huge! Just think that you are trying to sell a house and the deal is at hand, but you might not achieve it because of the hesitation of the buyer. Now, say that at that point you leave and relocate your LR (what I call *aiming the LR* or doing an *ALR, Aided Lunar Return*) placing, say, Jupiter of LR closely conjunct the Descendant of LR (possibility of promoting agreements). Well, maybe you spend a thousand dollars for the travel to Europe from the U.S., but by doing so you also earn 300,000 dollars!

C) The third huge resource that comes from the study of Lunar Returns is the possibility to help you fix (i.e. *rectify*) a time of birth, through a wise and adequate use of the LRs themselves. Say for example that you are in doubt with your own time of birth. With a couple of ALR – even with modest relocations that may cost you only a few dozen dollars – you can place, say, Mars of LR close to the cusp of two Houses. The following month, by simply comparing your recent events with the chart of LR, any good astrologer who's not a seller of hot air will be able to determine with absolute certainty if that Mars really occupied the previous House, the following House or both houses (i.e. if it really was exactly over their cusp). He will consequently be able to rectify your time of birth, and by repeating this experiment for a few dozen times, you may find out your true time of birth!

The fourth, very important function in the study of the Lunar Returns is that they help you dating the events within the frame of the 12 months covered by a Solar Return. I would like to offer you a practical example, and also a very substantial one, of what I'm writing. You are about to read the complete astrological analysis of the terrible saga of death of the Gandhi's family. It is the chronicle of the high number of violent deaths that stroke that family. You will see how LRs would have let man foresee the timing of those tragic events. Therefore, in the next chapter, you will find dozens of pages devoted to this subject.

# 2.
# The unconscious roots of my passion for the Aimed Solar Returns

Perhaps I have found out the unconscious – and that goes back quite a long time – roots of my irrepressible passion for ASRs. Be assured that my main motivation is their unquestionable value: ASRs do work perfectly (despite the disagreement of a few) thus representing a reality which is very close to pure mathematics: almost at the same level as Relocations.

We all know the value of symbols, and it hasn't been impossible for me to keep trace of the starting point of my profound interest towards this subject. I might remark, with certain bemusement, that nothing of this had ever emerged during three long-lasting sessions of depth analysis which I undertook approximately from the age of 20 until the age of 40. Only in recent times – within the frame of a magical period of my life – has it popped out in my mind; the clear, the crystal-clear, the impressively limpid memory of the very moment in which the trigger of the 'aimed birthday' clicked inside me.

I do not expect that everybody believes it – only those who have studied or read much of psychology.

I was three or four years old – no less and no more – it was my mother's birthday.

Keep in mind that the day of our birthday or the day of the birthday of a dear one, is always an extraordinary day of good or evil.

It is needless to explain what my mother represented for me. I am a Cancerian with my Ascendant also being Cancer (even though, having the Sun in my First House I am also an Aries to all intents and purposes): hence she was my everything, for me she was the world spinning around me, the air I used to breathe, love, tenderness, protection…

It is not by chance that I was her favourite son, the third of four.

I used to spend many hours of the day with her. As any good Cancerian, I absorbed all that she said without loosing a single word.

That day she upset me with her words, «Today is my birthday.» «What does it mean?», I asked. «It means – she answered – that your mum today gets a little older. Every year, on the day of her birthday, mummy gets a little older...» I got into a panic. I remember it as if it were yesterday. Disproportional emotional reactions broke out inside me, and I felt a sort of menace, a danger in those words – the fear that somebody or something could take her away from me.

I instinctively thought of an expedient, and that cruelly immature age made me exclaim, «No, mum – every year on the day of your birthday I will tie you to a chair with ropes so that you are not going to grow (in my childish mind getting old was a synonym for growing, also in the length of bones). This is what I'll do and you won't get older!»

It was very soothing for me to remember that episode, for it explains in a very simple and exhaustive way the fundamental direction of my life.

Let us repeat once again that the symbol is not a mark written on the paper with a pen – no, it is actually a dinosaur living inside us. This dinosaur might even devour us if we didn't grab it by the horns.

Later on I my life, other symbols would strike by force before my path, forecasting the precise route of my destiny.

By the age of 8 I used to be a pupil in the primary school of the Barnabite in Posillipo. Every morning a claret schoolbus would stop just before our door to take me to the top of the most picturesque hill of Naples. During the trip, in turn, little boys and girls used to sit by my side to express their personal, familiar, delicate problems. I did not understand that situation, yet I was already able to realize that something was going on – although I could not recognize that it was a symbol pressing strongly from inside myself, urging me to understand which direction my life would take.

Approximately four years later, as a student of junior secondary school I used to trace strange drawings with a little mitre square and a stencil with circles of different dimensions. I would cross circles and triangles and colour them in a particular way. Several times my teachers sent for my parents and asked them what those strange drawings represent. Several years later, at the age of 22, I started drawing freehand astral maps of people, and I used a little square and a stencil of circles: then I connected the two things.

# 3.
# Why and how do Solar Returns and Lunar Returns work

There is a question that I've asked often to myself. Several times I have also been asked the same question by my readers or by people attending my seminars and lectures. The question is, in what physical or universal principle is it possible to set the functioning of Solar and Lunar Returns, thus accepting – already seen to be working in their theoretical formulation – that they actually operate in practice?

Let us forget for the time being what I have repeated several times – i.e. that an astrologer should not really care for the theoretical justification of the functioning of the Aimed Solar Returns and of the Aimed Lunar Returns, after having successfully experimented thousands of times that ASRs and ALRs do really work in practice. Yet over the years I do have developed a theory of my own, a theory that seems to have been validated by different schools of thought, some of them strictly scientific and some others, non-scientific.

For example we know that Carl Gustav Jung discussed for long the question of astrology being considered under the principle of cause and effect or under the principle of synchronicity. He also worked together with Wolfgang Ernst Pauli, a Nobel laureate in physics, and all his doubts on this subject started to pervade his works, beginning with his study on synchronicity[1] through all the following publications in which he faced such subjects. Almost until the day of his death – as described by Emma Baumann Jung[2] herself – he continued being uncertain about 'that strange thing called astrology', but he never doubted its validity: he was simply uncertain about how to classify it – as a 'causal' or as a 'synchronistic' phenomenon. Unfortunarely the great Swiss psychologist and thinker left us with this doubt.

Personally, for some years now I have been developing the conviction that our discipline should be explained in a causal way.

Before exposing my whole thought on this point, particularly referring to the Solar and Lunar Returns, I would urge you to read something important (at least in my opinion). It's a series of articles that appeared between 2005 and 2007 in my quarterly *Ricerca '90*. It is my belief that the following articles have an exceptional importance, especially if you consider that they contain certain coherent aspects that characterize them all in a sort of cross-party or bipartisan alignment.

I believe that the 3$^{rd}$, 4$^{th}$, and 5$^{th}$ of June 2005 are bound to be historical days for astrology. Those days, in the *XII Yearly Congress of Astrology* promoted and organized by *Ricerca '90* in Vico Equense (not far from Naples), some scientists 'out of the halls of power' held exceptionally interesting lectures.

I wish to express my gratefulness once again to those extraordinary researchers for their highly valued contributions – a special acknowledgement to my master and friend, engineer Vincenzo Di Napoli who has left this life. Now those scientists sat down at the same table without knowing each other. They exposed some aspects of a possible vision of the world and its laws: a sort of *Weltanschauung* that you may consider following a criterion which I'll explain later on. This idea picks up a little bit from each of the following lectures and may become the ground for a general theory on a possible functioning of astrology – a new theory never conjectured before, which in my opinion may be of particular interest and a quite convincing one.

Please read their lectures and also what they wrote on *Ricerca '90*: I will comment upon them later on.

### It's science that should validate itself – by Renato Palmieri[3]

As it always happens in the conferences of 'heretical' disciplines, when you face the problem of their relationship with 'official' science they show a disposition of reclaiming their own validation on the basis of principles taken from the disciplines currently in force – whereas we should overturn the question and ask the academic science to show 'its own' credentials on the basis of heretical principles. The paradox is only apparent: in fact, it is precisely the anomalies presented by the so-called 'scientific heresies' that are the 'heel of Achilles' of the normal paradigm, which is unable to explain them and therefore – simply denies them. An emblematic example is given by 'cold fusion': in 1989 it marked the beginning of a series of experiments on a global scale, each of them confirming its validity, followed by a progressive wave of resistance at a theoretical level – or rather at an 'economical' level, and at the level of the power of the Establishment.

Two considerations can be put on the table in the frame of our congress. Astrology researches its effectual motivations in two orders of influences: those of a gravitational kind, and those of an electromagnetic kind. Let us consider then what current science really 'knows' of the essence of gravitation and of electromagnetism. Well, it can be easily shown that it actually knows absolutely 'nothing'.

1) In this congress the Zodiac is your daily bread. Zodiac implies ecliptic. The plane of the ecliptic is that of the whole solar system, with an axis centred on the Sun and a vast equatorial plane on which the planets rotate: the giant planets with their whole parade of satellites, Saturn with its rings, and so on. This structure, in its whole, has a discoidal shape similar to that of the immense galactic discs, and a general rotation which is prospectively anticlockwise or clockwise as regards the two poles – North and South – of the central axis. Such an immediately evident feature has a very clear name: it is called *dipolarity* and it is present without ambiguity in any celestial body having enough size. However, gravitation is incredibly ignored from this scheme. It is ignored in every book of theoretical physics, of cosmology and of history of science, starting from the theorems of Kepler and of Newton throughout the experiment of Cavendish for the measurement of the gravitational constant and up to Einstein. Even more: it is even denied when they talk about the 'spherical symmetry' and the 'unipolar field' of gravitation (cfr. Phillips, *La Geofisica*, Biblioteca EST Mondatori, page 168). This implies that all the discussions and the calculations that have been made or that they are making about gravitation are approximate: the proof being that the so-called G-'constant' or gravitational 'constant' is reckoned with only three significant figures (6.67), while other cosmological constants have eight or nine figures.

2) Here are two pieces of magnetic chess: a queen and a king. They have the same polarity, being opposite to the polarity of the magnetic board. Let us pull the two bottoms of the pieces closer. Immediately it becomes evident that the so-called 'repulsion' between them does not manifest along an axis – as it is shown in any book of physics – but with a sort or rotational 'sliding' that no theory is able to explain to us. Now,

such a phenomenon is exactly identical to the behaviour of a comet with a very stretched-out ellipse: when it reaches the perihelion, it also 'slides' rotating around the Sun and then it goes back to outer space with an overall movement which nobody would ever define 'repulsive' as regards the Sun.

As a consequence, the general scene of the pieces of knowledge 'proven' by current science with respect to the so-called 'heretical' notions is similar to Pieter Bruegel the Elder's painting *The Blind leading the Blind*. The roped-party leader, who's already fallen into the ditch, is the academic science – despite Popper's 'falsifiability', which Professor Emilio Del Giudice has rightly criticized in his previous lecture. The following blind men, unless they resolve to leave the roped party as soon as possible, will follow as the heretical disciplines do looking for the support of science.

And to sum up with a general proposal, may I invite you to found the CCCONS as a counterpart to the notorious CSICOP (TN: today's CSI, *Committee for Skeptical Inquiry*): where the latter is the *Committee for the Scientific Investigation of Claims of the Paranormal*, the former would be the *Committee for the Control of Claims of the Normal Science* – it should pass judgment on many of the most sensational articles of the academic magazines like the *Scientific American*.

Vico Equense, the 4th of June 2005

## On Fibonacci, pyramids and environs – by Vincenzo Di Napoli[4]

This lecture can be seen to be the continuation of what – some time ago – I happened to claim on the implication of the fatal Fibonacci number on architecture. The dimensioning of the building elements according to the classical golden dimensions, both on plan and on elevation, implies an important consequence in the field of hertz microwaves: a building element, with its planoaltimetric conformation, builds up a volume; as regards to microwaves, this volume behaves just like a resonance box – it resonates on frequencies corresponding to the frequencies of the various colours of the Helmholtz spectrum. The induction of such frequencies is of a cosmogeographical kind; their value not only depends on dimensions, but also on shape as well as on the orientation of the building element in space. At his point let us add that such frequencies, when dimensioned in accordance with the golden elements, fall in the band corresponding to orange yellow. How could ancient architects reach such results? It is a mystery.

In order to understand the importance of what we are talking about, we must notice that, according to the medical theories of chromotherapy, all the colours ranging from orange yellow to red are bioaccelerator, while all the colours towards violet are bioretardant[1]. Hence, we have a standstill in correspondence of orange yellow. Thus, we have opened a new chapter of environmental health: a chapter that considers even the nature of building materials as a corollary – this is particularly true with the sands used as a component of the different kinds of concrete, and those used for colouring the internal walls. So, during the design of new objects or the renewal of existing ones, there's the need of a technique that allows to determine and to measure the following elements:

1) Sensibility to cosmogeophysical radiations of the premises for their planoaltimetric conformation.

2) Nature of the materials with which we intend to build.

3) Colours of the walls delimiting a room.

If the volume of the room can be inscribed into a sphere, the accumulation of energy can be studied also on a diagram, representing its planimetry. This I have personally carried out by using the Callegari machine as a hertz-microwave detector – see the previous issues of our quarterly. In a following issue we'll describe its technique of employment.

At this point let me make a digression, due to its historical character within my studies and because of its astrological implications.

Originally I focused my attention on these subjects when I resolved to investigate certain, still unknown aspects of the Egyptian pyramids.

I built a model on the same proportions (i.e. the same ratio between its perimeter and the double of its altitude) of the Great Pyramid of Giza, and I found out that its volume was resonating on a frequency around orange yellow, and that it changed in plus or minus depending on its orientation and on the day. This implied important considerations:

1) Its builders knew very well that the entity of the inductional cosmogeographical energy was a function of its planoaltimetric dimensions...

2) ...and that it was variable with the orientation as regards to determined constellations – which testifies the perfect knowledge of astrology[2], if not something else.

Searching for the meaning of this all, I assumed that the explanation might hide in the aim those mastodontic objects had been built for, which was undoubtedly the conservation of the Pharaohs' mummies. Now, the conservation of a corpse implied a struggle against the enemies of the flesh provoking its putrefaction, namely water and micro organisms (fungi). Against water they performed a biopsy that allowed withdrawing all the inner organs from the corpse; and substituting them with cotton wool drenched in perfumes. The corpse itself was wrapped up in cotton bandages drenched in sea salt. Against micro organisms, there was the energy accumulated inside the pyramid: as we have seen, it fell in a colour range close to the orange yellow; hence it was also able to keep them sedated, therefore inactive.

This justifies, for example, the mishaps of the French archaeologists who first violated the pyramids and withdrew some mummies, now exposed at the Louvre in Paris. In fact, as they entered inside the pyramids they became victims of the micro organisms; once outside, the micro organisms resumed their virulence provoking even the death of certain members of the expedition – the death later on explained as 'the Pharaoh's curse'.

An astrological consequence is that it would be helpful and interesting to analyze the levels of geocosmic energy depending on the day and the hours, taking photographs of the celestial vault using the Callegari control unit. It would be another piece of corroboration, if needed, of the physical-scientific fundaments of astrology.

I propose to develop a research on this, hoping to be able to report some positive result on the following issues of this quarterly.

In mathematics, the **Fibonacci numbers** are a sequence of numbers [...] The first number of the sequence is 0, the second number is *1* (NT: F0 =*0* and F1 =*1*), and each subsequent number is equal to the sum of the previous two numbers of the sequence itself, yielding the sequence 0, 1, 1, 2, 3, 5, 8, etc. [...] The sequence extended to negative index *n* satisfies $F_n = F_{n-1} + F_{n-2}$ for *all* integers *n*, and $F_{-n} = («1)^{n+1} F_n$ [...]

The sequence is named after *Leonardo of Pisa*, known as Fibonacci, who introduced this sequence in his 1202 book *Liber Abaci*. Fibonacci's intention was to describe a law describing the growth of a population of rabbits. It is assumed that each rabbit takes a month before it becomes fertile, and that each couple of fertile rabbits produce a couple of bunnies each month. So if we start with a single couple, after the first month we have two rabbit couples, of which only one is fertile. The following month we have 2+1=3 couples, because only the fertile couple delivered: and of the three couples, only two are fertile. Thus the following month we have 3+2=5 couples. Thus the number of rabbit couples each month describes the sequence of Fibonacci numbers. The first 41 Fibonacci numbers are:

0, 1, 1, 2, 3, 5, 8, 13, 21, 34, 55 (=F10), 89, 144, 233, 377, 610, 987, 1597, 2584, 4181, 6765 (=F20), 10946, 17711, 28657, 46368, 75025, 121393, 196418, 317811, 514229, 32040 (=F30), 1346269, 2178309, 3524578, 5702887, 9227465, 14930352, 24157817, 39088169, 63245986, 102334155 (=F40)

Fibonacci sequence is called sequence A000045 in OEIS. Fibonacci numbers possess an amazing wide range of properties; they can be found in the mathematical models of several phenomena, and they are used in many computational procedures. Moreover, they possess several interesting generalizations. A scientific magazine, *The Fibonacci Quarterly*, is specifically devoted to these subjects.

**(Partly quoted from English Wikipedia and partly retranslated from Italian Wikipedia)**

**Notes of the Author**

1) Those who ever dealt with chromotherapy know very well that if you suffer, say, from a molar toothache, wearing a red scarf would be like adding fuel to the flames. On the other hand, any garment whose colour tended to violet (i.e. the opposite direction in the spectrum of electromagnetic-waves frequencies) would certainly relieve your pain.

2) In my opinion, this is another topical passage of engineer Di Napoli's lecture: it has a great importance also considering what he and his esteemed colleagues have been telling us on these pages in the last few months. I believe that they have been disclosing cores of an extraordinary truth in the field of Knowledge: such Knowledge that is not polluted by the blind fundamentalist hatred of certain pseudo scientists who are moved by prejudice or – even worse – perhaps they're in somebody's pay... Here the author refers generically to 'constellations' while we astrologers know that it has to be referred to the transit of celestial bodies along the ecliptic. These few lines are pregnant with extraordinary importance, for they allow us to understand wonderful aspects of how the universe, the Earth, and the stars work – not to mention their mutual interactions. Anybody, let me underline *anybody*, can prove with his/her own eyes that if you build up a small pyramid with the figures suggested by engineer Di Napoli, he/she would observe, for example, the 'prodigy' of the split apple. Let us cut an apple in two halves and put one half into a pyramid made of transparent Plexiglas, made according to the ratios of the Great Pyramid of Giza. Now let us place the other half of the apple under another pyramid – built up with *wrong* measures. After a few days you'll see that the first half preserved perfectly, while the other one putrefied completely. I am perfectly convinced, at this point, that fundamentally important things have been written down in the recent issues of *Ricerca '90* – extremely important for the understanding of astrology as well, of how astrology works. Suggested by Pino Valente, by the engineer Giuseppe Callegari and others, the grounds have been established for a possible test of the frequencies of the different celestial bodies in the Callegari scale and using the Callegari Control Unit, and any possible future employment of such frequencies. The notion that one day you may deploy an aimed birthday in a laboratory is much closer to reality than to a science-fiction novel. Once again let me express my gratefulness to engineer Di Napoli for such pearls of knowledge!

**Callegari radionics and astrology – by Giuseppe Callegari**[5]
I fully agree with those, like professor Palmieri and others who held their lectures before me, who claim that ASTROLOGY has its own life and it has no need for the official consent from whomsoever. Emilio Segré, Nobel laureate in physics, the discoverer of the antiproton, in a congress titled «The Physics of the XX century» declared in public, «[…] without the bravery of men capable of thinking and reasoning in an unconventional and untraditional way, detaching from the so-called 'fundamental laws' we would not have today the radio, the television, the telephone, the airplane, the space missions… So any time that the practical experience suggested not to consider some of the 'consolidated' certainties of the Official Science, or even to consider them as questionable…» This Science even today wants to ignore, or at least it pretends it ignores, the existence of the Other Science, parallel to itself: that science that amazes and excites you; that makes you rejoice at the beauty of the Creations; that makes you dream and fancy; that elevate the spirits; that should be taught to everybody from the very first years of school. The father of radionics, Giambattista Callegari warns, «[…] The incontrovertibly established results of experience are authoritative upon the theoretical propositions… Theories in general can be considered with certain detachment, leaving to time the task of affirming them, of perfecting them or burying them according with the results of further experiences… **Theories may change, but the facts and the results of experience remain still, and cannot be ignored…**» But as you can easily guess, there's a precise will, tenaciously working against the common man, to keep tight the strings of profit, cost what it may.

What's systematically going on in the world is before everybody's eye. The most absurd wars, the most dissolute abandonment (despite the frenetic consumerism of many) of suffering populations that run the risk of disappearing. The foolish clearing of trees and the huge deforestation, having the consequence of eliminating the great present that God has given to us. The green of plants and trees not only is a pulsing tank of oxygen and chlorophyll: it is also a natural defence against the constant, unceasing bombing of neutrons from outer space.

So I ask, where have all the Mighty, the Chiefs of the Nations, those 'in the know' gone? They are actually absent, minding only of their own – political and financial – business, careful not to loose their own power, cost what it may… You'll forgive me for this digression, but I believe that it's not a bad thing to keep our eyes on these subjects, especially when you are facing other subjects, so pleasant and fascinating ones like what Astrology offers today to us, in this gorgeous day in Vico Equense. So let us stick to our subject: «**Possible hypotheses on how Astrology works**» Six thousands of years ago Fo-hi, a Chinese enlightened mind claimed, «**Man is the synthesis between the Celestial Strenghts and the Earthly Strengths.**» In particular, «[...] *the celestial bodies [...] are points of reference for the motion of the earth in the Universe. Such motion corresponds to periodical variations in the energy of the space, affecting the phenomena that weigh both upon organic and inorganic substance – therefore affecting, in particular, Man. That is to say, there are variations in the fields of strengths that affect man.*» (Translated from G. Callegari's work: «La mia opinione, fondata sulla K-analisi, intorno al contenuto del volume: Mario Pincherle, *Fonti archeologiche della magia*, Edizioni Filelpo, 1977»).

Giambattista Callegari's radionics confirmed, after six thousands years, the transcendental truth expressed by Fo-hi. The discovery of the K-effect or Radionical effect, and the «Radionical principle» (1938-1945), together with the results of a relentless, unceasing experimentation confirm that, as the consequence of the 'Cosmogeographical Conjuncture' – i.e. the simultaneousness of natural phenomena weighing on the Earth and the Universe to which the Earth belongs – particular processes of natural ionization take place in space, and such phenomena make it possible the activation of the phenomenon called '**resonance**'. *In other words, in the non-impedant (i.e. more transparent) space it becomes possible for the exchange of energy between the radio oscillating-broadcasting structures (in our case **the planets, the stars, the constellations**) and man.* Anyway, such a phenomenon concerns all living beings: besides man, the animals and the plants, as well as the inorganic substances.

*Hence the manifestation – in that sky and in that time – of phenomena and events that interfere and interact with the 'earthly day' of the human being, both at a material level and at a psychical-emotional level.*

From the results of Callegari's experimentation, man is nothing more than a particular 'naturally oscillating circuit': a sort of Callegari circuit, with an antenna to pick up the waves arriving from the space surrounding him. In this natural circuit the **coil** is made up of nervous strands departing from the spinal cord, while the **capacitor** or **condenser** is made up of the grounds scattered all over the body. The average value of the radionical frequency of the human being, based on the original Callegari scale, is fk = 5.751. This value it is not expressed in hertz, but its value in hertz can be calculated. This value is the sum of the two following frequencies fk = 3.753 (biophysical wave) and fk = 9.001 (photopsychonic wave).

There would be so much to tell about the radiations arriving from the celestial bodies: to each wavelength and frequency corresponds a different colour and musical note – by the way, the amusing configuration and the equilibrium of our solar system are governed by a musical order. For example, our Earth 'colours in blue' and it 'sounds in sol'. Giambattista Callegari determined the radionical values of the energy of the Sun, of the stars, of Galaxies and Comets (fk = 8.001); of the interstellar, interplanetary and endoatomic space (fk = 9.000); of the planets, the satellites, the asteroids, meteors and sunspots (fk = 0.001). The Sun and the Moon influence man, having him participate of the masculine nature of the former and the feminine nature of the latter. Just consider that a red blood cell performs a complete tour inside our body while the heart beats 28 times and you breathe 7 times.

This ratio between the number of heartbeats and the number of breaths you take is constant, and it is equal to the ratio between the solar cycle and the lunar cycle. This means that the rhythms of man follow the same laws of the rhythms of our Galaxy – i.e., there's a perfect analogy between macrocosm and microcosm. As if that wasn't enough, all this is complicated (and enhanced, for our amusement) by the almost 'persistent' presence of certain figures, in Nature, in the Universe and in the artistic or non-artistic artefacts created by man. For example, the divine golden figure or Fibonacci number $Æ = \mathbf{1{,}618...}$ – we find it in the disposition of the leaves of plants; in the logarithmic spirals of sunflowers; in shells; in vortexes; in the spiral-shaped galaxies; in Leonardo da Vinci's, Piero della Francesca's and Albrecht Dürer's masterpieces... Incidentally, or strangely, the radionical value of water measured by Callegari is fk = 1.600... Another repeating figure is $ð = 3.14...$ – it can be found in the structure of the Great Pyramid of Giza. Callegari found that in correspondence of the radionical number fk = 3.333 – which is also close to the double of 1.618... – the images becomes stronger, i.e. they appear in natural relief. In fact if you have a light beam pass through a Callegari radionical circuit, thus creating a radionical channel, you have variations in the Fraunhofer lines. Unfortunately there isn't time to go into these facts now. The CRC (Callegari Radiobiological Central unit) that you can see down here on this table is the prototype of the new model called CRC 75/05 Super Original New. It is produced exclusively in the Laboratory of Callegari Radionics and Radiobiology that I direct and supervise. Today I introduce it officially for the first time. Now with this model it is possible to 'pick up' a substance in general – and in particular, the human being. In other words, it is possible (also with a photo) to establish a radionical resonance with the object or the subject, and to study its/his/her energetic status of that moment: surplus, deficit, equilibrium.

Once you determine the imbalance and you discover the causes of such phase-shifts, it is then possible to restore phase, i.e. to re-balance trying to re-establish the isoenergeticism of the individual being examined. From this table of the XII Vico Congress on Astrology I announce to you the birth of **Radionical Astrology**. As regards to that I am working on a new instrument of Callegari radionics: the first central unit for Radionical Astrology called 'PC/05 ASTRAL RADIONIC CALLEGARI', an equipment unique in its genre, especially developed for astrological applications. Through a holographic technique, this unit allows the radionical verification of the typical determinations of the astrological technique. It allows ascertaining the current status of resonance or lack of resonance between the subject and the result of the astrological calculations represented by the graphics. In case of negative result – namely, the lack of resonance – it will be necessary to determine the probable data of origin, for example the complete birth data of the subject: day, month, year, time, place, environmental conditions, relevant local and/or general events, etc. Subsequently you'll be able to perform the required corrections in order to re-modulate the astrological determination. In case of negative result – namely, the presence of resonance – you will be able to determine the complementary radionical frequency ($fkc$ or $fkr$) and intervene positively with the application of the K-method (Callegari's radionical method) on the energetic status of the subject in a natural way, using subtle, non-destructive and non-invasive energies without any collateral effect and which is absolutely not damaging. In other words, it will be possible to verify whether the 'astrological remedy' recommended by the operational protocol is really necessary and applicable, or if it is not compatible with the subject considered.

This verification will be performed by reckoning, with the already mentioned PC/05 Callegari unit, the value of radionical frequency $fk$ on the recommended astrological remedy; and checking up with the very same equipment whether such a frequency is complementary or not complementary for the subject. For example, if the astrological remedy implies an environmental-geographical relocation (a change of both spatial-terrestrial and energetic-magnetic co-ordinates) you determine the radionical frequency of the place recommended [NT, for an Aimed Solar Return] with reference with a time interval close to the foreseen one, and you verify whether such a frequency is complementary, that's to say, whether it is the right one for the overall re-equilibration of the subject. If this is not the case, you have to re-examine the proposed case and find out another astrological remedy. For example, it might be solved with the direct and unique application of the complementary radionical frequency (the already mentioned *fkc*) with the aforementioned CRC 75/05. It is time now for me to conclude my lecture, for I don't wish to take time from other lecturers at this table. However, let me express my deep approval and my special gratefulness to Ciro Discepolo. With his usual elegance and passion, he has been able to describe to you all some experiences of radionics that he personally had with my father Giambattista Callegari – and he has done it with conviction and with a wealth of affectional details. I am deeply grateful to him for that.

## Astrology, prejudice and a 'gem' on Guglielmo Marconi – by Emilio Del Giudice[6]

Let me begin with William Shakespeare, a quote from Hamlet: «There are more things in heaven and earth, Horatio – Than are dreamt of in your philosophy.» It has almost nothing to do with philosophy, but listen to me for five minutes and I'll be able to tell you a tendentious story of the birth of radio at the end of the 19th century.

Around 1870 Scottish theoretical physicist James Clerk Maxwell proved that, based on the functions of electromagnetism, it is possible that the field energy propagates in space through the electromagnetic waves, the latter not being the same as the electric field and the magnetic field; as it were, they are in fact its 'travelling component'.

In other words, the comprehensive field has this travelling component as well as the component called *near field*, which propagates much less, being the field closer to the source. How did this idea get into his head? As long as everything is static, nothing propagates. But let us argue that the field source is modified by somebody close to the source.

Since this field acts at a distance, and it acts over electric charges, the natural question is, how much time after the modification of the source does the charge receiving the action 'realize' that something has been modified? Does it realize it immediately or after a while?

Let us put this in a simpler way. Guess you have a pool full of water. A ball is floating on the surface. You wish to move the ball but you are at a distance from it. So what you do is take an oar and smash the water with it to create waves on the surface. Waves reach the ball and it moves. If you hit the water properly, you'll have the ball move.

In this example you modify an infinite medium and it takes a while to get a result at a distance. Which is the vehicle in this case? It's the propagating wave.

Now, the electromagnetic wave acts more or less the same way – to make a long story short, you have a field generated down here, with a charge, and it acts over there. So you take this charge and instead of keeping it still, you move it. As a consequence, also the acting strength fluctuates. The question is: does fluctuation appear at the same time or a little later?

Well, the answer given by Maxwell theory is that it takes a little time. The speed of propagation of this wave, according to the parameters of his theory, is equal to the speed of light. This arouses the suspicion of light being a particular form of the electromagnetic field.

About thirty years later, this appeared to be a mere theoretical construction. Then Heinrich Rudolf Hertz experimentally verified Maxwell's theories. In his studies, Hertz was assisted by Augusto Righi, an Italian after whom squares, street, and schools are named here in Italy – so that we can project Hertz to be a 'validated' person. So – by using electromagnetic waves it is possible to send messages at a distance. How come it took a number of years before the electromagnetic waves found their practical applications?

Because one of the consequences of the theory confirmed by Hertz's experiment was that the electromagnetic waves propagate along a straight line with lateral fluctuations – the so-called refractive effects – as large as the wavelength.

So if you consider the antennas available at the time, if you used electromagnetic waves whose wavelength is as long as a few hundred metres to one kilometre, the refractive effects made it possible that the waves overcame a hill – but not certainly the curvature of the Earth.

Hence the notion of transmitting an electromagnetic wave from Europe to America or vice-versa was a foolish nonsense.

Luckily Guglielmo Marconi wanted to try this foolishness out. He had a very rich family background. As a rich boy, he was also arrogant. So he resolved to carry out this attempt. He was certainly clever but also ignorant. In fact, he did not study because he was rich. So he confused the 'electromagnetic' field with the 'electric' field. He thought «In the books it is said that when an electric field is close to a conductor, it arranges itself parallel to the surface of the conductor. Hence, the Earth is a conductor and the electric field must arrange itself parallel to the soil. If so, the curvature of Earth is not a problem.» So did he rightly surmise – or better said, unrightly: because as an ignorant boy, he wasn't aware that the electric field arranging itself parallel is the near field – not the electromagnetic field which has nothing to do with that. Anyway he knocked at Augusto Righi's door who was teaching in Milan by the time. And if Hertz is the father of the electromagnetic waves, certainly Righi was its uncle. So Marconi addressed Righi more or less this manner: «Professor, I've found a way to transmit a radio signal from Europe to America.» As a successful scientist, Righi was arrogant too and replied, «Oh really? And how would this thing work?» Marconi confided to him what I've just detailed.

Then Righi replied icily, «Get out of here right now, I haven't got time to waste on these things, come back after having had some education!» kicking him out.

Luckily, Marconi had no need to ask for funds from the State – which would have been refused for sure – so he asked his mother instead, who would have certainly gouged Righi's eyes out had she known of Righi's negative reaction. So his mother sponsored the enterprise and Guglielmo left for England, where he placed an antenna in Cornwall. Then, considering that his mother's money was much but not endless, he rented a plot of land – and not buy it – in Terranova, Canada; and placed another antenna there. Meanwhile the press began spreading the news of an Italian young man working on a wireless telegraph.

Journalists started polling various scientists on this subject. On the front page of *Le Monde* (the most important French daily at that time) an interview with the most important theoretical physician of France, Henry Poincaré, was published. He was a great scientist. Those whom I am mentioning were not simple people, were not ignorant; they were not

Piero Angela [NT, Italian science journalist and a member of CICAP, the Italian council of sceptical organizations]; each of them had discovered something.

So back to Henry Poincaré declaring to *Le Monde*, with all his French condescension, «Has anybody explained to this Italian guy that the Earth is a sphere? Perhaps he thinks that the Earth is flat, like the ancients did? Haven't they told him?» (A note of the Author: This resembles, somehow, the story of the bumblebee – according to scientific calculation it should be unable to fly, yet nobody told it so that it flies anyway. See Ciro Discepolo's *I fondamenti dell'astrologia medica*, Armenia)

Marconi didn't care, the day arrived and he sent the signal, and the signal arrived! How embarrassing!

Then, if we were to take 'Popper the bighead' seriously we could wonder, «Did Marconi falsify the theory on electromagnetism? On one hand the theory says that the electromagnetic waves propagate approximately along a straight line; on the other hand the Earth is round. If you put these two things together, an electromagnetic wave starting from Europe cannot arrive in America.»

If it does arrive, according to Karl Popper one of the two statements has been falsified.

Which of the two assertions is correct? «Is it not true that the electromagnetic waves propagate on a straight line?» or «Is it not true that the Earth is round?»

It is absolutely true that the electromagnetic waves propagate in a straight line; and it is also true that the Earth is round (it is also proven by photographs now) – so what is the explanation?

The explanation is always the same: there's something unknown at the time of the events, something deceiving people – in our case, it's the ionosphere. At the time of the events neither Righi nor Marconi knew that there is an ionosphere – a layer of the atmosphere surrounding our planet at several scores of kilometres from its surface. The ionosphere is made up of gases that are ionized by radiation from outer space: the result is a layer of ionized molecules.

That layer behaves like a mirror with regard to those electromagnetic waves whose wavelength, let us put it this way, corresponds to the density of that plasma.

Therefore, with frequencies lower than the so-called plasma frequency of a gas, the ionosphere behaves like a mirror. That is to say that that layer of gas is opaque to radiations. So, luckily – fortune favours the brave – the frequencies that Marconi employed fell into the right range. Hence the wave of Marconi started from Terranova; proceeding on a straight line, it went up and up; it met the mirror; it was reflected down to Earth; and it eventually reached Europe.

So you can see that Righi's theory was absolutely right; Poincaré's statements were indisputable; yet Marconi was right despite them all.

Why?

Because of the intervention of a different circumstance, unknown to his contemporaries, that conspired to make things work as they did.

In fact there's a saying: If an old professor says that something is not possible he's almost certainly wrong, but if he says that it is possible he's almost certainly right.

That is, if you say that something isn't possible it is the greatest piece of nonsense that one can say, because there is always a way to overcome the obstacle.

I do not mean to say that the hypothesis that I'm offering to you is the right one; perhaps it isn't so, but in any case this makes you realize that it is not impossible to think of mechanisms that explain... Now that I think about it again, what is certainly impossible is to say, «it is not possible...».

Just to say that ignorance does not always help: the first time things went well for Marconi, but the second time they went wrong, definitely wrong. It was the case of the radar, whose idea first occurred to Marconi. In fact, during a conference held at the headquarters staff of the Italian Navy in 1922, he proposed to place an antenna on a ship to 'shoot' an electromagnetic wave which would glance off another ship, if it came across one, thus coming back and revealing the alien ship's presence. It is the same principle on which a modern the radar works.

But as we have seen, Marconi could not differentiate between an electrical field and an electromagnetic field. He lacked the knowledge about wavelengths.

He had a liking for long waves, so he projected a radar tool (or had it projected) based on a radio wave whose length was some hundreds of metres. It is therefore not true that the Italian Navy did not possess a radar instrument during the War – in fact the Navy had radar, and we called it 'gufo' (owl). But the Italian 'owl' was useless because the electromagnetic wave that it employed had a wavelength of some hundred of metres, while the ships were much shorter than that! As a consequence, the refractive effect, i.e. the lateral deviation, invested the whole ship and the result was that you could see nothing. The resolution of a radar instrument, that's to say, the length of the smallest object visible, is given by the wavelength employed.

Thus, the ships being shorter than the employed wavelength, the Italian Navy's 'owl' was a fiasco.

Two such equipment were mounted, one on the battleship *Littorio* and one on the destroyer *Lince*, but a few months later they got dismounted because they detected nothing.

The Englishmen used electromagnetic waves with a 10-centimetre length for their radar and they could see not only ships but also airplanes.

Although the very idea of radar first occurred to Marconi, thanks to the fact that he hadn't a clear notion of the undulatory theories, the equipment created by him proved to be ineffectual.

Coming back to Astrology and to many other related phenomena – I would say that usually a series of factors that would make the phenomenon plausible are not considered and worse: they are neglected. In fact during the last years we have seen the flowering of many impossible things: cold fusion is one of them, i.e. the posibility of conducting nuclear reactions at room temperature, and without huge machines. We also learn – and it is true – that the armies of a certain countries employ strange weapons, called depleted uranium weapons even though depleted uranium has nothing to do with them – it is only a sort of smokescreen operation. These weapons produce a flow of neutrons, a flood of nuclear reactions – let us put it this way – in an unconventional way. This is what the armies of the major countries do, such as the United States, leading me to suspect (among other things) that the hostility manifested by the Establishment against new discoveries is actually the wish – inspired by the armed forces – of avoiding a particular concentration of the public attention on them, so that somebody may exercise a monopoly on them.

You are right: I haven't talked about Astrology. But I did talk to you about conditioning and prejudice, about the reasons why scientists or the scientific community are not always worth being listened to. Sometimes, in fact, they rather deserve to be ignored or disbelieved.

**The miraculously healing water – by Nicola Del Giudice**[7]

Let me digress a little bit from the subjects dwelt upon so far. As a homeopath doctor, I happen to face paradoxical aspects, such as the miraculous healing water, the absence of molecules as a *condicio sine qua non* of a therapeutic phenomenon that science cannot simply explain – therefore I mainly refer to the actions and the events happening within my field of expertise.

Certainly, science has been meeting many strange phenomena: once they belonged to magicians and charlatans, now they are the fundament of science.

One of the interesting phenomena is cold fusion […]. I know Ciro since we were kids, so several times we have discussed about things that are going on; certainly one of the most important features of any researcher should be – being curious. Curiosity means not to deny *a priori* any phenomenon, and not to look for a scientific explanation at any rate. I've seen many scientific theories falling before an empirical event, but I've never seen an empirical event falling because of a theory.

Let's accept empirical events then without the need of denying them later on, or as you can see some times, without the need of a self-objection, as it were, just because we do not want to devaluate the physical theory.

This is precisely what happened to me some time ago. One of my female patients with a disease, she was discovered to have a serious disease: multiple sclerosis. As it happens quite frequently, her condition developed a month after a pregnancy. It affected the lower parts of her body, and she was desperate. She was a good acquaintance of mine; she told me that the diagnosis had been made in a famous medical centre in Milan. Of course, she was very fond of homeopathic medicine, and she also had an undeserved faith in me; she asked what we could do, considering that traditional science could do nothing.

Then we treated her with specific magnetic fields for six months. At the end of this treatment she went back to that medical centre in Milan: after a session of nuclear magnetic resonance she was told that her scars had totally disappeared, and she had recovered movement and sensitivity.

Perhaps this case is peculiar compared to other ones, because it just happened a little time ago. But the thing was striking. In fact I remember that at the first session of electromagnetic field therapy I tried testing her sensitivity by piercing a needle on her foot, and she had no reaction at all.

After some treatment I repeated the test and the lady immediately reacted to the stimulus, showing that she had recovered sensitivity.

When my patient went back to that diagnostical centre in Milan, the person who had previously diagnosed her disease (he was a good friend of hers, too) could not deny the facts. Yet, in an attempt to stick to the traditional theory and medicine, he claimed he had made a wrong diagnosis initially: she had never really suffered from multiple sclerosis.

In other words, he preferred to make a fool of himself rather than admitting that a homeopathic treatment could have really given any benefit to the lady.

I might enumerate several cases like this. There are also cases of mutual irradiation with our neighbours, people we meet, and such exchange may also have a therapeutic function. It may be the case of a guru or Jesus Christ healing the cripple or it may be somebody healing a headache with the imposition of his or her hand, or whatever. We irradiate in any case, and we can have a practical demonstration of this too.

As an example, let us take a Kirlian camera and take a picture of a patient and of his/her therapist. You'll see that the photographs of their aura are different if you take them before and after treatment. Paradoxically the therapist's aura after treatment tends to assume the patient's characters – as if the negative influence of the patient affected the therapist, as if there was a resonance.

And this is another amazing fact that would need to be analyzed.

For sure, official science denies itself the possibility of facing such themes, although – let us put it bluntly – when the problems touch their personal spheres they don't hesitate to ask even for the homeopaths' help secretly crowding their clinics – like a famous pharmacologist from Naples who used to pontificate against homeopathy in his classes.

One day a student went to a homeopath doctor; where he noticed – guess who? – his professor of pharmacology and asked him, «Professor! How come you are here now, if you keep on denigrating homeopathy?» The professor looked into the student's eye and answered, «My son, bread is bread but skin is skin!»

Another case happened during a confrontation between the adherents of allopathic medicine and homeopathic medicine, the former represented among others, by professor Garattini. First the allopaths spoke. I don't wish to repeat everything that was said against us the homeopaths – that we are swindlers, magicians, charlatans and you name it. [...] In particular, Garattini spoke ironically on the lack of understanding about how molecules recognize each other within a living organism. Although it has been ascertained that molecules move to find an appropriate equal to react with, the manner in which they accomplish this is still unknown.

How can molecules recognize each other among millions of molecules within an organism? How do they know which one of them is their 'soulmate', their second self with which they can mutually entangle giving an oncological effect? They don't explain it.

Of course we too would not have an answer to this question. So I said, «You see Professor, if you give me an explanation on how molecules move, I swear I'll stroll in the very centre of Naples with a poster saying, 'Homeopathy is nonsense, and I am a fool'.»

He answered, «Are you bull****ting me or what?» and I said, «No, I am not».

Said I, «On the contrary, let us suppose, that you take a plane and fly to the United States to take part in a congress. There you browse a newspaper and you see a short article saying that 'a certain professor…' has died in a car accident: at that point your hand goes to your breast and you fall down to the ground due to a heart attack. Then Professor Garattini, can you explain to me which one was the molecule that hit your eyes from the paper? The molecule that through your eyes arrived to the midollary zone of the suprarenal gland, that activated the production of adrenaline there, the adrenaline entered into circulation, it caused the vasorestriction and you had a heart attack? Could you explain this to me, doctor Garattini?» […]

Of course I had no answer from Professor Garattini. But I can attempt one and give it to you now. Here is an evident example of it. There are two people suffering from the same pathology, they go to two different homeopath doctors. Both doctors know homeopathic medicine perfectly, both prescribe the treatment correctly – the same treatment for both patients – but one patient recovers while the other does not.

Could you explain to me why one patient recovers while the other doesn't? It is because homeopathy recognises an effect – the therapist-medicine effect. Even the therapist is a medicine, and a powerful one! So the very same drug does not have an affect if provided by one doctor, but it does if provided by another. The reason is that a resonant irradiation exchange has been activated, and this exchange is the first source of healing. The same happened, for example, with a patient of mine suffering from asthma: he arrived in the surgery breathing in a horrible way; he took a seat in the waiting room and started chatting with the others.

When the time arrived to see him, he simply told me that the crisis was over.

That is, the very fact of discovering inside the clinic the possibility of opening himself to others and exchanging information – therefore important feelings, sensations and emotions – had made it possible for him to relax his body without any need of taking cortisone or other drugs.

So what we are learning – in conclusion – and we are trying to enhance by means of homeopathy are those apparently strange aspects that this science proposes. We find similar underlying notions in astrology, in acupuncture and other such disciplines. Interestingly these concepts not only provide an acceptable basis for the subjects but they are also able to explain the great discoveries of the official science. In other words, perhaps it hasn't been possible to demonstrate, for example, how molecules meet – but it's a matter of fact that the molecules do meet.

If we are able to advance this thought process further it would be a big step forward for science and diseases would no longer need the types of drugs we are using nowadays.

Thank you all (AN, audience applauses).

## A scientist's thought on Astrology – by Renato Palmieri

Sirius rising, a leaf moves on my balcony. Of course it does not move only because of the influence of Sirius, but for the infinite magneto-gravitational components coeval to the rising of Sirius. They change every moment in a non identifiable way, therefore the leaf palpitates at every puff of wind and it rustles together with all the other leaves.

Although it is true that it is impossible to sever all the innumerable influences of the astronomical firmament, yet many of them possess a cyclic nature as regards to the position of the Earth in the solar system and the 'other stars' – as Dante Alighieri used to call them – and their cyclicity may determine sensitive, periodical variations of those influences in quantity and mode, thus contributing to imprinting those who were born under the light of the birthday with different characters.

This is what a man like me can recognize in Astrology: one who is not a scientist, but one who knows – from history – that this is a branch of learning whose students were thinkers and scientists. Moreover, I do not exclude *a priori* a symbolic and supersensitive value of the astral references on the human experience. *Homo sum: humani nihil a me alienum puto*, as Terence said..

Anyway, it is a matter of fact that – as it has been proven very well somewhere else – that as far as knowledge is concerned, academic 'science' is as qualified as the roughest of the astrologers. This is particularly true for those subjects, such as gravitation and electromagnetism, whose essential nature science completely ignores, yet using these subjects for its arrogant refutation of the loathed astrological 'heresy'.

## A few notes of remark – by Ciro Discepolo

Instances of two interventions from unbiased and open mided scientists whose research into normal phenomena is branded to be paranormal only because they are not accepted by the Establishment.

We thank professors Vincenzo Di Napoli and Renato Palmieri very much for the elucidation of knowledge and wisdom they bestow upon us each time they accept to collaborate with our quarterly magazine.

It is my opinion that in the past year we have hosted extraordinarily interesting articles by them, as well as other articles having similar content. I am referring to several articles and brief essays of scientist who made us reflect on certain contentious subjects which I would like to mention in a concise list:

- Engineer and professor Di Napoli, together with engineer Callegari and other students of Giambattista Callegari's method have taught us – among other facts – that when two bodies in the space are in resonance (i.e. their energies are in resonance), impedance (in the 'transmission between the two energies') is equal to zero. This means that distance hasn't value any longer. The consequences of this fact are enormous, for it explains, among other things, how is it that Pluto may have the same astrological value as the Moon or Mars.

- Professor Palmieri has made us notice that modern physics does not take into consideration the question of polarity of the gravitational field of the Earth and of other planets. Moreover, in his *Unigravitational Physics*, professor Palmieri unifies the nature of the electromagnetic and gravitational waves, with the insertion of fundamental distinctions where most other physicists are in a confusion claiming, for example, that Pluto cannot have an influence on human beings because its gravitational strength is virtually zero.

- Scientists and researchers Emilio Del Giudice and Nicola Del Giudice has made it clear – with several very clear details – the notion of the memory of water, and the fact that a newborn baby, before developing a magnetic filed of its own, takes the magnetic field that is 'gravitating around it' at the moment of its birth. That's to say, the water molecules are oriented by the magnetic field and they preserve 'forevermore' such orientation – and this may help us very much explain how astrology works.

Yet in these pages our friends have written this and much more. Do not forget it, for in my opinion, *Ricerca '90* made it possible to seal up an important chapter of history in the huge book of philosophy of science.

**cd** (Forgive me for my excessive vulgarization; perhaps it was necessary for a non-insider audience.)

As you can easily understand, we are really facing a topical milestone in the heuristic path in general and in particular in the study of astrology. The three notions that I have just recollected for your attention may be the fundaments for a universal theory that we might call the **Callegari-Palmieri-Del Giudice's theory**. This theory may be sufficient to explain a possible way of the functioning of astrology from a purely physical point of view, without mentioning either Jung's synchronicity or the so-called paranormal phenomena that amuse the minds (?) of the member of CICAP (TN, the Italian CSICOP).

The points that have been discussed so far are constitute just the tip of the proverbial iceberg. I believe that compared to the day prior to this *XII Congress of Astrological Studies* in Vico Equense, a new and extremely important *Weltanschauung* has been established before the world and particularly for open-minded people.

It will be necessary to come back again and again several times in the future, to study and to have a debate in this field. For the time being, considering the subject of this book, we can consider this question closed in order to say something even more specific about Solar and Lunar Returns.

Approximately fifty years ago the scientific study of biorhythms started to spread among medical doctors.[8]

In fact, even after the end of WWII, medical doctors went on giving medicines to patients without giving any particular importance to the moment of the day in which it was administered[9] that resulted in wasteful consumptions like concentrates of vitamins and dietary minerals at night just before going to sleep; or melatonin in the morning.

When doctors got aware of the importance of biorhythms, they could avoid most of such mistakes.

Today we are aware that there are different biorhythms, among which the following three are the most important:[10]

1) A circadian rhythm lasting, as its Latin etymology says, approximately one day. Obviously this corresponds with the time that the Earth takes to rotate once around its own axis. We have innumerable evidence of such biorhythm associated with the life of human beings, animals, and plants. For example, it can be easily proven that there is a precise reproducibility of the peaks in the curve of certain biological functions of the human being as observed during the day: such as the frequency of the daily peaks of urination, of arterial pressure, of the index of blood flocculation, and so on. For example, we know that our body produces melatonin constantly, but there's a peak of 'overproduction' about half an hour after sunset. This is why – among other things – melatonin induces an antidepressant action, which is extremely important when the sun lights up our day no more; and melatonin also induces sleep. Hence you can understand why it was a mistake on the part of certain doctors to give artificial melatonin early in the morning. Let me mention at this point poor professor Luigi Di Bella, the physiologist who developed the so-called Di Bella therapy, an unorthodox cancer treatment which caused collective discussions during 1997 and 1998 in Italy. He was literally 'slaughtered' by the Medical establishment because his therapy went against the interests of pharmaceutical companies. In fact Professor Di Bella, together with other alternative scientist, believed that it was extremely useful to give patients – as well as healthy people – 'industrial' quantities of melatonin and vitamin C. (It's for similar sentences that I have to go to the stake. See the shameful episode of the Italian Wikipedia at this website: http://www.cirodiscepolo.it/wikipedia.htm. Don't be surprised then, if one day some supporter of CICAP or of the *Italian Wikipedia* would manage to have cocaine found on my writing-table in order to get rid of such an uncomfortable and unpleasant person like me.)

2) A monthly rhythm of about 29 days clearly connected with the complete passage of the Moon around the Earth. We have incontrovertible evidence of this too, despite the opposite opinion of 'scientists': even children can see them, such as tides, or the menstrual cycle.

3) A yearly rhythm linked with the complete orbit of the Earth around

the Sun. Examples of this are the animals hibernating always during the same period of the year; others migrating or being moved by sexual desire always in a precise period of the year. Trees bear fruits always in the same time of the year, and so on.

Now consider the sine wave below and pay attention to point **A**. This sine wave can represent the development of any biorhythm. Let us consider two of them in particular: the wave could draw the development of the lunar biorhythm and of the solar biorhythm. Let us start with the solar one. In the very moment of our birth, with our first breath, our first yearly biorhythm starts: it begins at the point **A** and it ends at the point **A**.

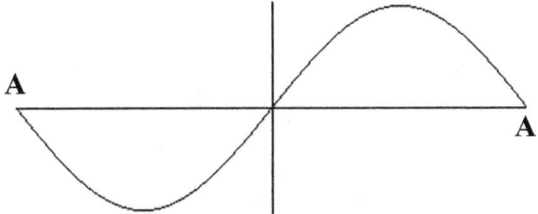

So we should not be surprised if somebody (i.e. me the Author) claims that in the moment of the yearly solar return, exactly at the point **A**, the imprinting that we receive from the sky is not the same as that of the rest of the days of the year. In fact it is very special, not because of analogies, but because the moment A is a sort of 'reset' or zeroing of a whole yearly cycle to start with another yearly cycle. In my opinion this widely justifies the importance of each of us being under that particular sky of the world in that moment and not in any other moment – according to criteria whose real literature (I mean the literature originated by practice, not by theory) suggests that thus our year might be qualitatively enhanced – but also spoiled if we are not careful.It seems quite obvious to me that the same may be said about the sine wave of the monthly cycle, where point **A** corresponds to the return of the Moon to the precise point it was in at the moment of birth with regard to the native in focus.

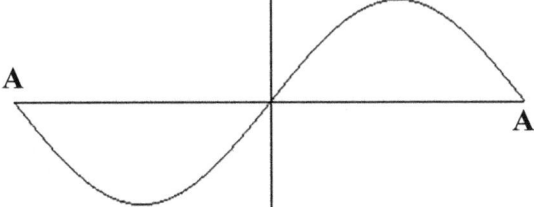

I believe that such an explanation is plausible. Nevertheless it is left to the students, pupils, colleagues and denigrators to use or not to use such wonderful tools of quality enhancement to one's life: namely, the Aimed Solar Returns and the Aimed Lunar Returns.

**Note**

1) Carl Gustav Jung, *La Sincronicità [Synchronicity]*, Editore Boringhieri S.p.A., Torino, 1980, 124 pages.

2) Gret Baumann-Jung, *Alcune riflessioni sull'oroscopo di Carl Gustav Jung [Some considerations on Carl Gustav Jung's horoscope]*, Ricerca '90 #5 of January 1991, translated into Italian by Enzo Barillà

3) Renato Palmieri is an excellent physicist from Naples. I had suggested to the Italian Institution of Philosophical Studies [Istituto Italiano per gli Studi Filosofici] – a wonderful institution of Knowledge conceived, founded, and directed by Gerardo Marotta – to publish Professor Palmieri's precious volume: otherwise it would have never seen the light of day. There was no special need in urging them to it, because when I talked to the secretary general of the institution Professor Antonio Gargano and my friend Professor Aldo Tonini, they immediately accepted my request, and this way they added another gem to their already huge list of Cultural works. Thus, at last his book *La fisica unigravitazionale e l'equazione cosmologica [Unigravitational Physics and the Cosmologic Equation]* is a reality now, and certainly one of the things I am most proud of.

4) Engineer Vincenzo Di Napoli died in Novembre 2007. He was a great researcher; his life crossed mine several times. He used to be my teacher of electronics in the school «Augusto Righi» of Naples. He was a simple man, who used to reach the core of any subject; everybody used to understand his lessons immediately. Later on, we met again when he was the president of the Association of Ham Radios of Naples. I was trying to get a CB licence then, but I did not succeed because by those times they required a quite difficult exam on radiotelegraphy, and my lack of 'an ear for music' for such things, was a hindrance in distinguishing 'dots' and 'dashes' of the Morse code. We met yet again when he was the president of the Centre of Studies «Callegari» concerning Callegari Radiobiology. I have written of this latter event in a brief note in my book on the interpretation of the natal map *L'interpretazione del tema natale*, Armenia editore, Milano, 2007, 350 pages, in pages # 87-90. And to conclude, I would like to add – it doesn't seem a mere coincidence – that Professor Di Napoli had always lived not farther off than fifty metres from my place. I remember him with gratefulness and affection.

5) Engineer Giuseppe Callegari is the son of Giovanbattista Callegari. I have written briefly about the latter in my book *L'interpretazione del tema natale*, in pages # 87-90. I am very glad to see that Engineer Callegari is trying to further develop his father's great discoveries.

6) Emilio Del Giudice is professor of Physics at the *Istituto Superiore di Fisica* in Milan, Italy. Together with his brother, homeopathic medical doctor Nicola Del Giudice, he has written books of great scientific interest. They also tried (in my opinion, with great efficiency) to develop the question of the memory of water – a subject of extraordinary interest that may help in understanding the mechanisms of the influence of the sky over the life of terrestrial creatures.

7) Apply to him the same considerations about his activity together with his brother. Nicola Del Giudice is a well known and appreciated homeopathic doctor, endocrinologist and researcher in a broad sense. He wrote together with his brother the book *Omeopatia e bioenergetica. Le medicine alternative: dalla stregoneria alla scienza [Homeopathy and bioenergetics. The alternative medicines: from sorcery to science]*, Cortina editore, Verona, 1999, 302 pages; and also the volume *Omeopatia. Un ponte tra biologia e psicologia. Vent'anni di ricerca della Fondazione omeopatica italiana [Homeopathy: a bridge between biology and psychology. Twenty years of research of the Italian Homeopathic Foundation]*, edizioni Nuova IPSA, Palermo, 1998, 334 pages.
8) Lyall Watson, *SuperNatura [SuperNature]*, Rizzoli editore, Milano, 1974.
9) *Ibidem*.
10) Ibidem

Left to right: Nicola Del Giudice, Renato Palmieri, Emilio Del Giudice, Ciro Discepolo, Andrea Rossetti, Massimo Troise, Giuseppe Callegari

Callegari Radiobiological Central unit and Vincenzo Di Napoli

# 4.
# Lunar Returns

Lunar Returns have a fairly high value in predictive astrology, provided that you are able to read them correctly. In particular, they help date the events in a highly precise way.

I am often surprised because some readers ask me why I haven't written much about them so far.

Well, I do believe that no other author on Earth has written even a portion of what I have published on this subject.

For those who do not really remember, let me summarize my most important contributions in this field:

- Some articles in the magazine *Gli Arcani*, ed. Armenia, Milan, at the beginning of the '70s.
- *Guida all'astrologia*, 1979, Armenia, Milan
- *Guida ai transiti*, 1984, Armenia, Milan
- Several articles in the magazines *Astra* and *Sirio*, Milan, between 1977 and the early '80s.
- *Trattato pratico di Rivoluzioni solari*, 1993, Blue Diamond Publisher, Milan
- *Transiti e Rivoluzioni Solari*, 1997, Armenia, Milan. As it is explained in several passages of this volume, those sections may be used also for the interpretation of the Lunar Returns.
- Several articles on the quarterly *Ricerca '90*, ed. Ricerca '90, Naples, from 1990 onwards.
- *Nuovo Dizionario di Astrologia*, 1996, Armenia, Milan
- *Nuovo Trattato delle Rivoluzioni Solari,* 2003, Armenia, Milan
- *Nuovo Trattato di Astrologia,* 2004, Armenia, Milan. This is a volume of almost 800 pages: of them, approximately 500 pages are devoted to the dating of events. Within that section of the volume, there are several examples of Lunar Returns and how to read them.

- *L'interpretazione del tema natale*, 2007, Armenia, Milan
...and many more.

Everybody knows my opinion on the usage of LRs, yet it may be good to repeat it in short. I believe that LRs should mainly help us dating the events within the frame of the 12 months covered by a Solar Return. While SRs may be aimed, I find it much less useful aiming LRs if you have already aimed your SR. In fact, no matter how much daunting or alluring may be the Lunar Returns within the year, they could never overcome the limits imposed by their ruling Solar Return.

In other words, if you protect yourself with a good Aimed Solar Return, within the frame of the following twelve months even two or more apparently frightful Lunar Returns wouldn't be able to produce devastating effects, if there is no trace of them in the Solar Return. The same can be said on the other side as well: if a SR announces a detrimental year you wouldn't be able to overcome the predicted events of the SR even if you aimed every single Lunar Return of the following twelve months.

If anything, we could talk of 'modulation' – a slightly positive and/or negative effect which might be algebraically added to the effect of the relevant Solar Return.

So, in what circumstances is it convenient to relocate, or better said, to aim a LR?

Certainly it is not expedient to do so to counter the misjudgement of not having aimed your Solar Return: for you could face such a negative experience in the next twelve months, that the conviction would grow strong in your mind to relocate for every single aimed birthday in the following years from then on.

Nonetheless we could plan a sort of partial repentance. This would be the case, say, of a subject who had the chance to select among a range of possible locations for an ASR, and opted for the cheapest one and/or the closest one. Such a subject might wish to mend this decision by aiming the Lunar Returns of the most difficult months. Be clear that even so, this is not a completely logical thing to do, but one can try.

There is a third possibility: a good example of which is one of my only two aimed LRs in my life (up to summer 2007).

Please consider the following charts: one is my birth chart and the other one is my ASR of 2006 in Petropavlovsk, Kamtchatka. I must say that it was a really important and positive ASR for me.

On the 11th of February 2007 in Naples I would have faced the LR that you can see in these pages.

In that case, with a really negligible displacement, I could have enhanced that LR with two really positive results:

- keeping Saturn out of the 10th House, and
- considering that my birth time – 5:40 am – is almost certain, I could have placed Venus on the very cusp between the 5th and the 6th House.

I could have made all this by simply taking a flight to Genoa; I would have remained far from home for a few hours only, with not even the need of going out of the airport. In fact, there was a flight Naples to Genoa scheduled for the late afternoon on that day. Once there, I could have waited a couple of hours at the airport and then flown back home, spending less than 200 Euros.

If I remember well, the flight was scheduled to take off at 9:30 pm while I would have had my Lunar Return at 21:59 pm. Now a consideration must be made for the fact that I have been flying more than a civilian pilot, and know that it's quite a rare event having a flight taking off less than half an hour after the scheduled time.

In order to avoid any intervention of the devil, who's always waiting in ambush in these instances, I resolved to fly Naples to Turin, and to take the return flight Turin to Naples at 9:30 pm. This way, thought I, my flight would almost certainly take off later; and if it took off on time, roughly reckoning I would have been flying over Genoa at the moment of my Lunar Return. But you know, the devil is always on duty 24/7 – and my flight took off from Turin at 9:30 pm sharp!

I was disappointed to see that the flight commander, who perhaps had a gallant meeting in Naples, resolved to speed up the aircraft southward at an incredible pace. Thus I noticed with great dissatisfaction that in twelve minutes of flight we had already overpassed the gulf of Genoa.

Quite upset, I asked the flight assistant to request the commander to let me know the geographical coordinates of the place that we would overfly at 9:59 pm. Needless to say, the hostess stared at me with a strange light in her eyes; yet she complied and asked the commander. The commander denied giving me such a precious piece of information, probably fearing that I was a terrorist aiming to have the aircraft struck by a surface-to-air missile exactly at 9:59 pm.

I understood that I would never receive any assistance in this. So I opened my notebook and zoomed on a map of the area over which we were flying. I thought that the lights of the isle of Elba and of the town of Piombino would help me locate the exact place of my Lunar Return at 9:59 pm. I was right: at that time we would fly – roughly – somewhere between Piombino and Elba. Hence I realized, as you can see for yourselves, that the operation had been a partial success. Saturn had remained on the cusp between the 10th and the 11th House, while Venus had hit the centre, namely the cusp between the 5th and the 6th House.

It was a calculated risk: had I wanted my ALR in Genoa explicitly, I could have spent a night there and take the return flight the next day. But I took the exercise rather as an experiment than a serious attempt at aimed relocation. Saturn in the 10th House did not produce serious damage, while I derived some benefit from the position of Venus.

I think that this is a correct usage of an Aimed Lunar Return, with all the considerations already expressed in this chapter.

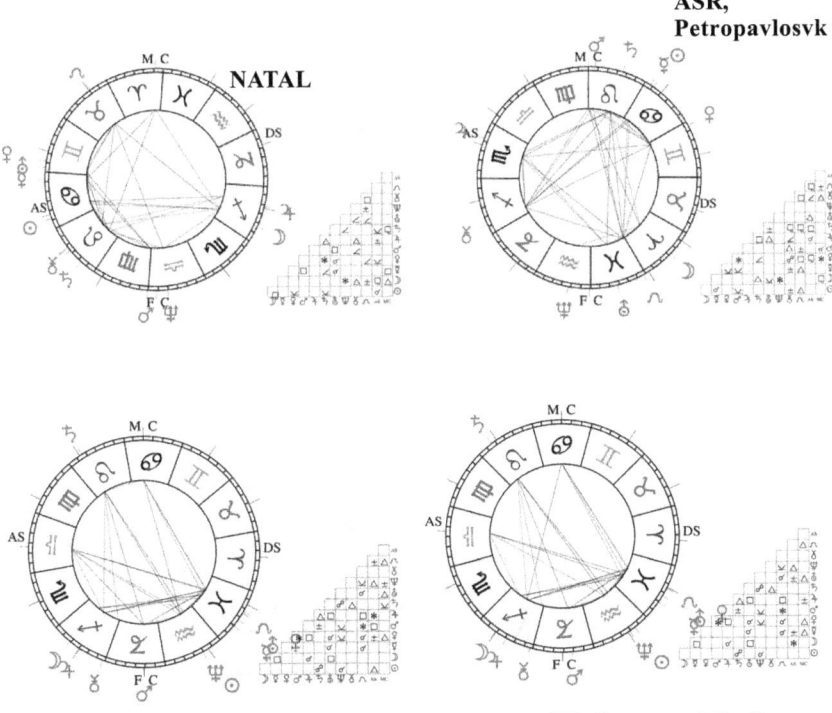

RL Napoli = LR, Naples          RL Genova = LR, Genoa

**RL Piombino = RL, Piombino**

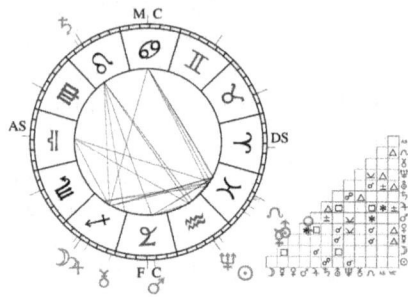

Now let us consider a more extensive example concerning the subject we are discussing. We'll make use of random data, but they could be real as well. Say that the subject to whom these data refer left in March 2007 for an aimed birthday and that the ASR is bringing good results. The subject wishes to further enhance the benefits of his relocation of March, and in August 2007 he asks me to help him aim his future Lunar Returns. In my opinion, this course of action may be excessively expensive and time-consuming and I would suggest it only for those special events in which the subject has got plenty of time and money, or if he/she is in the absolute need of conceiving really special goals during a certain year. I am writing down a report on this hypothetical subject with short remarks of the subject's base sky and his LRs, month after month. In each of the following pages you'll see, on the left: his birth chart, and on the right: his sky of BLR (Base

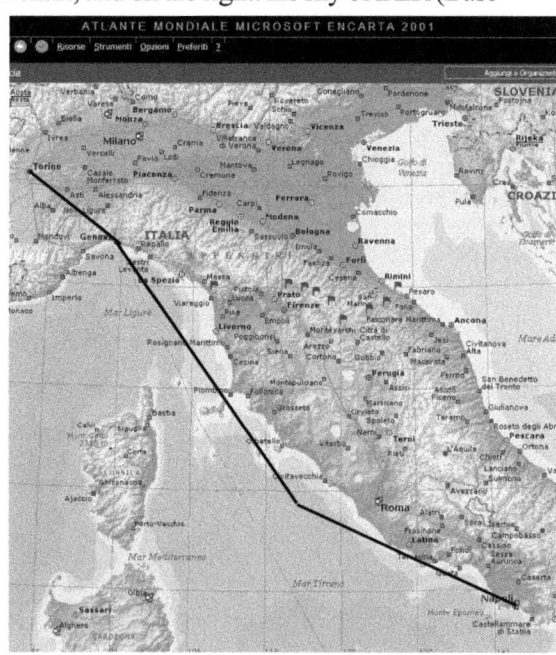

Lunar Return). Below them you'll see his natal chart once again, and on its right: the sky of the ALR that I suggested to him. In the first case I asked him to relocate to Oslo, thus avoiding two positions detrimental for his health and for any sort of trouble in general. Moreover, I have also placed a gorgeous Venus on the cusp between the 1st and the 2nd House. All this could be attained spending that LR in Oslo, Europe.

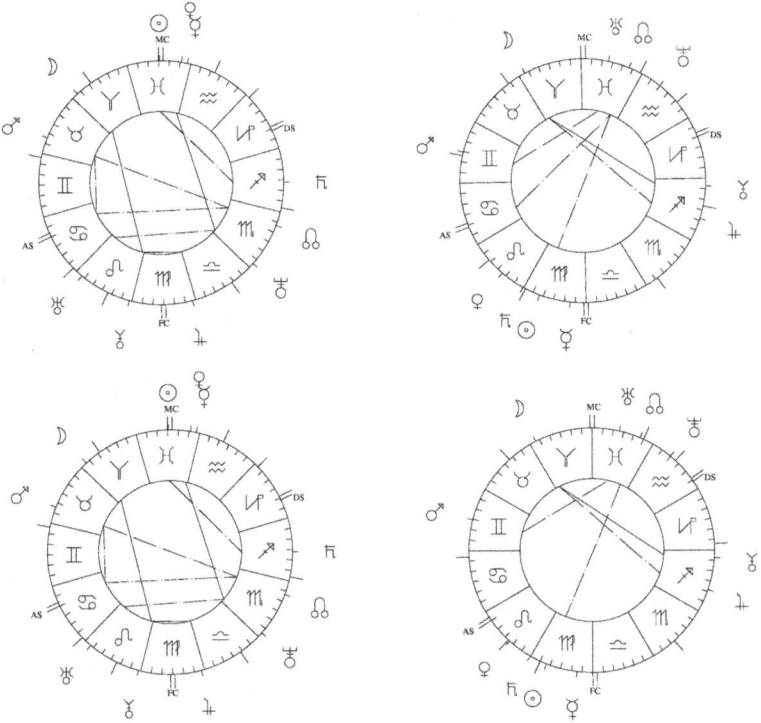

Below you can see the subject's ALR for October 2007: in Karachi not only do we avoid a Mars sticking to the Ascendant of the LR – we can also get two wonderful cusps, namely Venus on the delimiter 1st / 2nd House, and Jupiter on the 4th / 5th House! For the scope of this exercise it is not important to consider the ASR of that year: we have already explained that compared to the LRs, the SR is absolutely overriding as far as the events of the year are concerned. Possible supporting ALRs would only perform the task of not hindering the ASR and of enhancing the effects of the ASR. Any other consideration or speculation follows well behind, as it is something absolutely ancillary in the scope of this volume. Please note that in this case I also suggested to the subject to aim the LR with a modest level of travel. The effort to reach Karachi (which is the largest city of Pakistan, but not its capital) is minimal – compared with a travel to North Canada or to Alaska or to Micronesia or Polynesia.

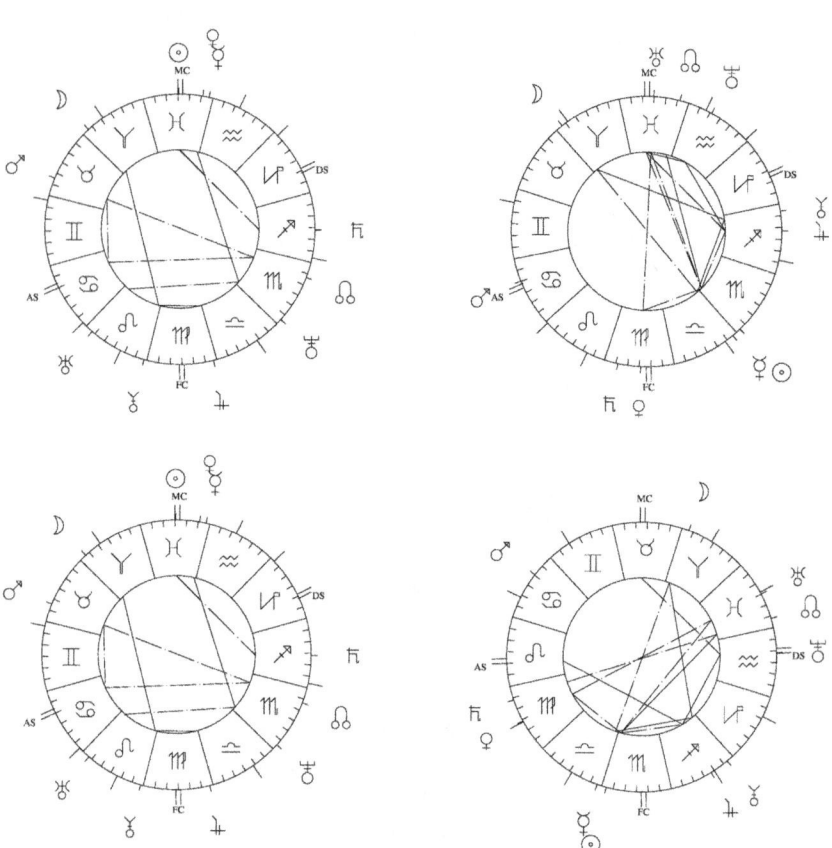

ALR of November. The Base LR would have the Sun in the 12th House, the Ascendant in the natal 6th House, and a stellium spanned over the 12th and the 1st House. The SR aimed in Mauritius (similar to the previous one, in Karachi) completely shuffles the celestials. All the detrimental or even dangerous positions of the BSR are gone with the wind. The Sun moves to the 10th House, we have a splendid cuspidal position of Jupiter between the 10th and the 11th House and – the cherry on the cake: Venus in the 8th House, certainly announcing incoming money.

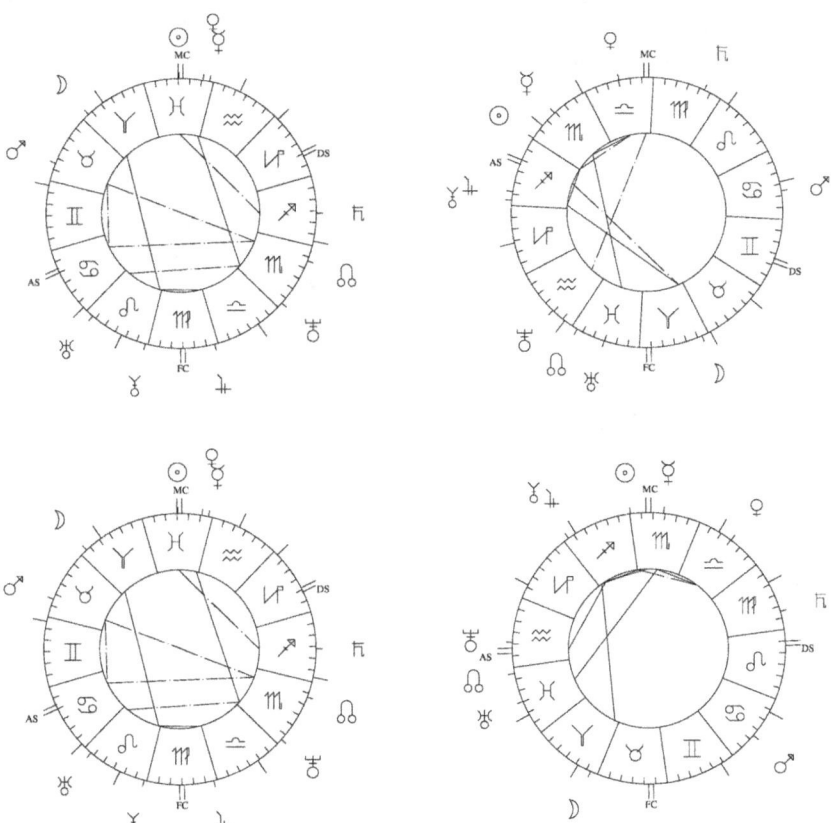

ALR of December. Mars is once again very close to the Ascendant, and there is a strong stellium with the Sun in the 6th House. Yet, since his ASR is good, nothing would happen to the subject even if he didn't relocate. I had a Mars in the 6th House of a LR myself recently. But I had protected my year with a good ASR, so the only problem I experienced during that month was three-four days of colic on account of bad food.

Nonetheless, for the same reasons already expressed – and I hope, almost definitely clear – I suggested the subject an ALR in Caracas in order to place that magnificent 'lining up' exactly over the Medium Coeli, besides Venus in the 8th House. Also in this case, travel was not particularly expensive or demanding.

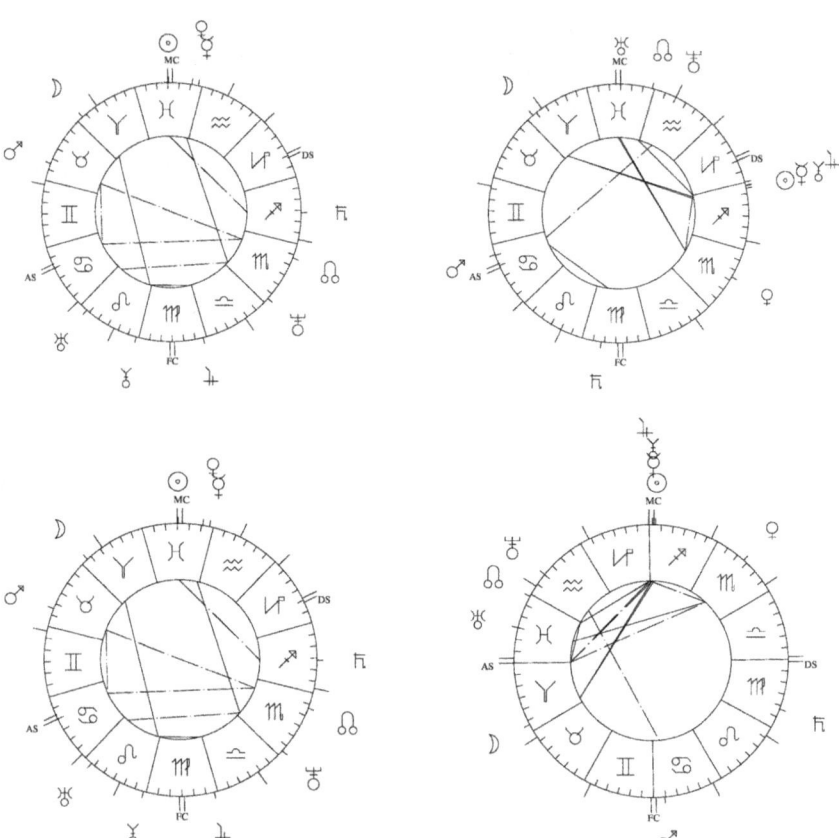

BLR of January 2008: no reason at all to have it changed.

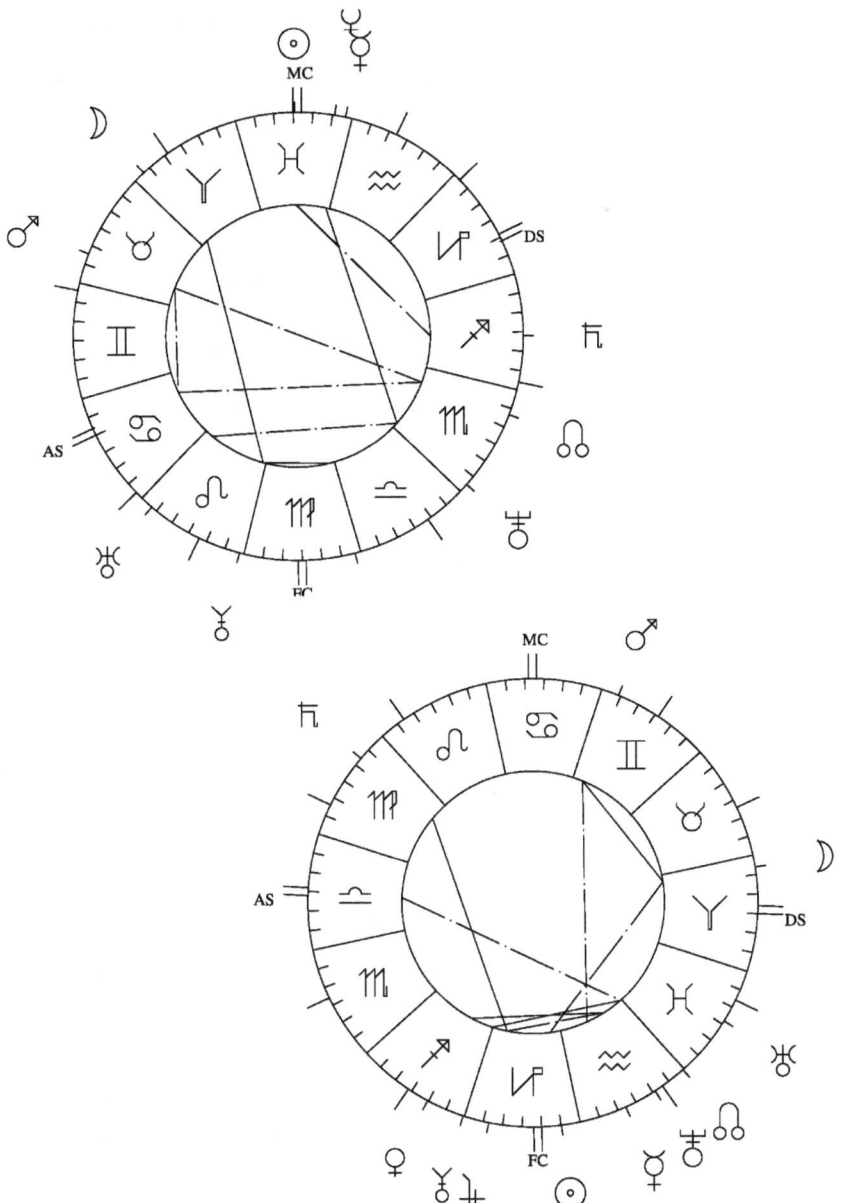

ALR of February 2008: a massive stellium over the 1st and the 12th House, as well as Mars in the 6th House. By relocating to Reykjavík, Europe, the whole stellium moves to the 2nd House and we keep Mars out of the 6th House.

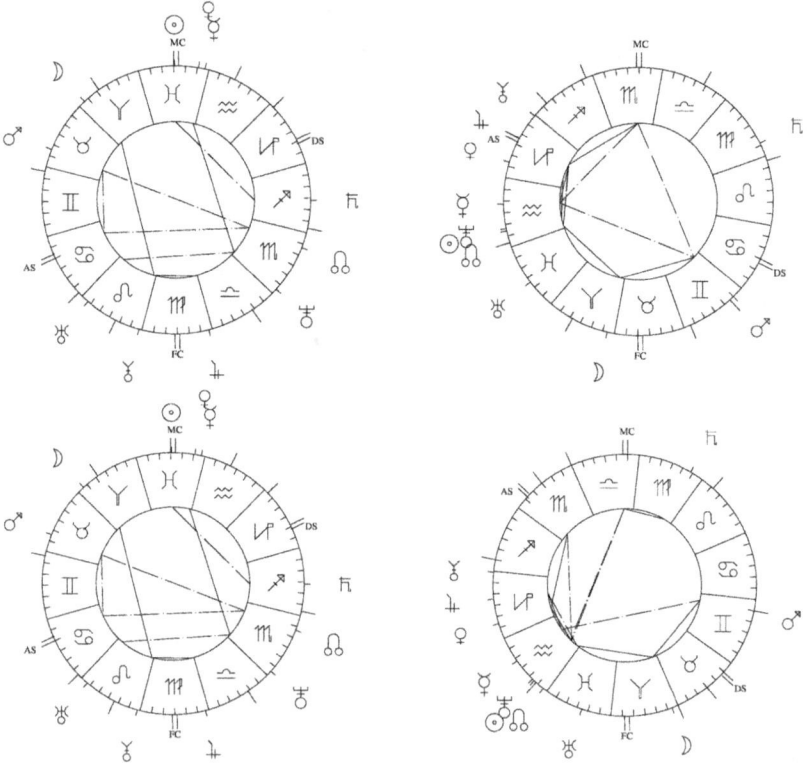

# 5.
# Twenty trustworthy rules

The rules you are about to read, similar to the 'sibling' rules that you can find in the volume *Transits and Solar Returns*, haven't been written as a Bible or a Koran or any other scripture – they simply descend from my own experience on the field.

The reduction of their explanation to a sequence of single sentences allows you to avoid useless sophistry, hot air and haughty descriptions that explain nothing. By means of them you can also nail the author to his responsibilities: for you can study your own natal chart and that of your closest relatives and their Returns of the last, say, five years – and verify whether the following rules do work or not.

If these rules are trustworthy, you'll get several instances of corroboration and you might also suggest your friends and colleagues to follow them. If not so, I myself suggest that you burn off this book.

1) In terms of operational and expressive power, the effects of Lunar Returns are much lesser than the Solar Return under which they take place.

2) A Lunar Return can never overturn or subvert the general reading of the Solar Return under which the LR takes place.

3) The Lunar Return can only act as a modulation – see the following chapter – of the current Solar Return; or as the enhancement of a specific aspect of the SR, referring to the month of validity of the LR.

4) The Lunar Return helps us very much in dating the events within the frame of the current Solar Return (see the almost 500 pages of practical examples in my volume *Nuovo Trattato di Astrologia*, ed. Armenia)).

5) An Aimed Lunar Return can not replace the Aimed Solar

Return. So if subject *A* does not relocate his SR and repents later on, he can not flatter himself with the illusion of replacing the missed aimed birthday with 12 or 13 Aimed Lunar Returns.

6) By exploiting the effect of synergy as explained in the innumerable examples of my volume *Nuovo Trattato di Astrologia* published by Armenia editore, it is possible and useful, too, to perform a single Aimed Lunar Return for a specific month in harmony with good transits and a previously performed ASR. This way it is possible to achieve – during that month and not in other months – what we most expect from this combination of active relocations.

7) Those who can afford it and have enough time to do so, can certainly achieve wonderful results by performing a good ASR and aiming all the LRs of the following twelve months.

8) Rule #7 is certainly true, nevertheless it must be underlined that – for the reason already mentioned – in the majority of the cases it is quite useless, superfluous, and redundant to aim all the LRs.

9) Even the most apparently awful LR can not imply serious damage if it takes place in the twelve months following a good SR.

10) Even an apparently wonderful LR would imply very little results if it takes place in the twelve months following a feeble SR.

11) As a consequence of rule #9 we might even perform an Aimed Lunar Return in order to place, say, a wonderful conjunction of Venus and Jupiter in the 5$^{th}$ House of the LR even if by doing so, say, the Ascendant of the LR would lie in the 12$^{th}$ natal House. In fact, if the reading of the current SR allows to forecast so, such a LR might announce the arrival of a new and happy love affair, while at most its Asc. in the 12$^{th}$ House might imply a bad cold – certainly not a stay in hospital.

12) With the exception of the rules listed in these pages, reading a Lunar Return is basically the same as reading a Solar Return: thus – with the exception of the rules listed in these pages – the relevant sections of my volume *Transits and Solar Returns* can be also applied to LRs.

13) A Lunar Return, just like the Solar Return, is always 'aimed' – even if you make up your mind to spend that moment at home, i.e. in the place where you usually live.

14) For an ASR it is enough to stay in the place of the Solar Return for a single minute; and for an ALR it is also enough to stay in the place of the Lunar Return for a single minute. If you aren't sure of your time of birth, you can reach the place one hour before the Return and you can leave one hour after the Return. There's no use in remaining there 24 hours or even longer (see my volume *A Few Facts on Aimed Birthdays*, Blue Diamond Publisher: it can be downloaded free from my website).

15) In the volume mentioned in rule #14 you can also find several cases of criticism that may be directed both to ASRs and to ALRs, and my answers to them.

16) If an ALR contains exactly opposite elements compared with the SR under which it takes place, the aimed result would be virtually zero. For example, assume that the SR contains a strict conjunction of Mars and Saturn in the 4$^{th}$ House (I'd never leave it there!) and you try and perform an ALR to place Jupiter and Venus in the 4$^{th}$ House of the chart of Lunar Return because, you possibly wish to buy or to sell an estate that month – the result would be close to absolute vacuum.

17) This rule is an attempt to explain better a notion that is not always easy to understand. I refer to placing, for example, Mars in the 4$^{th}$ House of an ALR. Many people refuse to do so, because they fear it might harm their parents. This is not possible! If it were, we should admit that it is possible to get rid of a hostile subject by simply sticking pins into dolls. At most, with Mars in the 4$^{th}$ House of the Return, we enhance our level of concern towards our parents' problems – not their real, practical problems. The same can be said, on the opposite side, for Venus in the 4$^{th}$ House of a Return. Having clarified this, let me add that if my parents lived, and if I could do so without it being detrimental to other elements of the Return, I would place Venus in the 4$^{th}$ House…

18) As with ASRs, ALRs too can help you to correct (i.e. rectify) your time of birth. Assume that we have a map of LR with Mars on the cusp between the 3$^{rd}$ and the 4$^{th}$ House. Don't you think that one month after, analyzing the events that happened, any astrologer would be able to understand whether that Mars was actually in the 3$^{rd}$ House or in the 4$^{th}$ House?

19) Nevertheless, remember that one swallow does not make a summer: a single event is not enough to rectify the time of birth. Rectification should be done following the protocol that I have defined in

the first hundred pages of my volume *Nuovo Trattato di Astrologia*, Armenia. So, placing a celestial on a cusp of an ALR may help you very much in this sense, but in my opinion its possible implication as regards to the time of birth should be added to – not replacing – the mentioned protocol of rectification.

20) In this volume you'll find examples of two Aimed Lunar Returns of mine in which I was in mid-flight at the very moment of the Return. I hadn't planned so, it was by mere chance: but they have helped me rectify my time of birth.

*Ciro Discepolo*

# A Few Facts on Aimed Birthdays

*Blue Diamond Publisher*

# 6.
# The concept of modulation

An example that we may well define 'biological' will help me explain to the Reader how – from my point of view and above all, according to my experience – an Aimed Lunar Return stands a chance of interacting with the current Solar Return.

Everybody knows that the human body produces melatonin: it is a substance that favours sleep and helps fight against depression. The production of melatonin in human beings has a peak – in a cycle of 24 hours – approximately half an hour after sunset. This is quite logical, if you think that one hand, the lack of sunlight should prepare the body to sleep, and on the other hand it can also induce a slight depression in human beings.

99%, this reflects the situation regarding the production of melatonin in the human body – a situation that can be verified with laboratory analyses.

Now – for the sake of simplicity and clarity – let us suppose that our melatonin production draws a perfectly sinusoidal wave as in the illustration below:

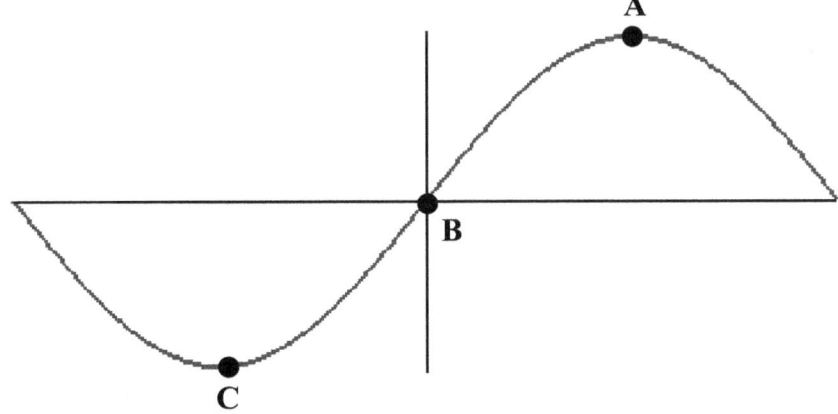

The peak marked with a capital letter A corresponds to the maximum endogen production of melatonin approximately half an hour after sunset. As I said, for the sake of simplicity you can take this wave to be perfectly sinusoidal. In this case the trough marked as C approximately corresponds to dawn which would have been roughly 12 hours earlier (if you were on the Equator and close to the equinox of autumn). It's the time when you wake up and your body does not need to produce melatonin: it 'knows' that it doesn't have to do so, for if it did it would spoil its own circadian cycle that induces, at that time of the day, a sharp awakening and a state of euphoria induced by sunlight. The medium point marked B corresponds to ca. 6 hours before the peak A.

The next day and all the following days, a similar situation would repeat itself.

Now let us assume that the subject whose melatonin production wave we are considering, resolves to take a small pill of artificial melatonin at the time of the day marked A. The content of melatonin of the pill would be a very small portion of our natural production.

Yet it would be enough to modify the perfect sinusoidal wave like this:

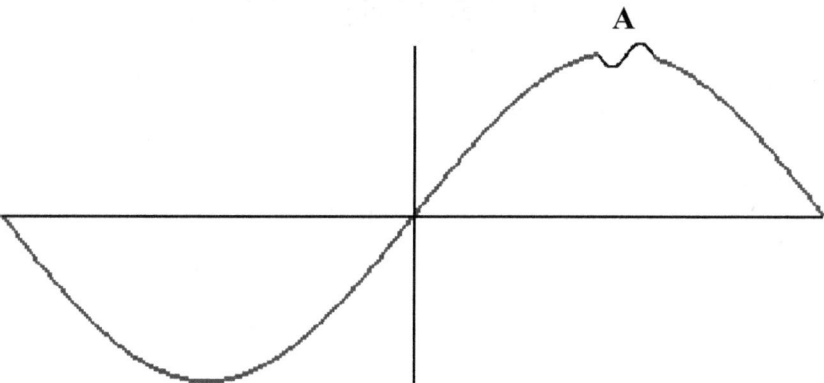

As you can see, the point marked A has slightly moved upwards. Perhaps the following diagram would make things even clearer:

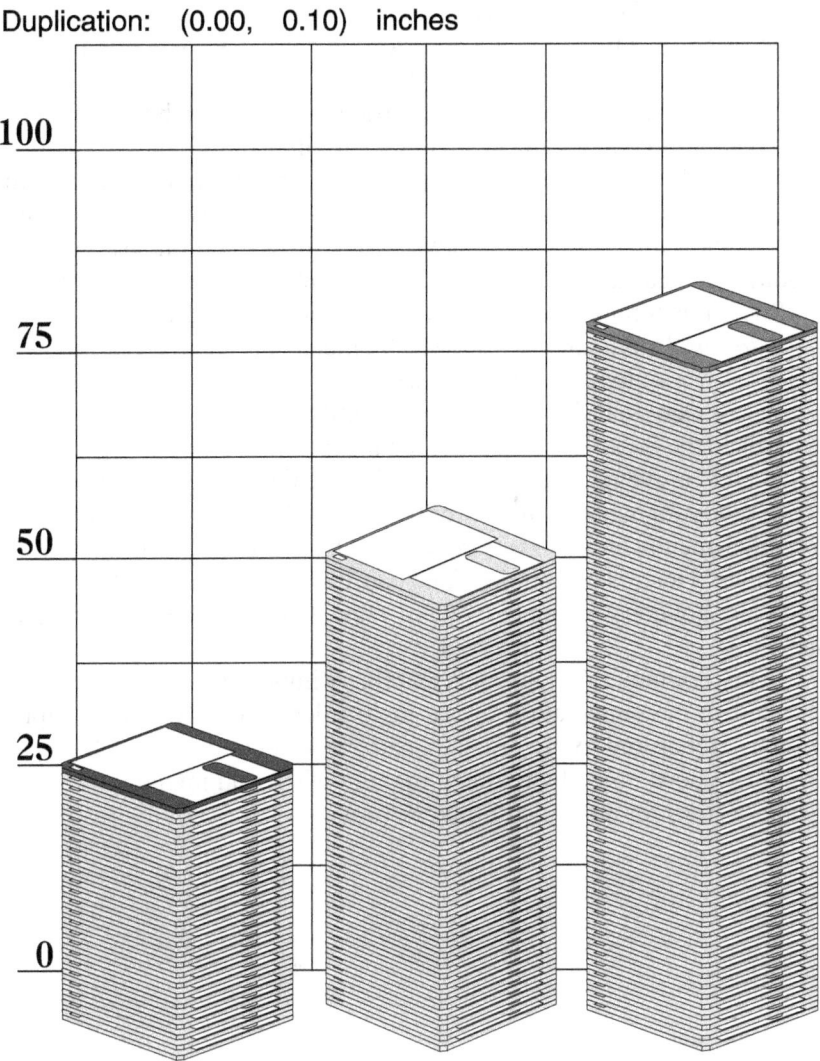

This chart is called a 'bar chart'. Now do not consider the numeric values of the three bars of the diagrams, but concentrate on their relative height, that represents quite well what I am trying to explain. The highest bar on the right may represent the point A after taking a pill of melatonin. The lower central bar may represent the point A before or without the assumption of the pill. In this diagram the central bar corresponds to a value of 55, but please make an effort and imagine that it is actually around 73.

Now it should be clear that I have tried to prove that the action of the drug has slightly altered the level of melatonin in our blood.

If the pill had had active ingredients other than melatonin, say for example stimulating ones such as caffeine and slightly depressive ones such as those that you can find in a variety of vegetal plants, the result would have been a slight reduction of the level of melatonin in our blood.

Such a general action, which I have simply outlined here, is called *modulation*. It indicates the process by means of which a little input is able to lower or to raise a certain threshold.

We can say that the Aimed Lunar Return work in the same way as regards to the Solar Return governing them during the year.

Let me be even clearer and say that if Helen's current SR is wonderful – especially for health – and one of her LRs of the same year is apparently very detrimental for her health, at most such a bad LR could only 'slightly modulate' Helen's current SR. The bad LR might simply give Helen a bad cold, but considering the overall year, Helen would have very good health.

In my opinion, this concept is extremely important. This is the notion that led to the enunciation of the main rules of the previous chapter, which – according to my practical experience and my research on past events – you should always keep in mind when you intend to change a Lunar Return for an Aimed Lunar Return.

# 7.
# Do ALRs work?

It is such a meaningless question that it would neither be worth an answer nor consideration. It is a matter of fact that all astrology – from the Western to the Vedic: considering all its variety – is fundamentally based on the principle of 'here and now', which is also the banner of Gestalt psychological analysis as well as the main subject dwelt upon by that wonderful movie starring Robin Williams and directed by Peter Weir: *Dead Poets Society*.

As I have written several times, in my opinion there are some aspects, in the study of Solar and Lunar Returns, that resemble pure mathematics – which makes it parallel to Astrogeography, the latter discipline being accepted even by those who question the effectiveness of the aimed birthdays (a term that I apply either to Solar or Lunar Returns). Yet both afore mentioned branches of astrology take their origin in the very same theoretical assumptions, and they do work in an absolutely identical way.

This time I'll skip the innumerable practical examples that I have given to my readers in at least a dozen of my books on these matters. I believe that such examples are so crystal-clear that nobody has ever tried to criticize them. So this time I'll propose one example only: an empirical one; one that any of you could fully manage independently; one whose starting point and whose point of conclusion is *you*; one on which you'll be able to give your unambiguous opinion.

It is such a clear and simple example – at least in my opinion it is so – that it can wipe away in one blow whatever residual doubt in both protagonists and antagonists. The latter will go on denying what I am writing, if that they have particular reasons to do so – but at least they might be convinced that they declare false things.

Now here is the experiment. Let us assume that Tanya, a female friend of yours, lives in Chicago, Illinois.

The following data are not real, yet they help us understand how the experiment I propose to you works; you can also use any other set of data, even real ones.

Now let us assume that Tanya was born in Chicago on the 24th of August 1968 at 11:15 am.

Consider Tanya's LR of January 2008, in Chicago: we can see Mars placed in the very middle of the 7th House.

Let us further assume that Tanya aims her LR and spends it in Denver, Colorado. Everybody knows that in the States it is possible to cover such a distance in very short time, spending less than $100 for a return trip. In the map of the ALR in Denver, Mars has clearly left the 7th House – it is in fact in the 8th House of LR.

This example is particularly directed at practising astrologers and students of astrology: if they decide to perform this experiment, a month later they would certainly be able to say whether during those 30 days Mars acted as a 'Mars in the 7th House' or as a 'Mars in the 8th House'. TThe effect of Mars being so utterly different in these Houses, even if an astrologer applies the most convoluted of rules – he would not mistake the behaviour of a Mars in the 7th House of Return with that of a Mars in the 8th House of Return.

Now, I believe that such a simple experiment will prove to you and convince you that this thing works... unless you intend to give evidence of it to a group of *fundamentalist scientifists* who would deny even the transit of the sun at the MC for the sake of running down astrology and astrologers.

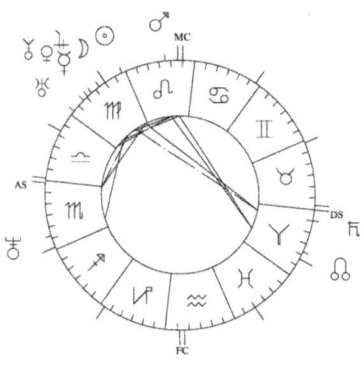

**Natal**                                                         **BLR, Chicago**

# DO ALRS WORK?

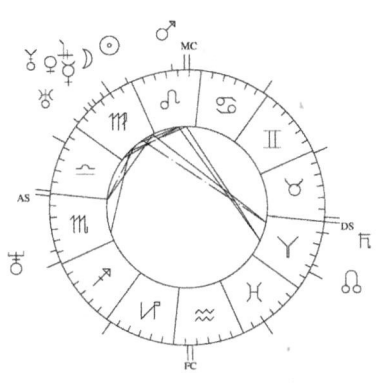

**Natal**

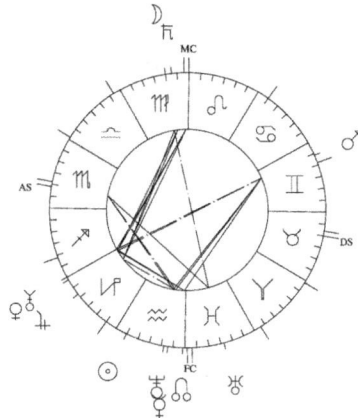

**ALR, Denver**

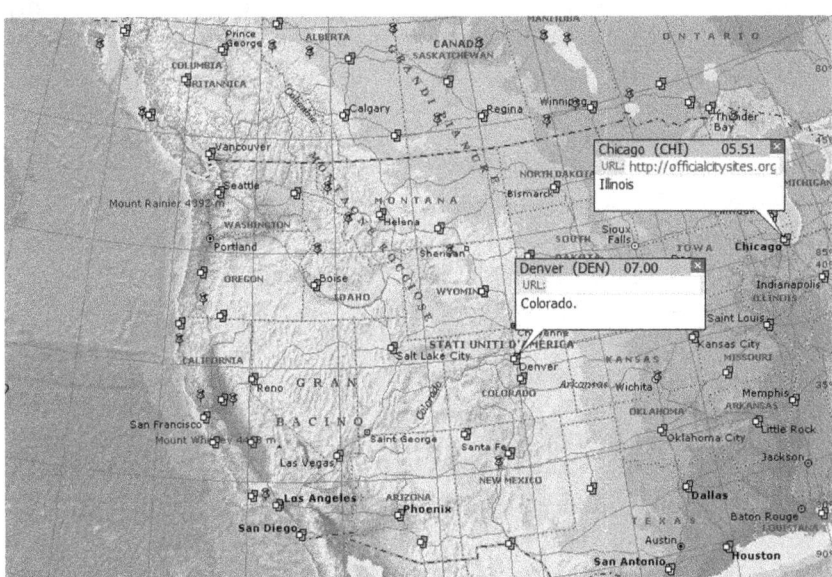

**Translator's note:**

*Scientifist:* I have tried to translate a non-existing Italian word which has actually been created by Ciro Discepolo to define a narrow-minded scientist.

In the Author's mind, a 'scientifist' is basically a scientist who scrictly follow a sort of *'scientism'* or *'scientifism'* consisting in a sort of religion, denying anything that he doesn't know or accept, despite any evidence, unless it's officially considered as 'scientific' by the scientific community – hence the word *scientifist*.

# 8.
# New fields of research for Lunar Returns

As I have written in another section of this volume, many students of astrology at different levels are showing a growing interest in LRs. As for me, I first started to study them in the early '70s. I am aware that at that time LRs could not have become popular among readers – the reason being that it took more than thirty years for me to convince most of my colleagues about the extraordinary importance and power of Solar Returns and of Aimed Solar Returns.

In this context, I would like to show you a new kind of research that I have performed with Lunar Returns thanks to a little but exceptional – at least I find it exceptional – modification to my already wonderful software *Aladino* (*also refereed to as Module for the Automatized Research of the Aimed Solar Returns 'RSMA':*

http://www.programmiastral.com/guide/rsma.htm).

For the sake of simplicity I'll show you an example using my own data of birth.

Let us consider my Base LR of February 2008, in Naples:

Now let us assume that I wish to attain extraordinary results, for that month, concerning the 5$^{th}$ and the 7$^{th}$ House. What would I do if it were a SR? Well, obviously I'd try to place Venus and Jupiter in the 5$^{th}$ House and the stellium with the Sun in the 7$^{th}$ House. Taken for granted that I know that my time of birth is absolutely correct to the minute, I'd also try to have the conjunction of Venus and Jupiter – one degree, that very day! – exactly on the cusp between the 5$^{th}$ and 6$^{th}$ House: this way I'd protect both Houses, the 5$^{th}$ and 6$^{th}$, as well as all the direct and indirect meanings covered by these two sectors of the sky. Now you can proceed with a series of attempts until you attain this result. Using the 'old' software Astral in fact, and after a number of trials, I could achieve it in Bordeaux, France. But if you really

# NEW FIELDS OF RESEARCH FOR LUNAR RETURNS

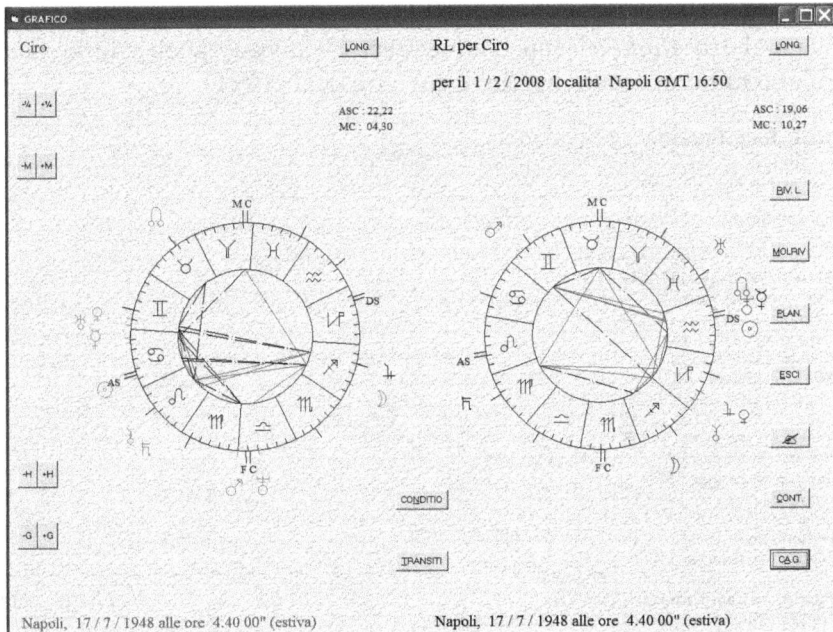

wanted to *choose*, and to choose freely, you should be able to compare a good amount of charts with the desired features: this way you'd be able to select a place where that LR could offer you an extra advantage.

This is exactly where *Aladino* can help you with its incredible power of calculations. Of course the example that we are considering can also be solved reckoning by hand (or by heart[1]), the advantage of *Aladino* being the fact that in its newer release, this application helps you spare hours, if not days of work. By the way the newer version of *Aladino* is freely available for its registered users. Of course, new users paying the registration fee will be given this newer version.

**Back to our experiment now.**

As you can see from the following illustration, I wrote my own data of birth in the section *Molriv* of *Aladino*, and then I selected the LR of February 2008. *Aladino* told me that the LR would take place on the 1st of February 2008 at 4:52 pm

Greenwich Time. The old *Astral* would have said 4:50 pm, but keep in mind that *Aladino* is much more precise – anyway, such a difference of two minutes would not have any practical effect.

**BLR longitudes listed by Aladino**
RS per prova , GMT: 01/02/02008 ore 16:52
RS per Napoli (NA) (IT)

Sole :in Aquario 12°12'10,8739
Sole :in Aquario 12°12'10,8739
Luna :in Sagittario 09°18'49,8420
Luna :in Sagittario 09°18'49,8420
Mercurio :in Aquario 22°29'36,1176  Retrogrado
Mercurio :in Aquario 22°29'36,1176
Venere :in Capricorno 10°17'18,7113
Venere :in Capricorno 10°17'18,7113
Marte :in Gemelli 24°05'50,3053
Marte :in Gemelli 24°05'50,3053
Giove :in Capricorno 10°03'46,2521
Giove :in Capricorno 10°03'46,2521
Saturno :in Vergine 06°54'11,1663  Retrogrado
Saturno :in Vergine 06°54'11,1663
Urano :in Pesci 16°39'57,8631
Urano :in Pesci 16°39'57,8631
Nettuno :in Aquario 21°21'39,1485
Nettuno :in Aquario 21°21'39,1485
Plutone :in Capricorno 00°12'00,9084
Plutone :in Capricorno 00°12'00,9084
Nodo Medio :in Aquario 28°39'50,7313  Retrogrado
Nodo Medio :in Aquario 28°39'50,7313
Nodo Vero :in Aquario 27°50'49,7316  Retrogrado
Nodo Vero :in Aquario 27°50'49,7316
Lilith(Apogeo Medio) :in Scorpione 22°19'40,4759
Lilith(Apogeo Medio) :in Scorpione 22°19'40,4759
Apogeo Osculante :in Scorpione 19°15'19,0544  Retrogrado
Apogeo Osculante :in Scorpione 19°15'19,0544
Terra :in Ariete 00°00'00,0000
Terra :in Ariete 00°00'00,0000
Chirone :in Aquario 15°32'08,6671
Chirone :in Aquario 15°32'08,6671
Pholus :in Sagittario 09°43'55,6753
Pholus :in Sagittario 09°43'55,6753
Ceres :in Toro 13°21'03,3248
Ceres :in Toro 13°21'03,3248
Pallas :in Pesci 19°09'59,5204
Pallas :in Pesci 19°09'59,5204
Juno :in Sagittario 17°10'29,8993
Juno :in Sagittario 17°10'29,8993
Vesta :in Aquario 21°46'40,2456
Vesta :in Aquario 21°46'40,2456
Casa 1 :in Leone 19°28'47,2689
Casa 2 :in Vergine 11°19'49,6739
Casa 3 :in Bilancia 08°15'28,7284
Casa 4 :in Scorpione 10°57'17,8303
Casa 5 :in Sagittario 16°45'59,8765
Casa 6 :in Capricorno 20°24'32,9715
Casa 7 :in Aquario 19°28'47,2689
Casa 8 :in Pesci 11°19'49,6739
Casa 9 :in Ariete 08°15'28,7284
Casa 10 :in Toro 10°57'17,8303
Casa 11 :in Gemelli 16°45'59,8765
Casa 12 :in Cancro 20°24'32,9715

Now let us input in Aladino the data of a baby born on the 1st of February 2008, in Naples, at 5:52 pm (Italian time corresponding to 4:52 pm Greenwich Time).

Something is still missing, but my brilliant programmer Stefano Briganti has added it to *Aladino* under my strict supervision: namely, the possibility of reckoning such an ASR (OK, this is an ALR – but *Aladino* doesn't know and it doesn't even need to know) in which a cusp, say the cusp of the 1st House, or of the 2nd House, or of any other House) is placed exactly where we want it to be.

I say that the amendment has been done 'under my strict control' because *Aladino* is a piece of software of incredible complexity: the risk is that by modifying a section of the programme any other section might begin malfunctioning.

In this case we bypassed the risk with a delicate sort of 'grafting'. Believe me, Dr. Briganti and I almost worked like surgeons, with a sterile mask on our mouth and the eyes glued to a microscope...

I am writing this at the beginning of September 2007: I won't give my OK to this new release of *Aladino* before one year, and certainly not before I have verified that all the other features of this piece of software haven't been damaged in any way.

Nonetheless there was still another problem left.

Wanting to position Jupiter and Venus on the cusp between the 5th and the 6th House and the stellium with the Sun in the 7th House, we should have accepted also an Ascendant of LR in the 12th natal House (of course the 'natal' of this LR is not my own natal chart, but this doesn't change what we are trying to achieve). Could we? Of course we can. In fact I have explained it several times: if the SR is good, even a bad LR taking place under that SR can not cause serious damage – not even if there is a Sun in the 12th House of LR. In the worst case the unfavourable elements of a bad LR within a good SR can simply announce some cold, with no detriment for its advantages given by the positive elements in the 5th and in the 7th House. Moreover – you should not undervalue it, although this refers to LRs only, not to SRs – we have placed a wonderful protection in the 6th House, the House of health.

Now all this shows the kind of open-mindedness that you need if you wish to create a condition of synergy between an ASR and an ALR. Nevertheless since its birth Aladino was programmed to block any possible 'solution to the equation' if it broke any of the 'taboo-rules' within the 'thirty rules' given in the volume *Transits and Solar Returns*.

So we performed a second amendment – together with the previous one – in order to be able to unblock the 'lock' of the 'thirty rules'. Now Aladino – only when we give it the desired longitude for a cusp – may also propose a Return with detrimental elements such as the Sun in the 12$^{th}$ House or Mars in the 6$^{th}$ House, or a stellium of celestials in the 8$^{th}$ House and so on.

To make a long story short, this is what the genius of the *One Thousand and One Nights* has been able to offer to us after a scan of a few seconds: a list of several dozens of places. We show you the relevant charts for few of these locations. Please consider them, study them and then try to understand which one I would have chosen if I had resolved to relocate this LR. Elaborate: why would I have chosen that place and not any other?

# NEW FIELDS OF RESEARCH FOR LUNAR RETURNS

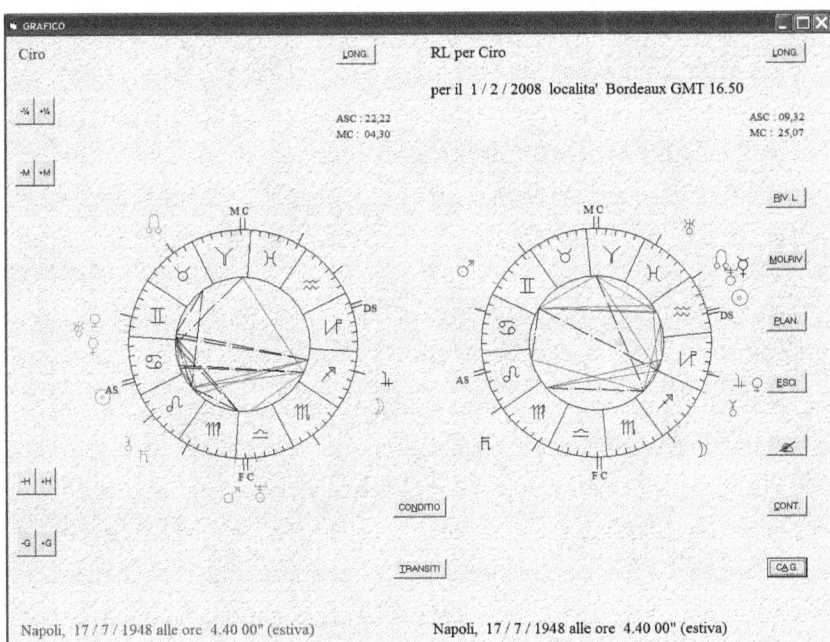

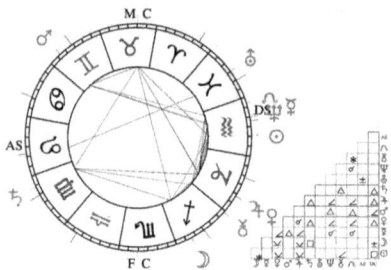
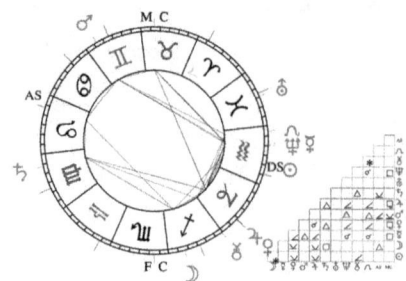

**ALR in Queenstown, South Africa**

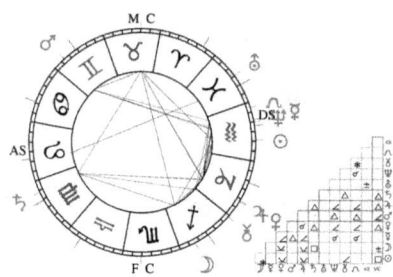
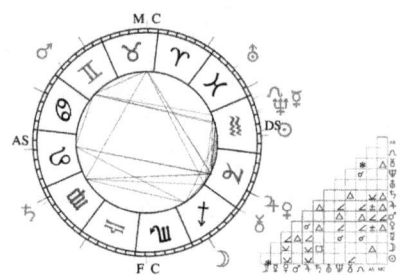

**ALR in Djanet, Algeria**

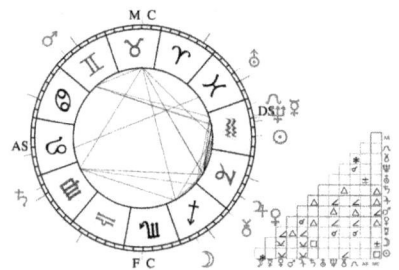
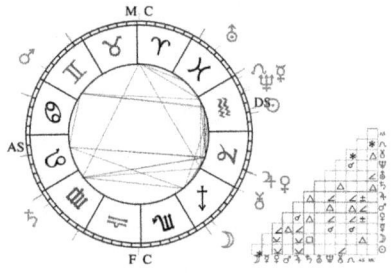

**ALR in Palma de Majorca, Spain**

# NEW FIELDS OF RESEARCH FOR LUNAR RETURNS

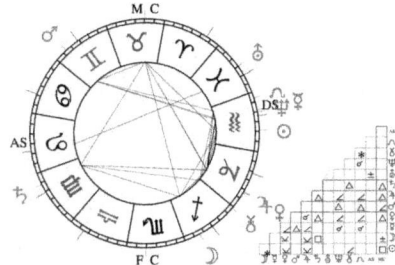
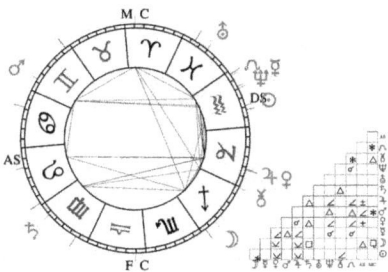

**ALR in Bordeaux, France**

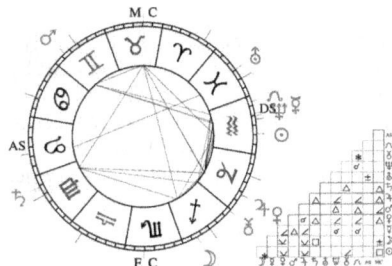
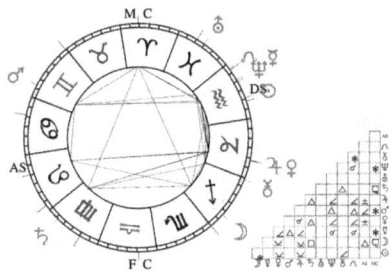

**ALR in Plymouth, UK**

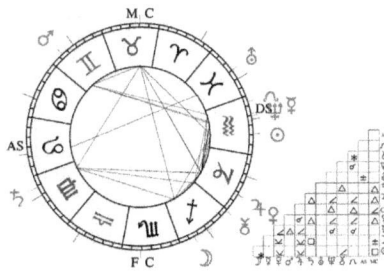
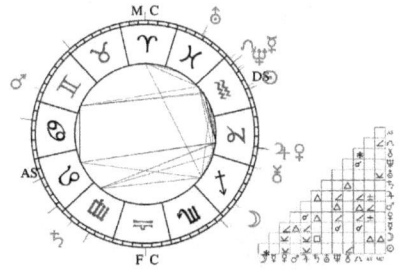

**ALR in Carrickfinn, Ireland**

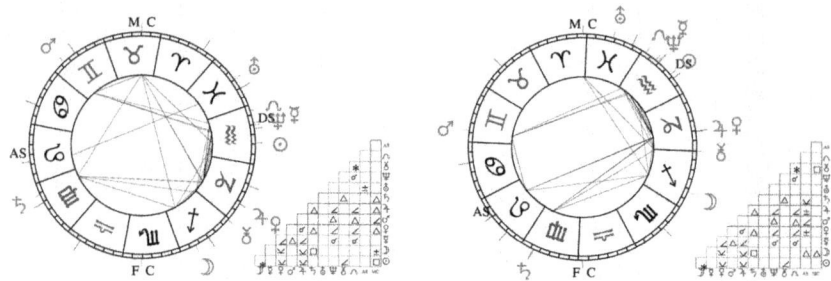

**ALR in Reykjavik, Iceland**

My choice would have been certainly Queenstown: there, relying on a very good 7th House and a very good 5th house, with Uranus also in the 7th House I would have increased the chances for the turn of events concerning the 7th House.

**Notes**

1) During a congress of Astrology in Lavagna, Genoa, in October 2006, half-jokingly I proposed to the audience that I select one subject among them to reckon his/her ASR by heart, and to modify it according to the rules of my school, still by heart. That day only a few good colleagues of mine did understand that I was not joking: it was in fact a piece of bravura that you could hardly witness in the future... The episode has been described with plenty of details in my volume on the interpretation of the natal map *L'interpretazione del tema natale*, Armenia editore.

# 9.
# A thrilling Lunar Return

With this Lunar Return of mine I wished to achieve a precise aim: to support with an appropriate astral configuration a series of publishing projects in which I would be involved during the second half of the month of October.

First of all, it is important to remark that in the overwhelming majority of my own aimed birthdays, I use the 3rd House and the 9th House of the SR as a recipient for the malefic planets, and this probably explains it well why my books have been published abroad so late. Nevertheless, in 2007 I aimed my SR otherwise and I spent it in Río Gallegos, Patagonia, Argentina: where I placed Venus exactly on the cusp between the 2nd and the 3rd House of SR – this way I would achieve important goals in the field of publishing during the following twelve months, especially with regard to publishing my books abroad.

In this case my goal was achievable because I would aim a LR that was already supported by a promising SR in the field of publishing, and a LR of this kind would work in synergy with the existing SR.

So it was easy for me to select a good location and I spent my LR in Istanbul, Turkey, where I placed Jupiter in conjunction with the Medium Coeli – immediately after the MC, in the so-called Gauquelin zone where the planet is supposed to be stronger – and at the same time I avoided the Sun falling in the 8th House and I also avoided possible harm to my daughters by putting Mars in the 4th House instead of the 5th House.

It is common knowledge that with low-cost airlines it is possible to relocate a Solar or Lunar Return with a one-day return ticket, with a relatively low fare.

II opted for this course of action as well but didn't know that I would have a thrilling Lunar Return… This is what happened.

My LR was to take place at 4:44 pm, local time of Istanbul; my flight back home would take off at 5:30 pm, local time.

I was in the airport already at 10 o'clock in the morning. With good anticipation, a flight to Milan Malpensa scheduled for 2 pm was announced to be rescheduled to 4:30 pm. But I had booked a seat on a flight to Rome Fiumicino, and there was no news about my flight. Usually, having no news of a flight is a bad sign: especially when Alitalia, our flag carrier, was facing a period of workers' union unrest because of its serious financial and corporate situation (still existing on the date I am writing these lines, on the 16th of October 2007). So I thought to myself, if it's 10 am and they already announce a two-hour delay for the flight Istanbul to Milan, when I'm supposed to take off in the afternoon there will surely be further delays and my flight to Rome Fiumicino might even be cancelled. So I resolved to take a seat on the flight to Milan, where I could catch an evening flight home to Naples. Of course I considered the chance that – with the devil's help – the 16:30 flight could actually take off on time, but the probability theory was against this remote chance, so I eventually determined that it would be a good decision to fly to Milan.

Of course things shaped otherwise. More than an hour before the scheduled departure, the aircraft was already connected to the terminal and 60 minutes before departure, two ground hostesses were already standing at the gate, ready to check the passports and the tickets.

Twenty minutes before departure we were embarking. The strangest thing of all is that, beyond any reasonable forecast everybody got on board immediately, nobody was missing.

Another incredible fact happened: the control tower gave an immediate OK for take off! It was as if Alitalia was making a demonstration of its own efficiency for a TV coverage…

Moreover, Istanbul has a huge airport, and in huge airports the aircrafts usually queue one after another on the runway. Well, not even this happened! There was no queue so that we took off at 16:30.

Now, I had the chart of my monthly Return clearly in my mind, and I feared missing the main goal that I intended to achieve by aiming it in Istanbul: namely, Jupiter in the 9th House in conjunction with the Medium Coeli. For if the aircraft had moved westward in the following minutes, Jupiter would have been placed very clearly in the 10th House of the LR, which would have simply spoiled my Aimed Lunar Return.

At this point, while all my mental antennas were trying to capture any indication of the direction that our flight was taking, I understood that something was happening in my favour. We were taking off and, as it is logical in these cases, we were taking off keeping the sun *behind* the aircraft – in other words, we were flying eastward. I could not be mistaken on such an elementary thing; I only wondered whether the captain would make a large or a narrow turn in order to take the final direction – westward. Minutes ticked away and it was like being in a thrilling movie film: the airplane went on rising up in the sky, still going eastward. Eventually we started a slow turn in an westward direction. At this point, I was in the need to know over which part of the globe I would be at 4:44 pm. In this search I have been shamelessly lucky, I dare say. I switched on my notebook, opened *MS Encarta World Atlas* and I zoomed the window around Istanbul. The sky was slightly clouded but I could see the ground from my seat.

At 4:44 pm just under me, a little bit on the right side of the window by which I was seated, I could see the portion of the Black Sea – a bay of an unmistakable shape (you can see it in the following maps). More or less we were flying somewhere between Igneada and Avcýlar, approx. 41°54' N and 27°56' East. Without loosing a minute, I immediately opened my astrology software and after typing the information in its module Molriv I got the chart reproduced down here. Ironically, this Lunar Return might even be better than the one planned for relocation in Istanbul. In fact I had Jupiter glued to the Medium Coeli but still in the 9$^{th}$ House, while Venus was touching the borderline of the conjunction, two and a half degree below the Descendant. The Sun as well as the Ascendant of the LR hadn't fallen into the 8$^{th}$ House. I had one doubt left: perhaps it was closer than 2.5 degree from the cusp between the 4$^{th}$ and the 5$^{th}$ House, what I had wished to avoid not to cause any harm to my daughter, nor to have troubles related with them. Nonetheless we have to remember that this LR and all the LRs of the period June 2007 to July 2008 stood under the frame of an ASR that contained no dangerous element of this kind: so, even if something would take place related to my daughters, it could not be anything serious.

In fact as soon as I reached home I got to know that my daughter Luna had had a tumble on the street at around 3 pm in Naples – but she only got slight scratches on her knee and on her lower lip. Those who haven't fully understood how LRs and SRs work would cry out, «This is the proof that the Mars of your LR was in the 5$^{th}$ House!» But it is not so – in fact we are talking of an event that took place in Naples at 3 'o clock pm, that is to say, *before* the Lunar Return of Istanbul. In fact at that time, the previous LR of mine was effective, the one I had spent in San Severo di Foggia – the one with Uranus in the 5<sup>th</sup> House and Mars in the 7<sup>th</sup> House!

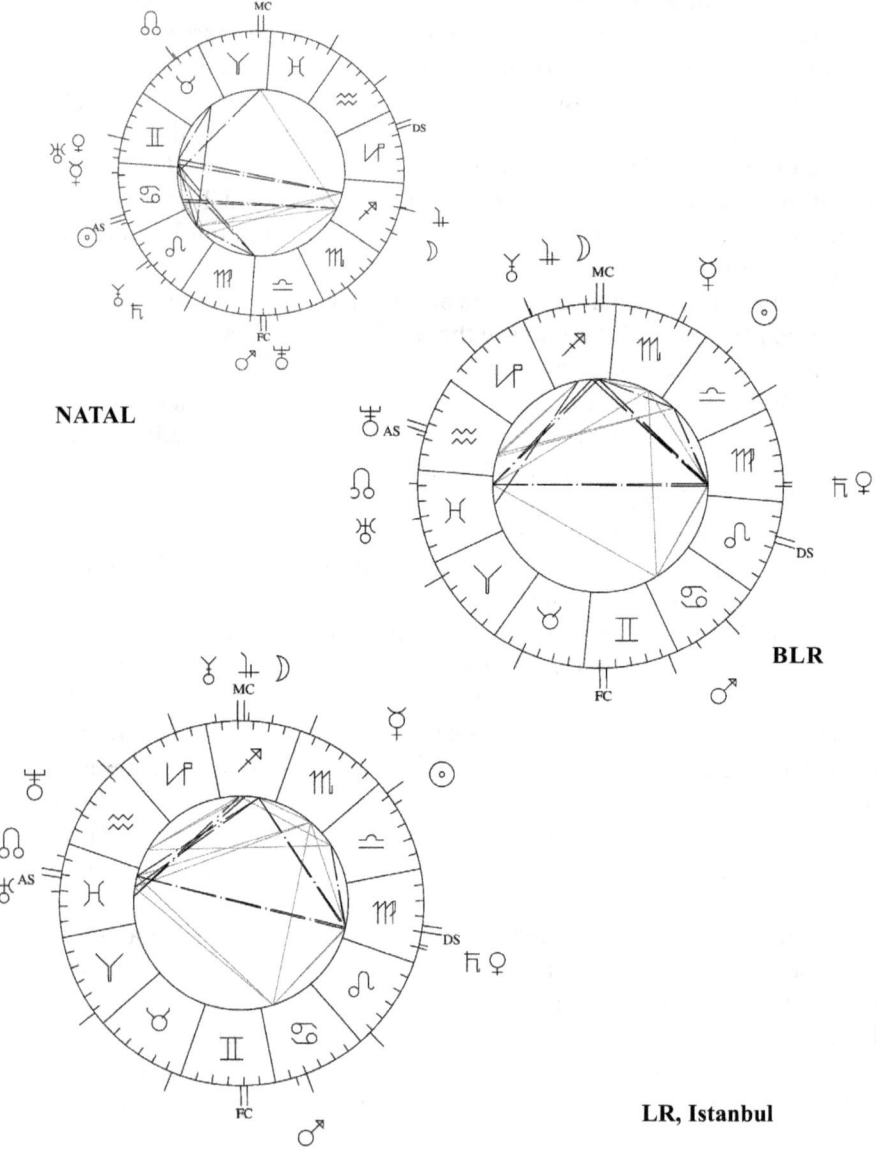

**NATAL**

**BLR**

**LR, Istanbul**

# A THRILLING LUNAR RETURN

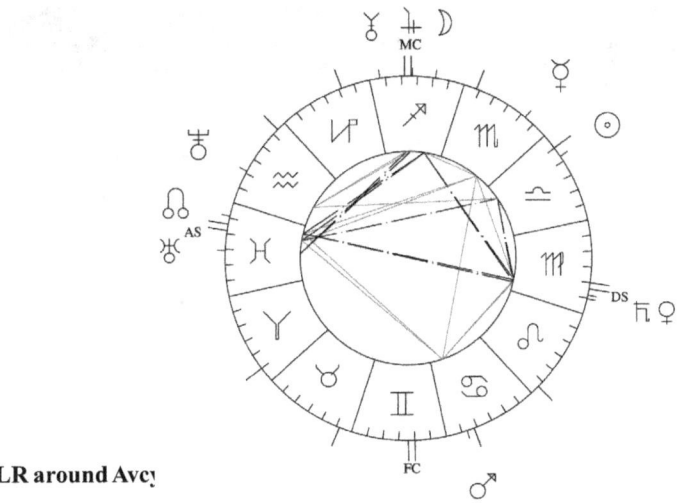

LR around Avcı

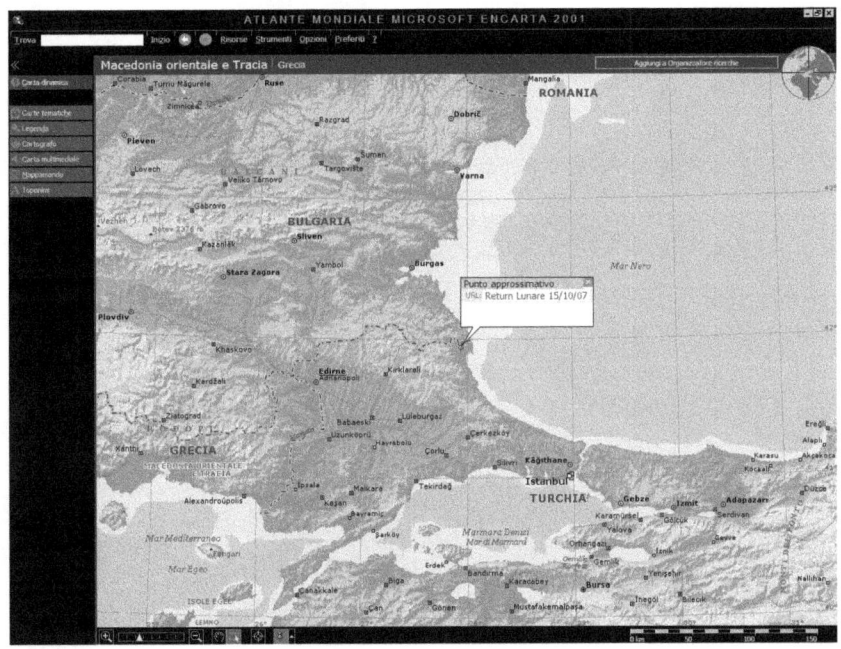

# LUNAR RETURNS

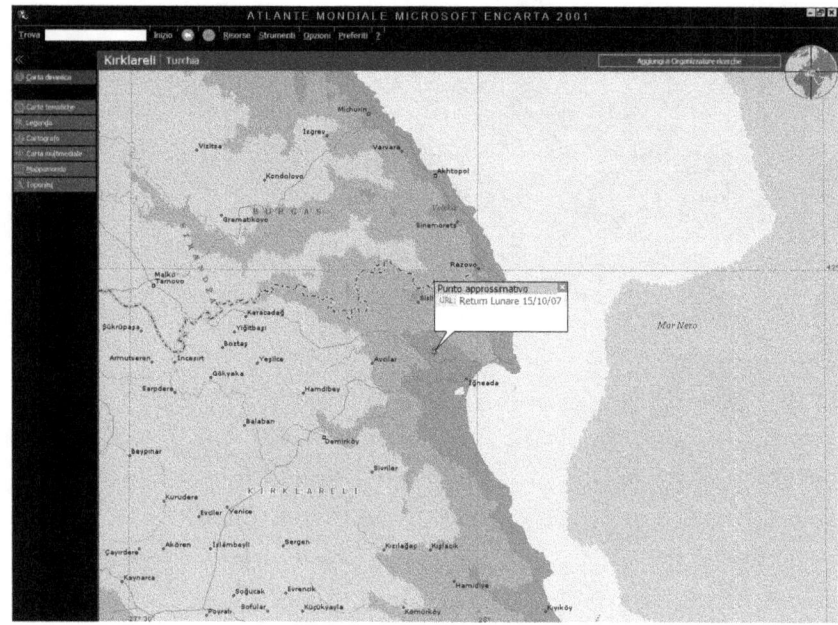

# 10.
# An Aimed Lunar Return for an intervention of rhinoplasty

While I am writing these lines, the subject to whom the following charts refer is having the Aimed Solar Return that you can see in the following pages: he had himself chosen the place to relocate it. Now the subject is deeply concerned because he would like to undergo rhinoplasty: not only for aesthetic reasons, but also for functional ones.

He asks me the following questions:

1) During such a SR can I undergo this kind of a surgical intervention?

2) Can I hope that such an intervention will have a favourable result?

3) Only one of the two candidate surgeons has given me his full data of birth: which one should I choose to perform the intervention?

4) Both surgeons wants to operate somewhere between the 10$^{th}$ and the 20$^{th}$ of December. Would it be helpful for me to aim a LR in order to achieve better results from this rhinoplasty? Keep in mind that I need it very much, but on the other hand it makes me deeply anguished.

These are my answers, the answers that I gave to myself and that I subsequently sent to the subject.

1) Obviously, I wouldn't have chosen *that* ASR knowing that I would have to undergo surgery; knowing that it would be an important operation for me, an intervention that would consist in liberation from the particularly annoying problems that prevent me from breathing and sleeping well. Considering that, such a SR is not the best one – because it has Saturn in the 10$^{th}$ House, which does not favour any sort of emancipation or liberation. Nevertheless we have certain elements in this SR that make me say «yes» to surgery. First of all, generally speaking, the SR itself is

not a bad one. Then we have Venus on the Medium Coeli, and Jupiter in the 2nd House: both favour specifically what we have enumerated so far.

2) Yes – especially if we sum the effects of the Aimed Lunar Return that I'm about to suggest you.

3) Not knowing the time of birth of one of them, I can only consider the other surgeon, the former being 'nothing' for me from an astrological point of view. Now I can consider the selected surgeon's natal chart, his LR and his SR and I can see that he's probably going to face huge legal troubles and/or troubles connected with his sentimental or marital life in the following months. Yet I would exclude that it could be a trial connected with the intervention that the querying subject wishes to undergo: in fact he is a famous surgeon, well known in this field; almost certainly he must be insured against the risks of errors in such a kind of intervention. Now, if he would make a mistake – a bad mistake – while operating Brad Pitt's nose, two or three insurance companies wouldn't be enough to cover the damage, and the surgeon would certainly undergo a sensational trial, resounding in all the media. My querying subject, however, is a rather modest man from the financial-professional point of view. It is not logical to think that if he resolved to bring a suit against the surgeon, such a 'war' would be announced so clearly in the surgeon's chart of Solar and Lunar Returns. Moreover, in my subject's SR there is no element announcing wars or battles of any sort, especially not legal suits – so I must think that the risks of mistaken surgery are quite reduced. Still in connection with the selected surgeon, the sinastry with my subject gives 8 points over 44 according to the algorithm that I have elaborated – the same that I use for the calculation of a sinastry that I offer free-of-charge to the visitors of my web pages. This result is soothing for me: in fact, if their index of sinastry would have been much higher, it might have represented a piece of common destiny between the two of them – and this would have been the case if they would face a long-lasting trial connected with compensation for damage. On the contrary, a low index of sinastry is typical of any person who enters in your life and goes out from it almost immediately, without leaving any significant track of his/her passage.

4) Certainly yes, because in this case we can sum a good Aimed Lunar Return to protect 'appearance' (especially following the subject's query) and, as the saying goes, the game is worth the candle. Below

# AN ALR FOR AN INTERVENTION OF RHINOPLASTY

these lines you can see the Base Lunar Return (a quite bad one) and the Aimed Lunar Return, relocated in the Cocos Islands, where we can place a wonderful Venus in the 2$^{nd}$ House with a tolerance of 12 minutes, just in case the subject had actually be born before the given time (although he assures that he is absolutely confident of his own time of birth). With these 12 minutes we would not loose the effect of Venus in the 2$^{nd}$ House even considering an extension of two and a half degrees beyond the cusp. Lastly you must consider that the Moon will be in Capricorn on the date chosen by the surgeon for the intervention. This is not the ideal position in these cases; I would have avoided Scorpio above all (there are different schools of thought about it, but I think that Scorpio is the Sign which is more strictly related to the nose), as well as Aries (the face) and Capricorn (the bones). On the other hand, the greatest percentage of surgical interventions has to do with bones, so it's OK.

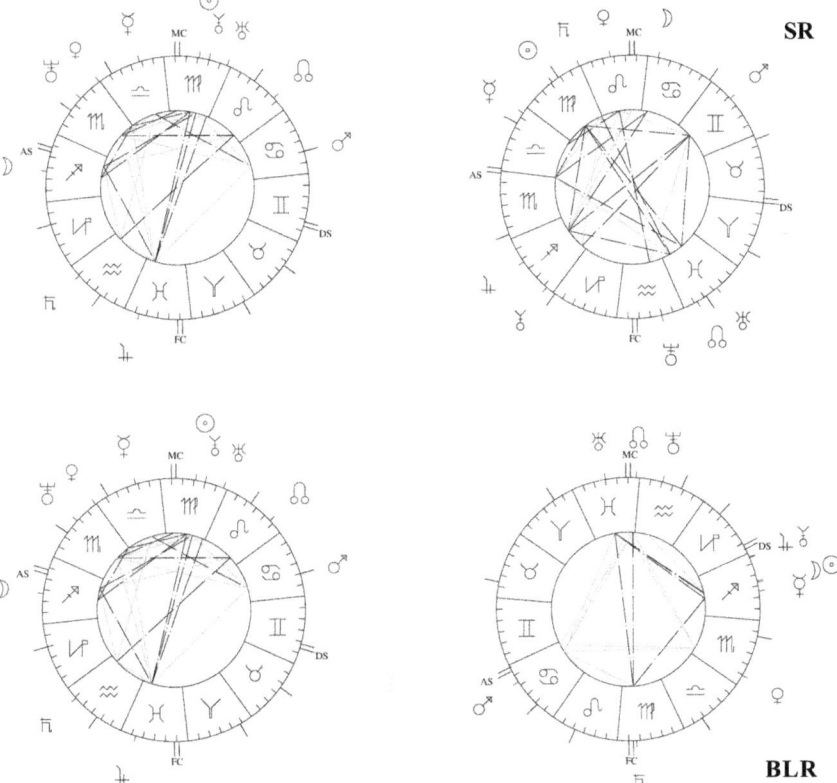

96 LUNAR RETURNS

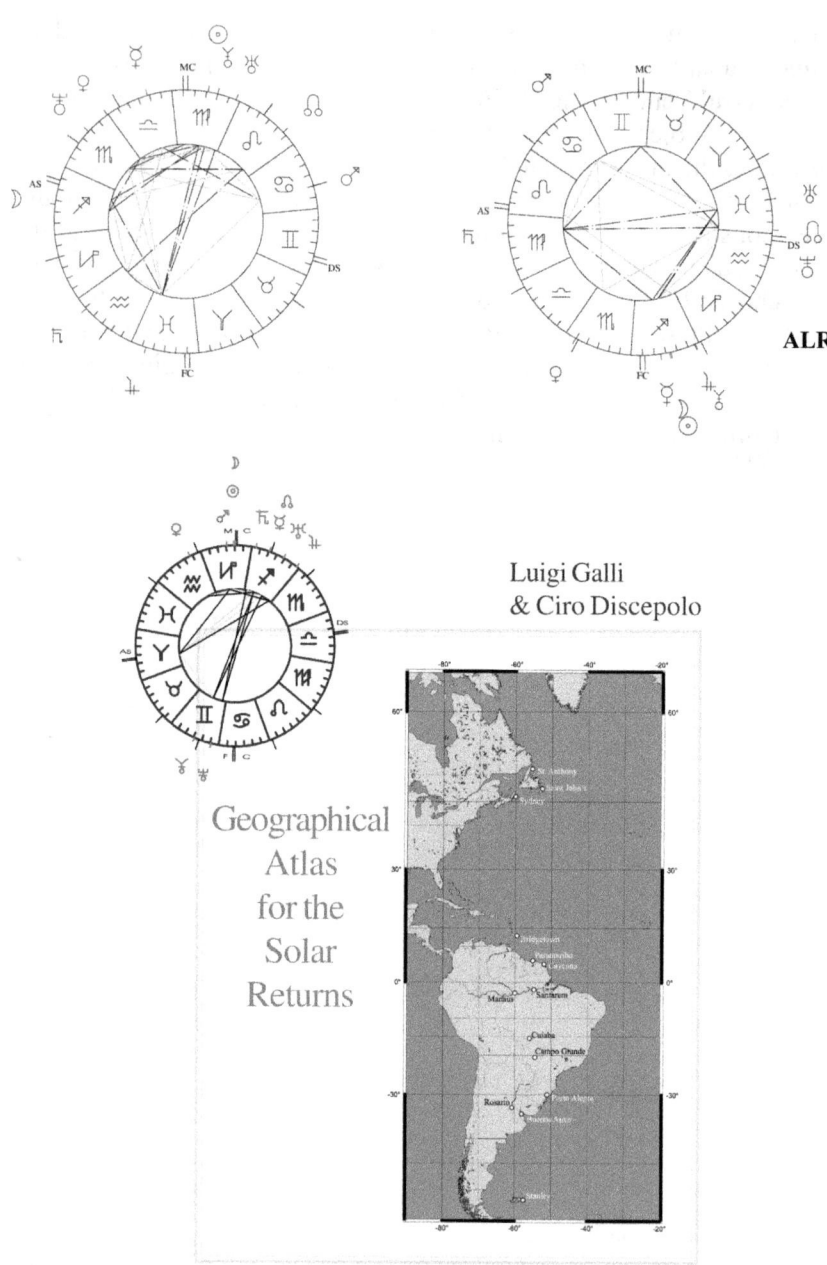

# 11.
# Lunar Return in San Severo di Foggia

The chart shows my LR of the 18th of September 2007, at 7:03 am Greenwich Mean Time, corresponding to 9:03[1] am Italian time.

The drawing itself doesn't change much if you cast it for Naples or for San Severo di Foggia, but the latter place is where I actually went to, that morning. I'd say it's almost impossible to see the difference in the distance of Sun and Saturn from the cusps. In Naples I ran the risk of having a LR with the Sun in the 12th House or with Saturn in the 10th House, considering the rule of the 2.5 degrees from the cusp – see Ciro Discepolo's *Nuovo Trattato di Astrologia*, Armenia editore. In such a case I detected a valuable place that was about 250 kms from home, where I could avoid both the Sun in the 12th House and Saturn in the 10th House – and not going there I would have felt like throwing a piece of good luck out of the window. After all, it was a matter of driving a few hours and staying there only five minutes. Moreover, a few days later two books of mine would be published: *L'interpretazione del tema natale*, Armenia editore, and *Transits and Solar Returns*, Ricerca '90 Publishing.

In other words, I was convinced then and I am still convinced now, that it was an alluring marketing action, because I could achieve the utmost result with the least effort.

So I selected the location with the help of *Aladino*, and I cross-checked the calculation by hand:
Longitudes of San Severo di Foggia:
- Sun: 25°00'01" Virgo
- Cusp of the 12th House: 28°13'57" Virgo
- Difference: 3° 13' 56" 00, that is to say much larger then the range of 2.5 degrees.
- Saturn: 1°56'43" Virgo

- Cusp between the 10 and the 11$^{th}$ House: 29°22'58" Leo
- Difference: 2° 33' 45" 00, not very much larger than 2.5 degrees – but larger.

Please note that in my case I am assured that there is no doubt about my real time of birth, having verified it several times in the last decades – nonetheless, if it had been a Solar Return I would have kept a much larger margin in order to avoid any risk of the Sun falling in the 12$^{th}$ House.

In this case, as I have already explained, the game was worth the candle. But if you work at such a level of accuracy, saying «San Severo» is not enough – you have to find out the very exact longitude of the location and you have to reach that very point inside the little town of San Severo corresponding to that longitude.

As you can see from the screenshots of Aladino reproduced in the following page, this piece of software is based on a huge database of localities that I have bought from American geographical institutions, which have obtained the coordinates directly from a satellite that has measured them. Now all this procedure assures me that the longitude of that place called 'San Severo' is 15°23' East and 41°41' North.

The next step was to open *Google Earth*, a wonderful tool for my work, and finding out that the point of my interest corresponds exactly to a shop called *Catalano* placed in Corso Amedeo d'Aosta #45. According to Google Earth the geographical coordinates of that point corresponded to the longitude of 15°22'59"86 E and to the latitude of 41°40'54"79 N: more or less, with the precision of a few metres, exactly the point that I was looking for, and where I eventually stayed during my LR.

At this point, I had only to drive my car and set up my GPS receiver to the address desired – all the rest was almost automatic...

**Notes**

1) If you cast my LR of September with the old version of *Astral*, the GMT time would result to be 7:00 am. If you do the same with *Aladino*, the result is 7:03. The slight difference is due to the different geographical coordinates of my place of birth in the different databases of geographical coordinates that have been published in Italy and abroad – but it's a difference of few hundred metres after all. In order to overcome even this non-existing problem, I remained before Mr. Catalano's shop from 8:45 to 9:03.

# LUNAR RETURN IN SAN SEVERO DI FOGGIA

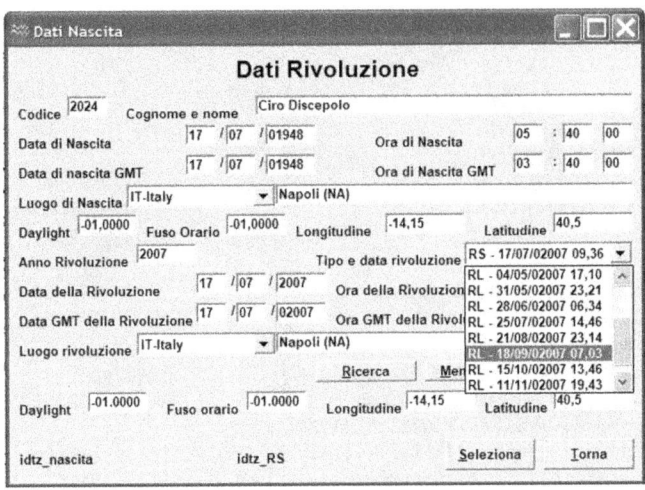

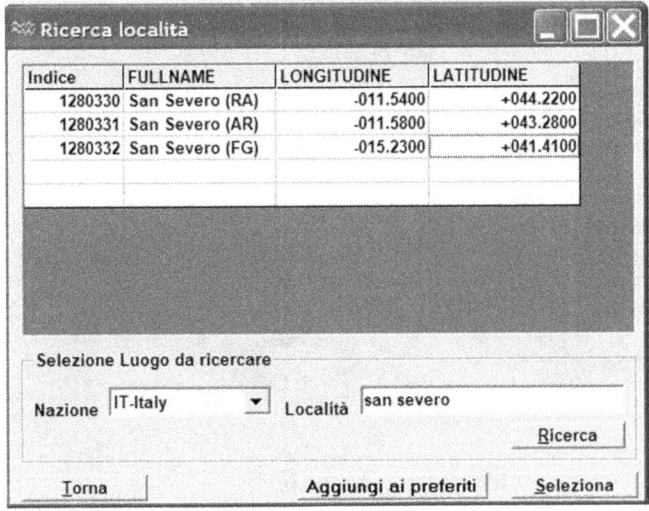

These are the two screenshots of *Aladino* that led me to casting my sky of LR for relocation in San Severo di Foggia.

RS per RL per settembre 2007, GMT: 18/09/02007 ore 07:03
RS per San Severo (FG) (IT)

Sole : in Vergine 25°00'01,4657
Luna : in Sagittario 09°18'51,9247
Mercurio : in Bilancia 18°40'59,5083
Venere : in Leone 18°17'03,7163
Marte : in Gemelli 24°48'11,4737
Giove : in Sagittario 12°32'36,0637
Saturno : in Vergine 01°56'43,5332
Urano : in Pesci 16°22'18,6200 Retrogrado
Nettuno : in Aquario 19°44'22,4983 Retrogrado
Plutone : in Sagittario 26°19'54,8911
Nodo Medio : in Pesci 05°53'11,6032 Retrogrado
Nodo Vero : in Pesci 06°54'31,0811 Retrogrado
Lilith(Apogeo Medio) : in Scorpione 07°03'29,7593
Apogeo Osculante : in Scorpione 11°25'45,9676 Retrogrado
Chirone : in Aquario 11°00'11,5014 Retrogrado
Pholus : in Sagittario 03°30'28,7015
Ceres : in Toro 23°55'01,6216
Pallas : in Pesci 06°18'09,3834 Retrogrado
Juno : in Scorpione 02°47'51,5418
Vesta : in Sagittario 17°13'10,4707
Casa 1 : in Bilancia 21°55'47,8647
Casa 2 : in Scorpione 19°28'24,9939
Casa 3 : in Sagittario 21°16'17,7155
Casa 4 : in Capricorno 25°58'02,5701
Casa 5 : in Aquario 29°22'58,0410
Casa 6 : in Pesci 28°13'57,2768
Casa 7 : in Ariete 21°55'47,8647
Casa 8 : in Toro 19°28'24,9939
Casa 9 : in Gemelli 21°16'17,7155
Casa 10 : in Cancro 25°58'02,5701
Casa 11 : in Leone 29°22'58,0410
Casa 12 : in Vergine 28°13'57,2768

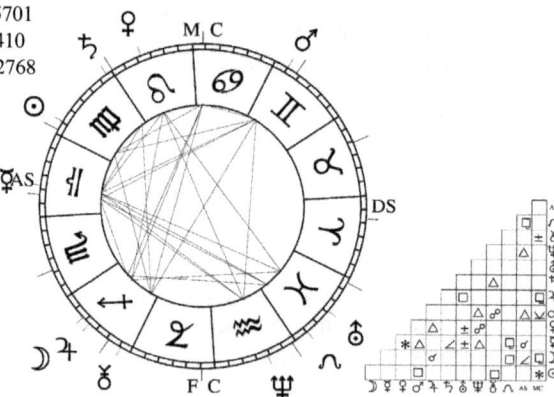

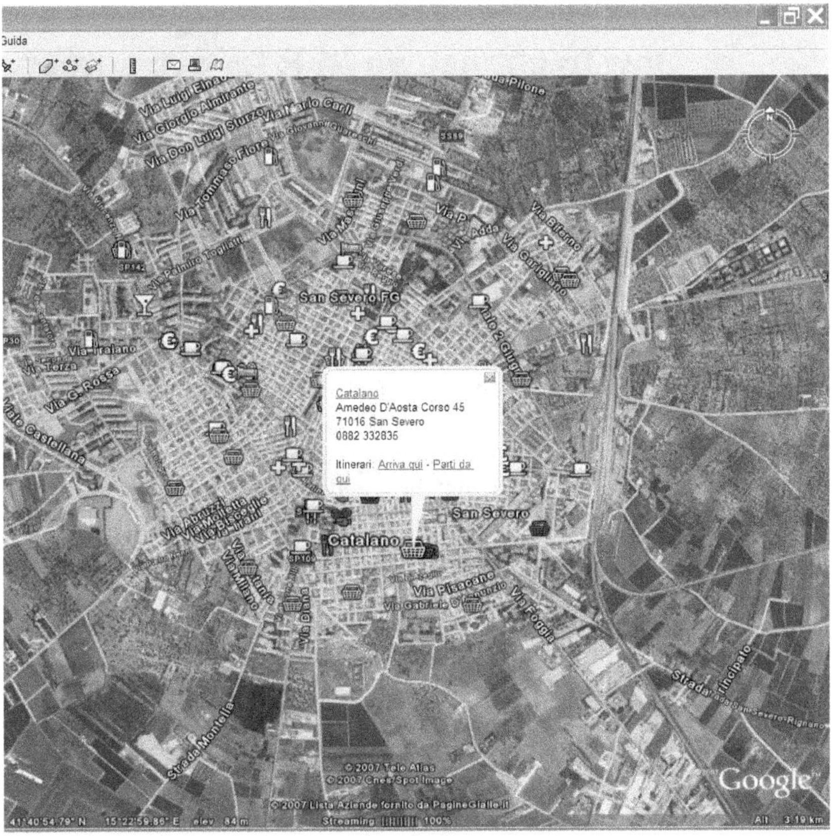

# LUNAR RETURN IN SAN SEVERO DI FOGGIA 101

This picture was taken before Mr. Catalano's shop in the very moment of the Lunar Return

# 12.
# How to choose an ALR for eye surgery

This practical lesson is about a subject who had recently spent his SR at home in Italy, but after a few days repented it because he had the Sun of SR in the 1st House of SR and Uranus in the 6th House of SR – not the very best for safety as far as one's health is concerned. And the very day of his birthday, he was told that he needed eye surgery not only to improve his health, but also to improve his sight.

So the subject contacted me asking in which period he should undergo such surgery. He also asked me for the most suitable month to found a commercial society with a female friend of his, before a notary.

The answer to this latter question is: never! In fact he had a quite dangerous Saturn in the natal 7th House, which we may compare to a sleeping dog. There was no reason to wake this dog up creating a new commercial enterprise while the subject's main activity is already a good, stable, and sure one.

So let us focus on the main scope of this practical lesson and let's begin with recollecting all the 20 rules already listed in another section of this book. First of all, the rule that says that you had better avoid any surgery during the 20 days immediately following one's birthday.

Now you'll see all his following LRs one by one. For each of them I'll write down some remark, without repeating what we have already discussed so far.

After this exercise we'll take stock of his general situation, also considering his transits as well as the subject's field of activity.

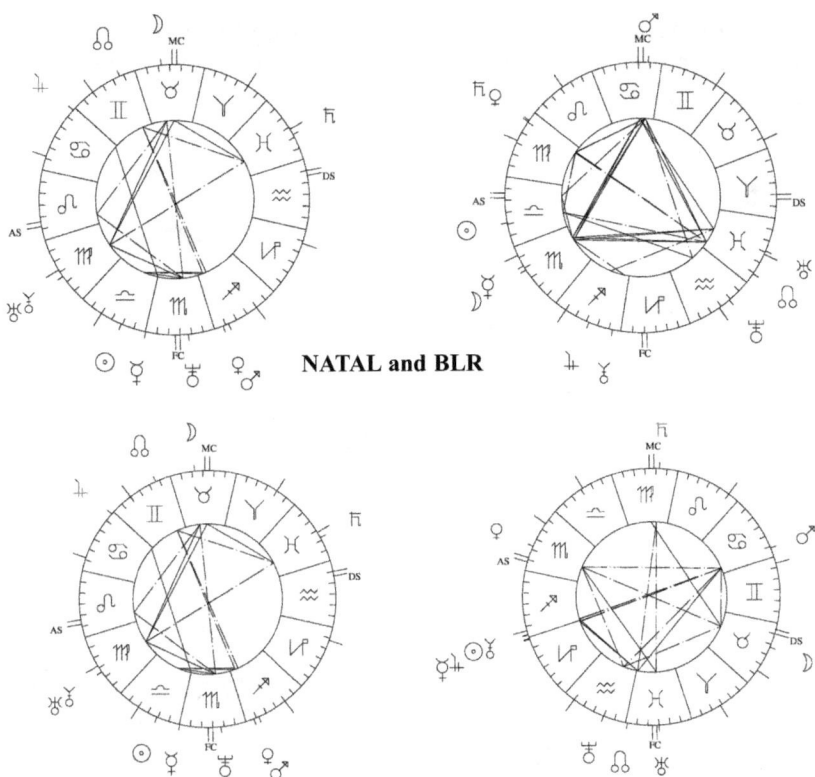

**NATAL and BLR**

The Base Lunar Return is quite detrimental, much in conflict with the subject's aims. With a low cost flight to Madrid, it's another kettle of fish... Remember that with Ryanair, for example, it is possible to reach several capitals of Europe with 25 Euro / ticket, and fly back to Italy for 1 •!

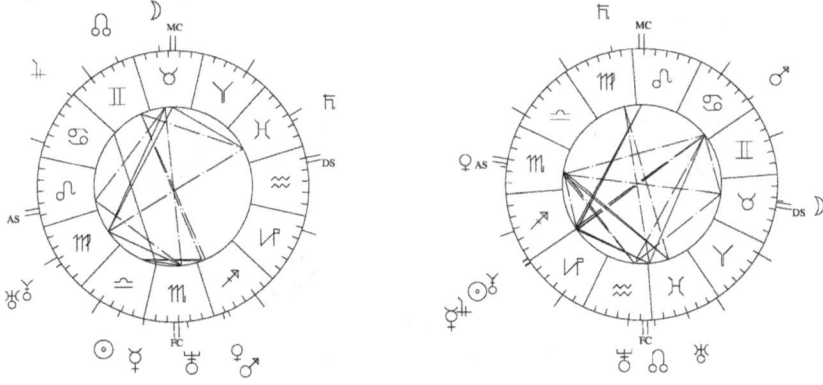

Almost the same can be said for his following LR: with a flight of a few hours, and a very cheap one at that, it is possible to improve his situation very much by spending the LR in Lisbon.

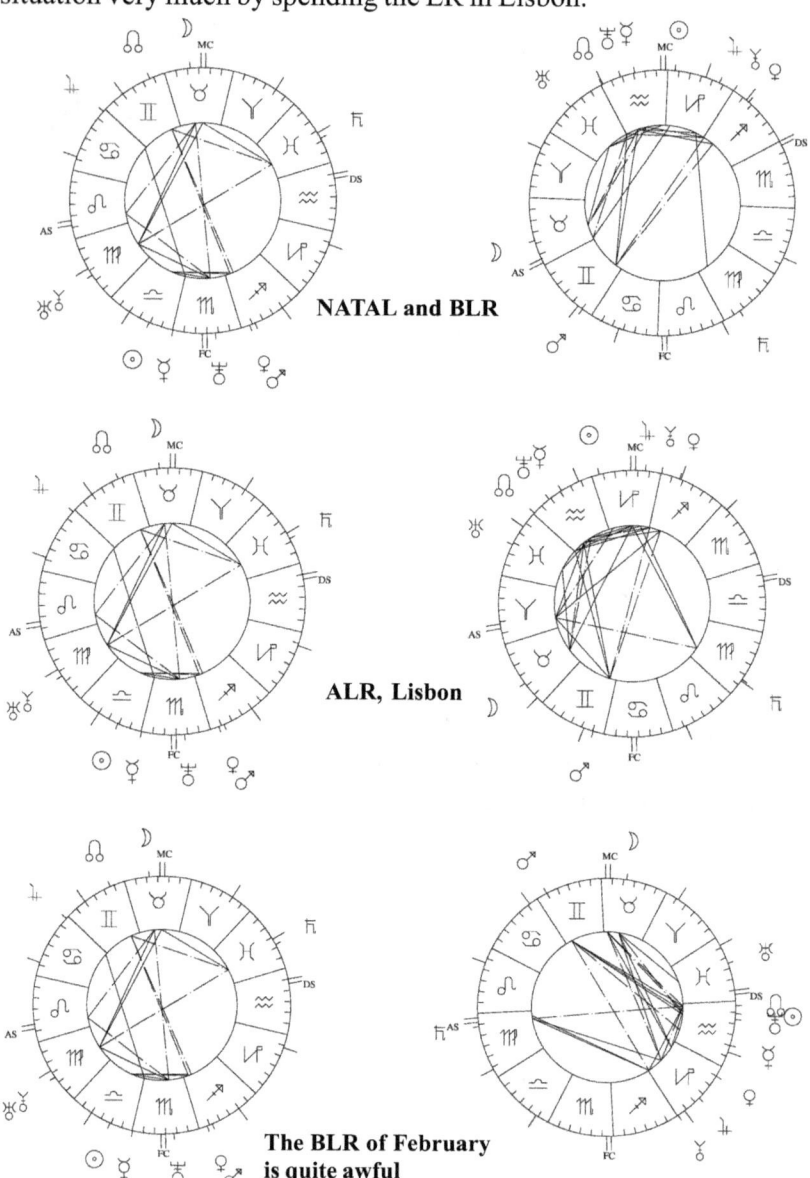

**NATAL and BLR**

**ALR, Lisbon**

**The BLR of February is quite awful**

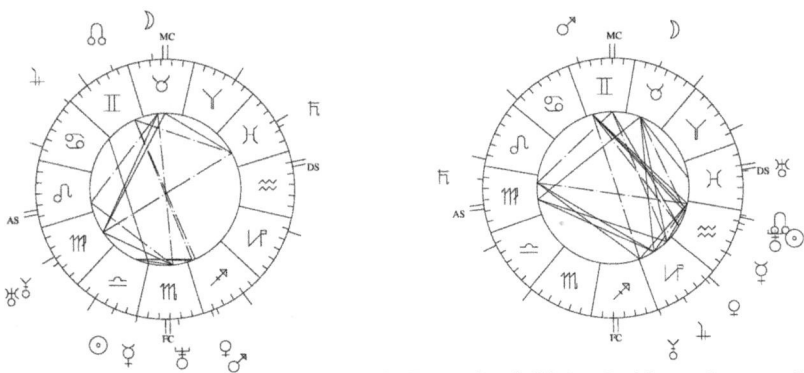

**But in Rovaniemi, Finland, things change a lot.**

**The following three BLRs don't need to be changed**

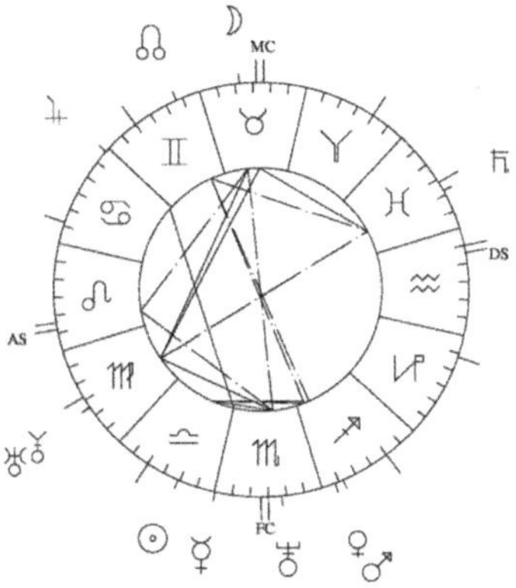

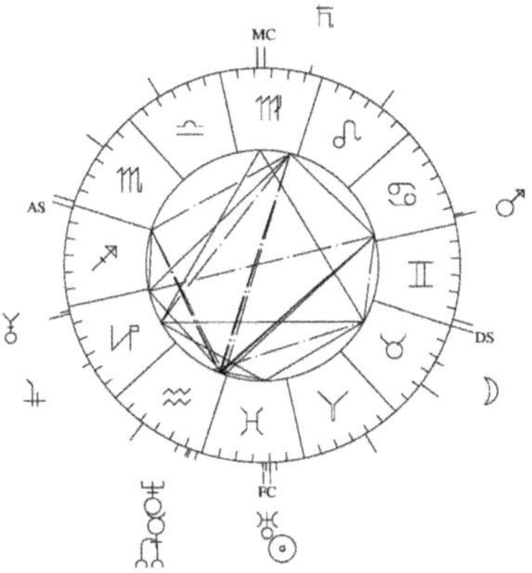

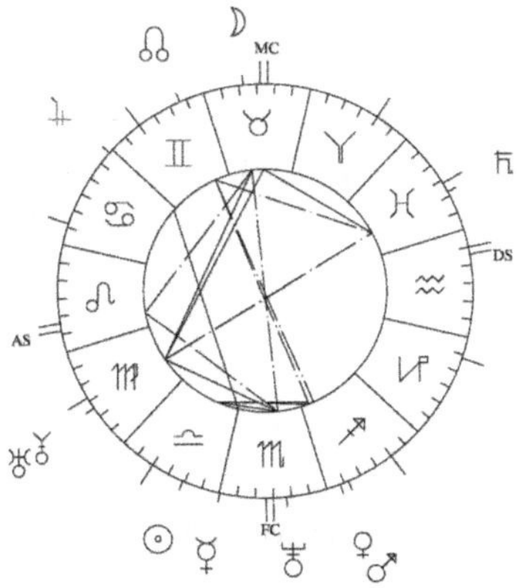

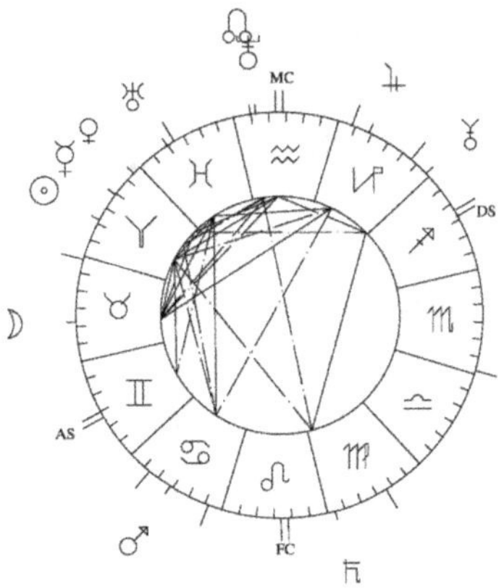

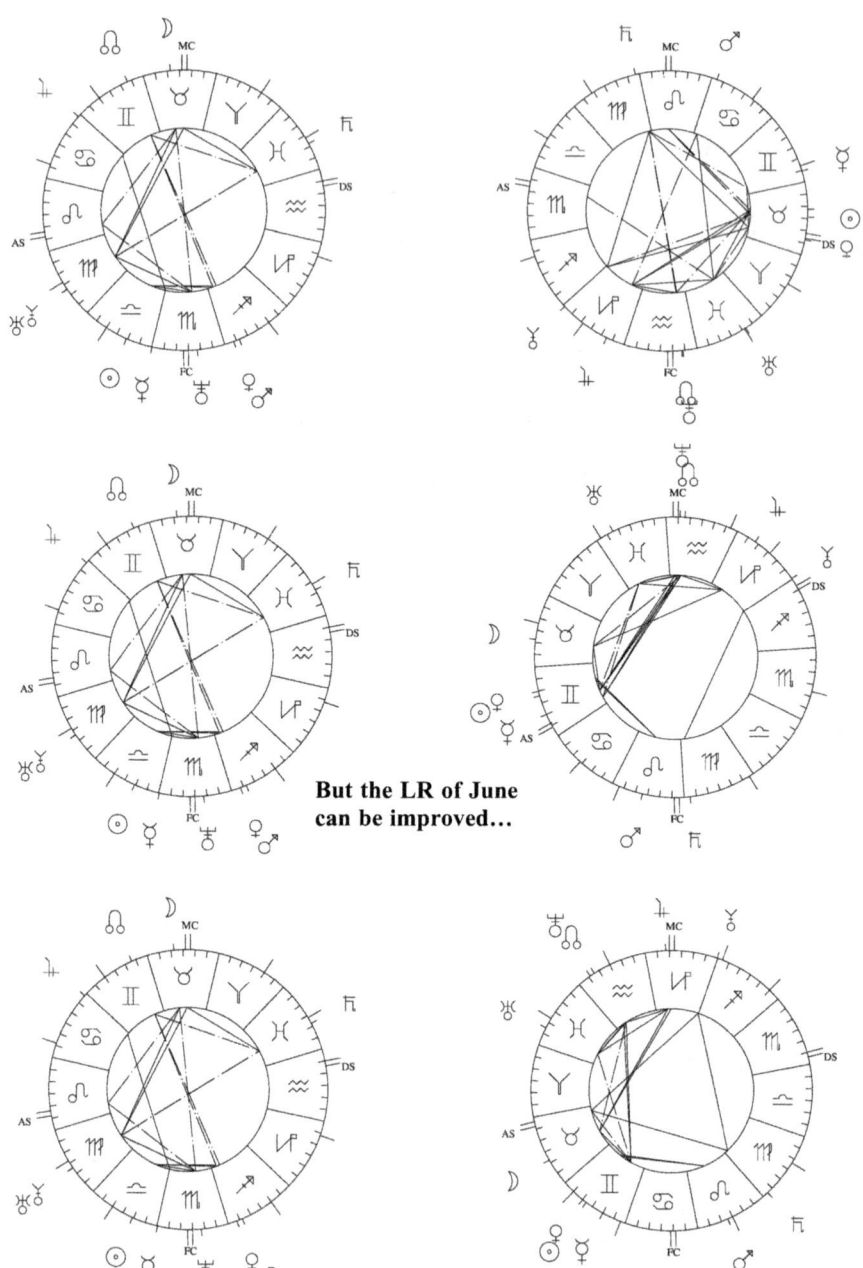

**But the LR of June can be improved...**

**..by relocating it in Ponta Delgada, in the isles Azores (Portugal).**

# HOW TO CHOOSE AN ALR FOR EYE SURGERY

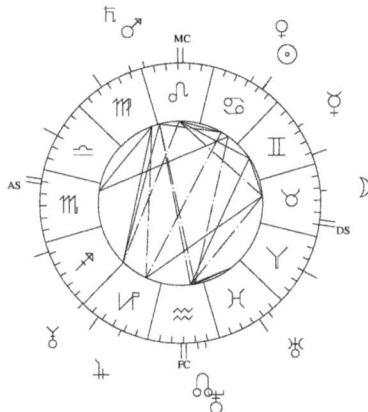

The above LR should be avoided because of its conjunction of Mars and Saturn in the 10th House. By relocating or aiming it to Madeira, Portugal, things become much better (see chart below).

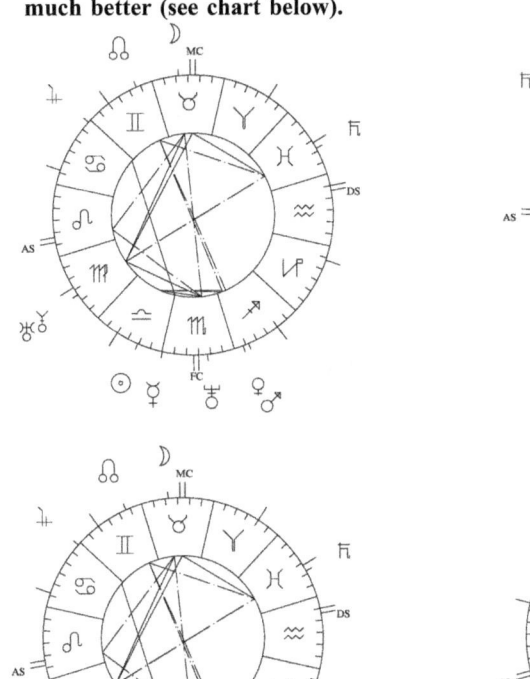

Ascendant in the 12th House and Sun in the 1st House: no good.

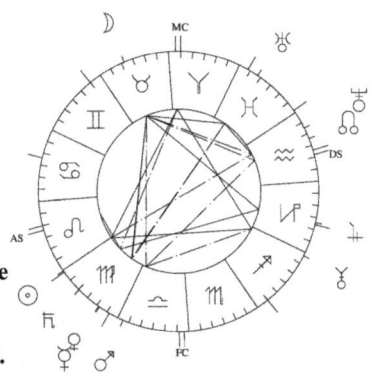

## LUNAR RETURNS

**In Lisbon it is much better.**

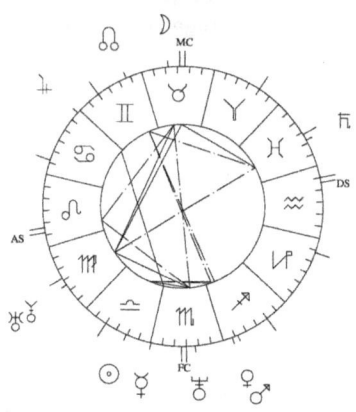
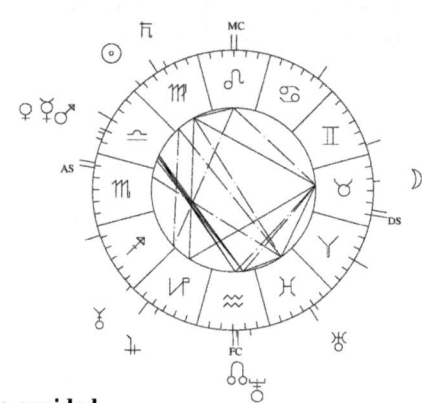

**The stellium in the 12th House should be avoided.**

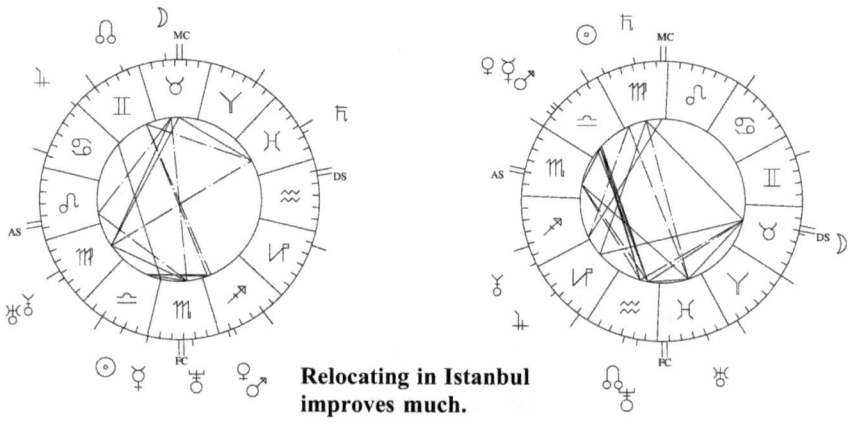

**Relocating in Istanbul improves much.**

Considering the rules expressed in this volume and those listed in my previous works; also keeping in mind that we should avoid surgery in the 20 days after the subject's birthday – but on the other hand it wasn't advisable to wait too long, otherwise it would be the stars who 'would cause any surgery, by chance' – I stated that the best LR within whose frame the subject should undergo surgery was the LR of the 21$^{st}$ of December 2007 in Madrid. I believe so also for the following reasons:

- We position Venus on the Ascendant of LR, thus protecting health very much
- The stellium of prevailingly harmonic celestials in the 2$^{nd}$ House is very good, because – as we stated before – surgery had also an aesthetical implication.
- In the days following the LR of Madrid, transiting Sun and Mercury would be trine to the subject's Medium Coeli, while Jupiter would still be trine to his Ascendant.

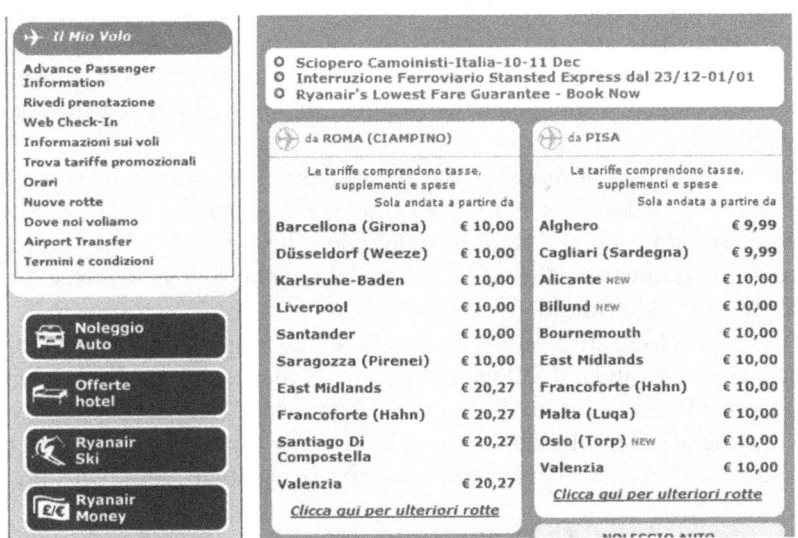

This is a detail from the website www.ryanair.com: try and test it!

# 13.
# A few practical exercises on the dating of events

Starting from the 70s to date, I have written plenty of material explaining how to use LRs for the dating of events: among them half a dozen books and several articles. In particular, about 500 of 800 pages of my volume *Nuovo Trattato di Astrologia*, Armenia, are devoted to practical exercises on the dating of important events: there you can find dozens of charts of LR that help achieving this goal.

Considering that, I'll include only a few examples here.

Let us start with the election of the current Pontiff: Pope Benedict XVI, born Joseph Alois Ratzinger, was elected on the 19$^{th}$ of April 2005, exactly three days after his birthday.

The most interesting this about this fact is that, according to all the expert Vatican correspondents, he became the Pope exactly on the day of his birthday.

In fact, still as a cardinal, on the 16$^{th}$ of April 2005 Joseph Ratzinger was asked to make a speech before the World: where he said exactly what his opinion was and what he would do if he was elected. By doing so he was convinced that he was actually deleting his own name from the list of the possible candidates to the papacy.

To make a long story short, he clearly stated – opposing the general trend – that he would not follow the stream of great ecumenicalism of his predecessor Pope John Paul II. Although he intended to respect the essence and the role of other religions, he said, he would virtually seal the borders among the different credo. He would not mix up Christians, Jews, Muslims and so on.

It seems that most of the voting cardinals in the papal conclave heartily agreed with him – almost certainly they would elect him thanks to the essence of his speech.

Now let us consider his SR, cast for Rome on the 16$^{th}$ April 2005. We can see there is a conjunction of the Sun with Venus, in the 3rd House. This shows his main asset for that year, namely – according to the experts of Vatican – his speech (the 3rd House). Now let us consider his LR covering the same period of the events we are describing: we can see that the LR also 'speaks' the same way. There we have the Moon and Jupiter in strict conjunction in the 3rd House, and the conjunction of Sun, Venus, and Mercury in the 9th House. So you see both Houses connected with communication are strongly occupied by magnificent celestials.

Unluckily I don't know the birth data of his family members, so I cannot use another software called *AstralDetector* to produce a graph on the most important events of his family – but in any case this graph would have simply confirmed what we have already described.

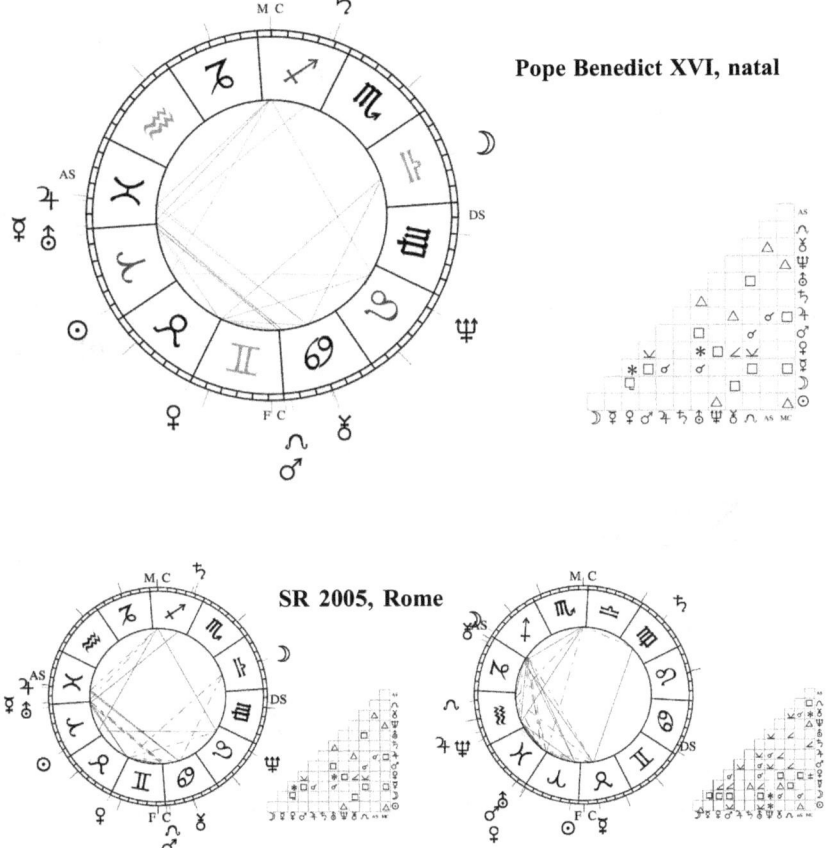

Pope Benedict XVI, natal

SR 2005, Rome

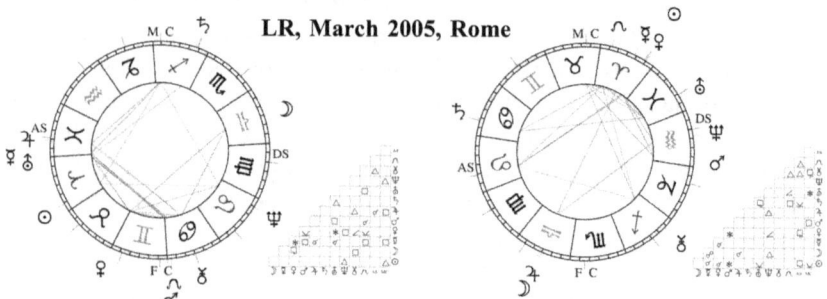

LR, March 2005, Rome

## Silvio Berlusconi announces the birth of a new political party

On the 18th of November 2007, without giving any prior notice Silvio Berlusconi announced the birth of a new political party: the People of Freedom. This took by surprise even his most intimate collaborators.

I am not certain about his SR – I know for sure that even his closest collaborators asked him where he had spent his birthday, but he replied with a laugh.

Nonetheless, you can cast his SR for Milan or Rome and there wouldn't be any significant difference. This SR seems to be the most representative of the events: Saturn is on the Medium Coeli is typical of a 'dismissal', the end of an activity, a 'discharge', as the one described in *The Missing Star*, an Italian film directed by Gianni Amelio in 2006. Nonetheless Jupiter in the 1st House and the Sun in the 10th House make you think that – from Berlusconi's point of view – it was a winning move.

His LR of October is clearly significant of the described event – without distinction if you cast it for Rome or Milan. In fact we see indication of a very strong radicalism (Uranus at the Medium Coeli and Mars close to the Ascendant), which induced a huge change of profession for him (Uranus at the Medium Coeli). While Jupiter and Pluto in the 6th House confirm what the SR says: a winning move at a professional level.

Last, let us consider the graph produced by *AstralDetector* based on a group of four birth dates: Silvio Berlusconi, Gianfranco Fini, Pierferdinando Casini, and Umberto Bossi – the leaders of the three allies of Berlusconi by that time. As you can see, the wonderful instrument of analysis of the dating of events called *AstralDetector* misses the real date by only two days: it draws a net negative peak in the graph on the 20th of November 2007. Keep in mind that the 'negative' or the 'positive' peaks cast by this software indicate important events for the subject –

# A FEW PRACTICAL EXERCISES ON THE DATING OF EVENTS 113

they can be favourable or unfavourable for the subject in both cases.

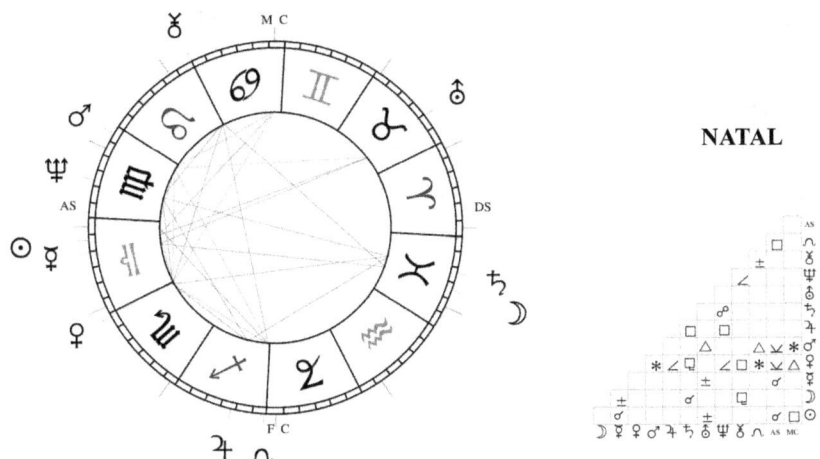

NATAL

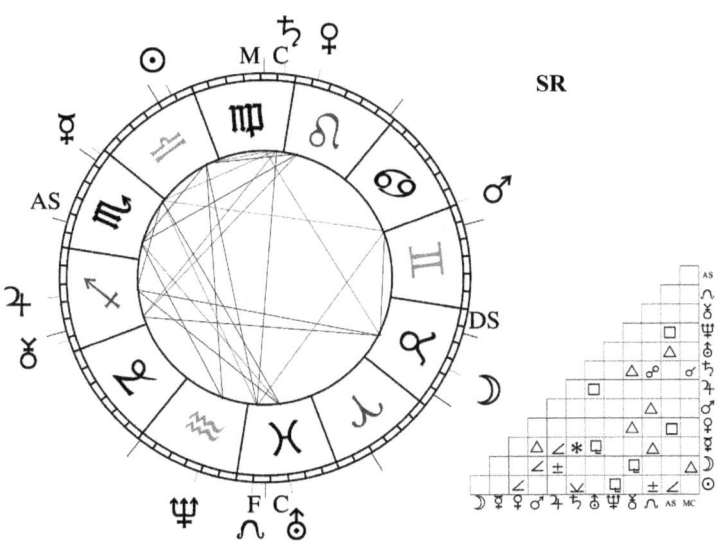

SR

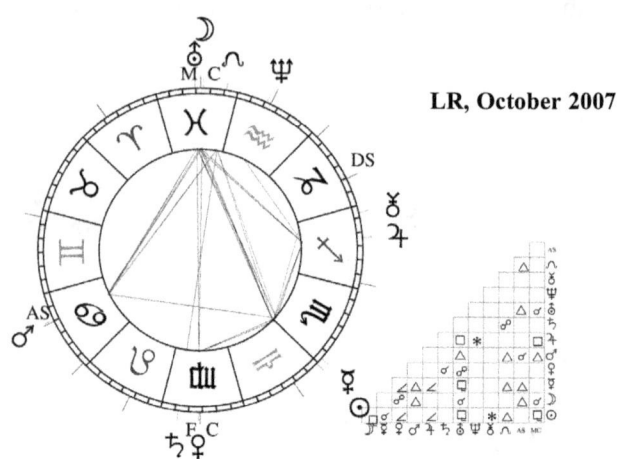

LR, October 2007

**The graph elaborated by the software programme AstralDetector**

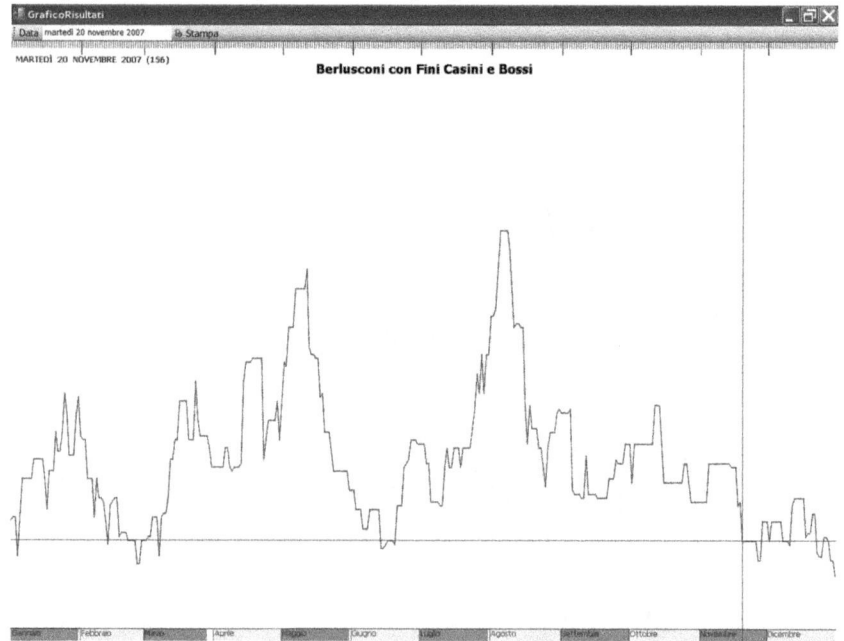

## The arrest of Stefano Ricucci

On the 18th of April 2006 all the Italian media reported in their first pages the arrest of entrepreneur Stefano Ricucci, accused of rigging the market and revealing classified information. He was involved in a process but this is not very interesting from the astrological point of view. What is really interesting in this case is the astral positions underlining his arrest in a very striking way.

Stefano Ricucci's SR of 2005 in Rome – where we suppose he spent his birthday – shows the Sun in the 1st House and the Ascendant of SR in the 6th Natal House. These are positions that, according to certain fellow astrologers, correspond to the growth of the chest in male subjects and of the breast in female subject. The followers of *Active Astrology*, on the contrary, believe that before certain positions of the SR it is better not to grow too much but avoid jail as well as other possible unpleasant situations instead – and they act in order to avoid such positions in the Return chart. Let us consider his LR of April 2006 – a few days before his arrest – and we realize that it is really striking in its precision. In fact the Ascendant of LR lies in his 6th Natal House, while Saturn is placed exactly on the Medium Coeli (announcing a very bad social fall) and the Sun is in the 7th House (possible troubles with law).

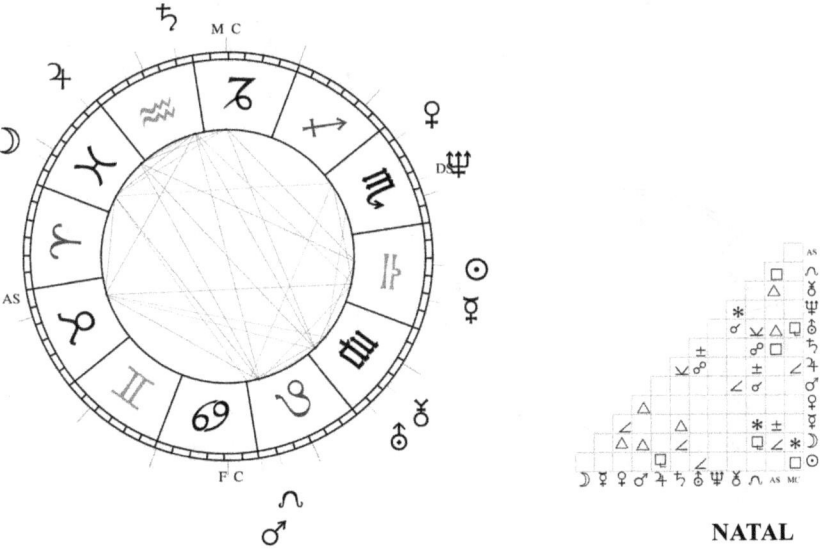

NATAL

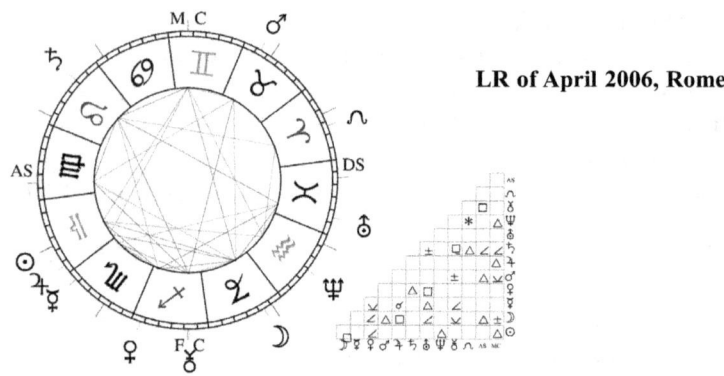

**LR of April 2006, Rome**

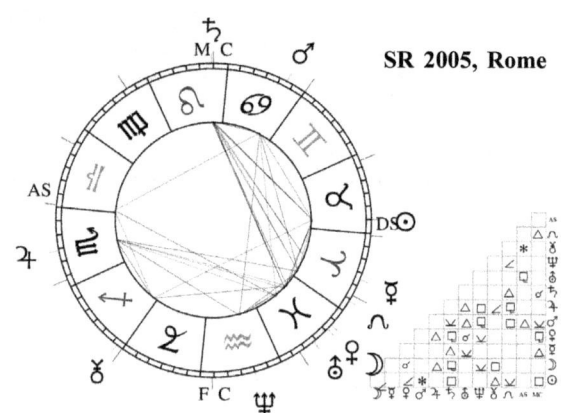

**SR 2005, Rome**

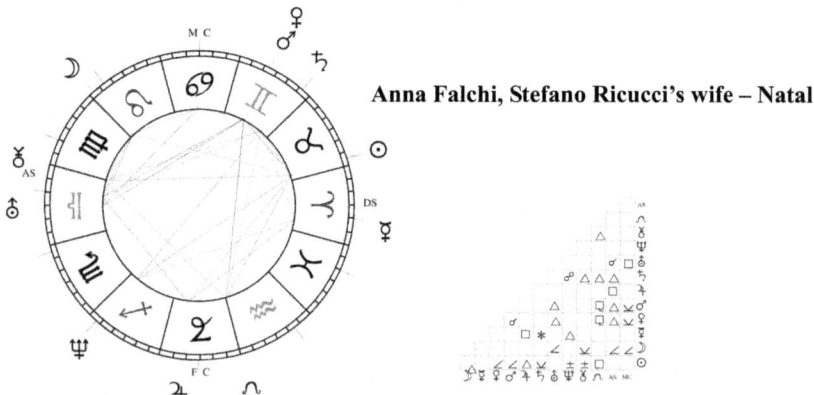

**Anna Falchi, Stefano Ricucci's wife – Natal**

# A FEW PRACTICAL EXERCISES ON THE DATING OF EVENTS 117

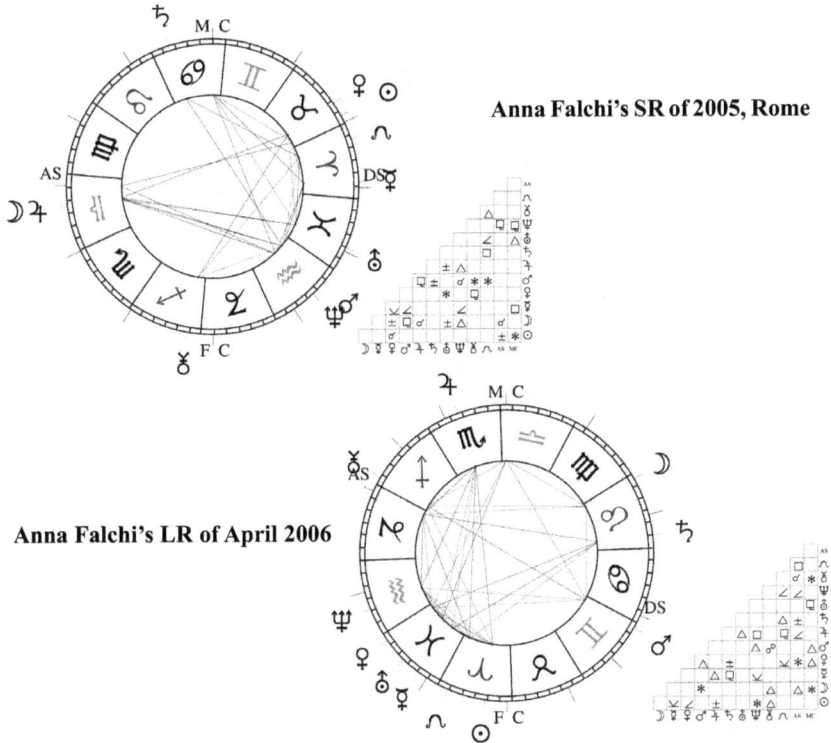

**Anna Falchi's SR of 2005, Rome**

**Anna Falchi's LR of April 2006**

If we consider his wife's celestials, the event becomes even clearer. First of all, his husband is arrested four days before her birthday – see the rule #1 of the thirty rules listed in my volume *Transits and Solar Returns*.

Her Solar Return of 2005 has the Ascendant falling in her 12th Natal House; the conjunction Sun-Venus in the 8th House (rule #26 warns that similar positions have something to do with jail, especially if there are other 'dissonant' elements); and eventually the cherry on the cake: Saturn in the 10th House heralding a very bad, brutal fall in society.

Her Lunar Return of April 2005 is considerable as well, with its Mars in the 6th House and Saturn in the 7th House: a copybook LR, announcing legal troubles for her husband. In this case Jupiter in the 10th House and the Sun in the 3rd House acted as a megaphone – the media covering the event.

In the following lines you'll find four of the thirty rules published in my volume *Transits and Solar Returns*: they can explain in full what happened to the pair Ricucci-Falchi in April 2006. Needless to say that I wrote those thirty rules several years before the arrest of Stefano Ricucci, and that you'll be able to use them to explain any future event without any need for fixed stars, Chiron, Arabian Parts, secondary or tertiary progressions, lunar nodes, and other rules invented on the spot.

1) The twenty days before one's birthday and the twenty days after one's birthday are extremely important days, both positively and negatively. Often the most important events of one's year take place exactly on those days.

4) Remember that if the Ascendant, a stellium, or the Sun of the Solar Return lies in the 1$^{st}$, the 6$^{th}$, or the 12$^{th}$ House, with almost no difference of strength between them, you should expect to have a very burdensome, dangerous, critical and gloomy year in one or more aspects of your life – not just specifically concerning your health, work or love alone. Almost in 100% of the cases, it would be a bad year, a detrimental one – a year that you'll never forget even though you would want to. I realize that this way I underline, I stress, I emphasize it – but it's exactly what I want to do. It is my opinion that no author has ever declared this fact with such a stress, but I find it correct to write down certain rules with exclamation marks – and this is one rule that needs to be written down so, more than all the others. Some author expressed himself in a fairly negative way in connection with the 12$^{th}$ House, but no one before me has ever demonized this House as much as I do. And nobody else has also treated as a criminal the 6$^{th}$ and the 1$^{st}$ House as well. Simply try and follow this rule, and then let me know. When these three Houses play a role in the Solar Return, you can face trouble and unpleasant situations of any kind: in your affections, your health, with justice, money, possible mourning, and so on.

5) The very same rule applies to Mars in the 12$^{th}$, 6$^{th}$, or 1$^{st}$ House of the Solar Return. This position alone can spoil a year even if other elements of the Solar Return may be positive, and even if during the year there are other gorgeous transits.

26) Remember: often the 8$^{th}$ House refers to jail.

At the end of this chapter let me repeat something important for me.

As I have written several times, in other books and articles of mine, it is my opinion that all the branches of Astrology deserve respect and closer examination from any student of this discipline.

But if we talk about Predictive Astrology I believe that my colleagues making forecasts on the basis of different schools of thought other than mine, they should show their loyalty and transparency towards readers by stating, at the very beginning of their works, what are the rules to be followed in order to be able to follow them in their heuristic path. Otherwise, if there aren't starting rules, everybody can claim anything and its opposite at the same time, whatever private or public event they analyze under that method.

**Galileo Galilei watching the celestials through his telescope did so not only to study their shape and motions, but also to elaborate his astrological forecasts.**

# 14.
# SRs and LRs in the attack on Pearl Harbor

This exercise allows throwing further light on certain details of the reading of SRs and LRs.

Let us consider the attack on Pearl Harbor, where the Japanese navy and air force conducted a surprise military strike against the United States' naval base in Hawaii on the morning of the 7$^{th}$ of December 1941, destroying several ships and causing personnel losses in thousands. Thanks to those manoeuvres, the Japanese won supremacy over the entire Pacific Ocean during the World War II – at least, for a short period.

Let us watch that event in the eyes of the four main leading actors of the time: namely the President of the United States of America; Winston Churchill; Benito Mussolini, and Adolf Hitler.

Let us begin with the President of the USA.

**Franklin Delano Roosevelt** was born in Hyde Park, New York, on the 30$^{th}$ of January 1882 at 8:45 pm. Nowadays the President of the United States spends a large amount of time flying on board the presidential airplane, mainly for security reasons. There he holds crucial meetings all the time, always connected with the most strategic locations of the world. But you can be reasonably confident that Roosevelt used to spend almost all his time in the White House or not far from there. We can presume that he spent his birthday previous to the 7$^{th}$ of December 1941, there.

His SR is quite clear. Mars in the 12$^{th}$ House conjunct with the Ascendant clearly announces a year of war and heavy concerns in relationship with foreign people and foreign countries (Neptune in the 9$^{th}$ House).

There had been rumours in the States of a possible future Japanese attack, and if anybody had studied Roosevelt's LRs it would have been possible to forecast the time of the attack with good accuracy. The most important element of the LR cast for the 5$^{th}$ of December (two days before the attack) is the Ascendant falling in the 9th House radix (foreign people). There is also a very detrimental stellium spanning the 12th and the 1st Houses as well as the Sun in the 6th House. That's really too much! Also consider that Mars is in the 11th House of the LR. Its meaning is similar to that of Mars in the 7th House, only a little bit less detrimental: war, attacks, marked tensions.

The only favourable point of this LR is Jupiter close to the Ascendant from the stronger side, i.e. in the 12th House. We all know that the consequences of that attack were very serious. On the other hand, we may say that the United States was quite lucky because there was no American aircraft carrier in the harbour that day. Was it by chance – many historians suggest so – or is it the evidence that the USA let Japan attack them in order to push U.S. public opinion from isolationism to the acceptance of participation in the war being unavoidable. We'll probably never know. Anyway, President Roosevelt's LR announces a little moment of good luck within a period marked by a very potent celestial situation.

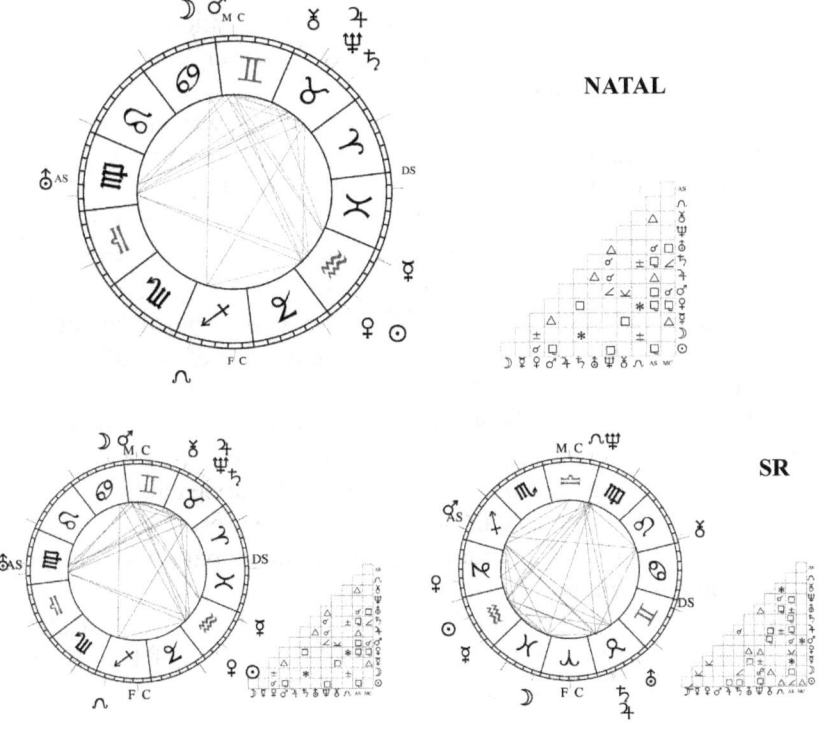

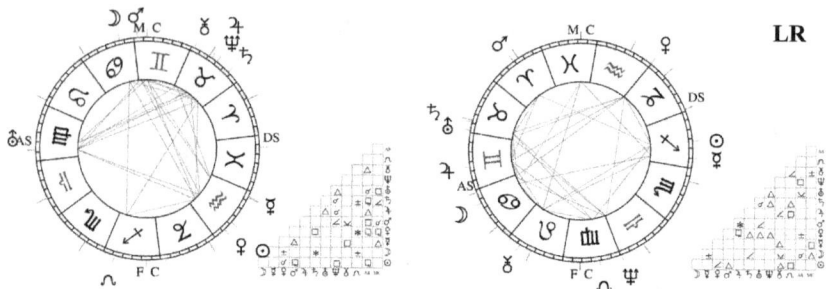

Let us consider now the same event through the celestials of the English Prime Minister. **Winston Churchill**'s SR took place a few days before the attack on Pearl Harbor: he was surely in London that day. In fact he was born in Woodstock on the 30th of November 1874 at 1:30 am. It is a matter of fact that things of an extraordinary importance take place during the days close to one's birthday. For example, Adolf Hitler died 10 days after his own birthday and got married somewhen between his birthday and his suicide. This fact is now accepted and reported by all my fellow astrologers. Unluckily they forget to mention who actually found out this fact – but luckily my books are preserved in the public libraries, and there is a date in each of them.

Now back to Sir Churchill's terrible SR. The Sun was in conjunction with the Ascendant of the SR, and it's not so important whether it lies in the 12th House or in the 1st House. There's also a stellium spanned over the 12th and the 1st House. Mars is in the 7th House and Saturn is in the 9th House, and they speak for themselves. Nevertheless there's something strange in it. Churchill knew that after such an attack, America's huge war machine would finally intervene giving an essential hand to the English, who had so far been the only nation struggling for the defence of Western civilization. So why was Churchill's SR so detrimental? The news arrived in London via radio, and probably made superoptimist Winston Churchill's blood run cold, because he probably feared that the USA had suffered such a terrible damage that had left Japan virtually unbeatable.

On the other hand, celestials are impartial: the presence of Venus in the 10th House of his SR announced a sort of emancipation for him and for the United Kingdom.

His LR of the 12th November 1941 is also significant: a strict conjunction of Saturn and Uranus in the 10th House of LR is very detrimental for the Prime Minister's position before the entire world, but on the other had Jupiter in the 10th House recalls the same reading of that Venus in the 10th House of SR.

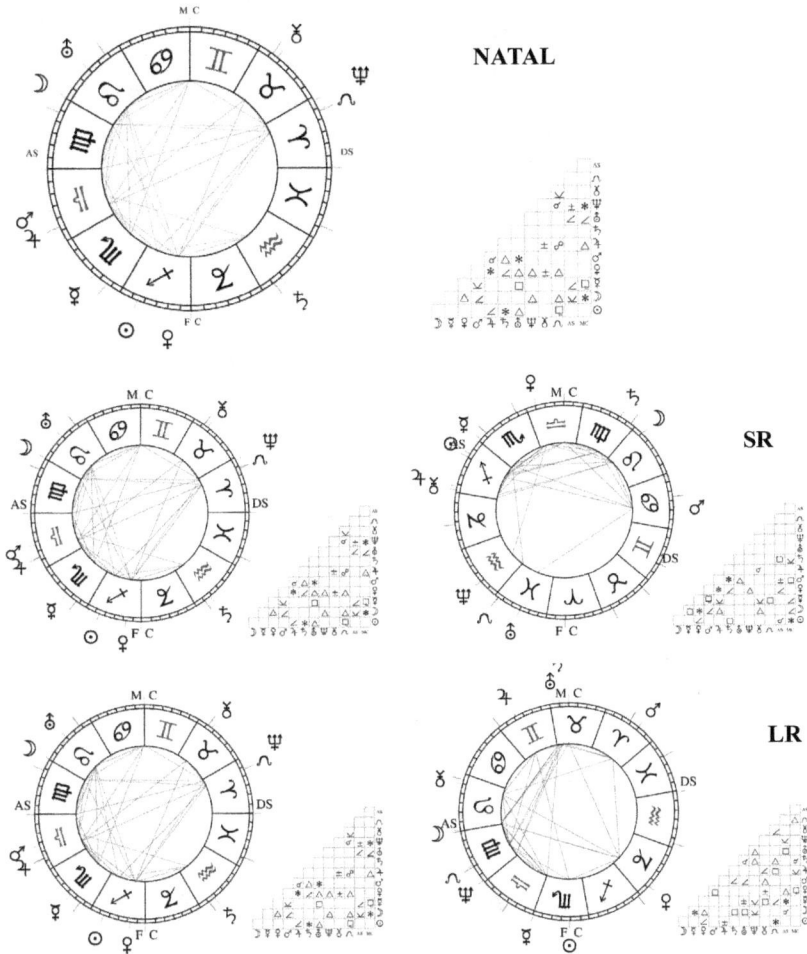

Let us study now **Adolf Hitler**'s stars. He was born in Braunau on the 20th April 1889 at 6:30 pm. Even in this case, there is almost no doubt on where he spent his birthday. We know that he had had his headquarters built on the Eagles' Nest, on a mountain peak from where he could see his birth village, Braunau. In astrological terms, there is a minimal difference between his spending his SR there or in Berlin.

Now Hitler's SR is remarkable. The Ascendant and Mars in the 9th House, but above all: a striking and quite positive stellium in the 11th House! It is evident for an astrologer that the *Fürher* – who in his madness believed that there were non-existing army corps ready to save him a few days before his final defeat – greeted the attack on Pearl Harbor as the sign of destiny of a very certain victory of the Triple, diabolic Alliance. The presence of Jupiter in the 1st House conjunct with the Ascendant in his LR shows the same kind of optimism. Venus might have been over the cusp of the 9th House.

Please note that other elements of this LR are really detrimental, but do not forget the rules already given in this volume for a correct reading of a Lunar Return: very dangerous positions of LR falling within the frame of a good SR – and Hitler had had a good SR fore sure – which can not and must not worry anybody.

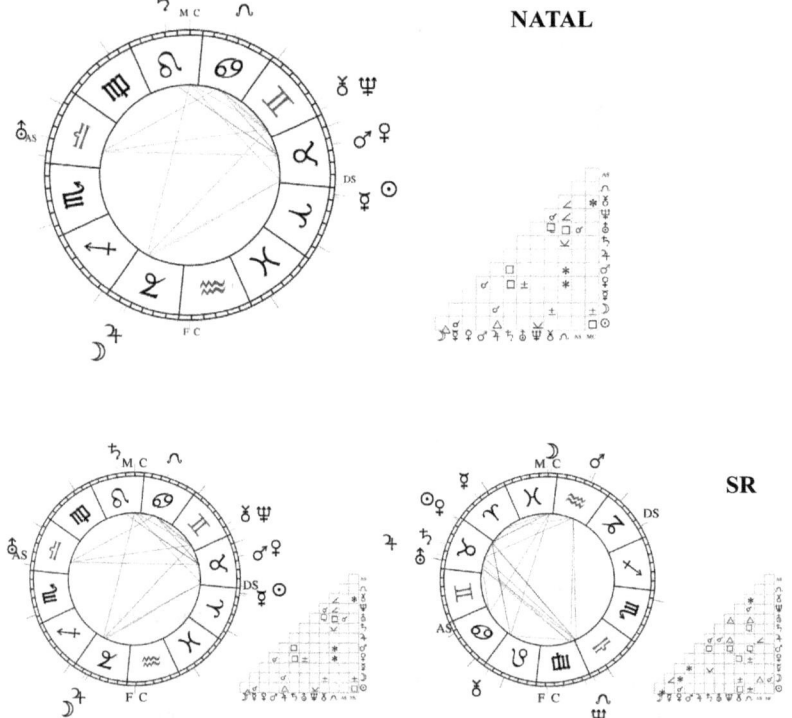

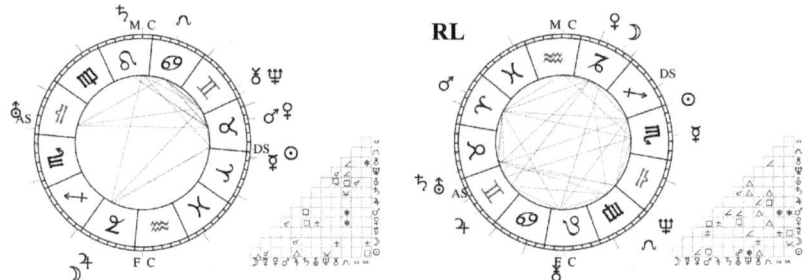

Now it's **Benito Mussolini**'s turn. Here we find ambivalence due to the fact that from certain points of view the Italian *Duce* was less mad than Hitler; in fact the former used to reason with more clarity of mind, compared with the latter. Also in Mussolini's SR we can find elements of joy for alleged victories abroad: the Sun, Pluto, and Venus are in the 9th House, and Venus is conjunct with the Medium Coeli. Yet the SR itself is still detrimental, due to its Ascendant falling in Mussolini's natal 1st House and because of a stellium in the 7th House of SR (announcing that a new, powerful enemy would soon arrive to fight).

We can cast similar considerations from his LR too.

And to conclude, consider the graph produced by *AstralDetector* for the year 1941 based on the birth data of the aforementioned subjects. It clearly shows a serious crisis on the 7th December, the day of the attack on Pearl Harbor; it is a net, negative peak. I mention it to arouse your curiosity, because the dating of the events through the graphs of *AstralDetector* is not within the scopes of this volume. To get to know more on this subject visit this webpage (in Italian): http://www.cirodiscepolo.it/AstralDetector.htm

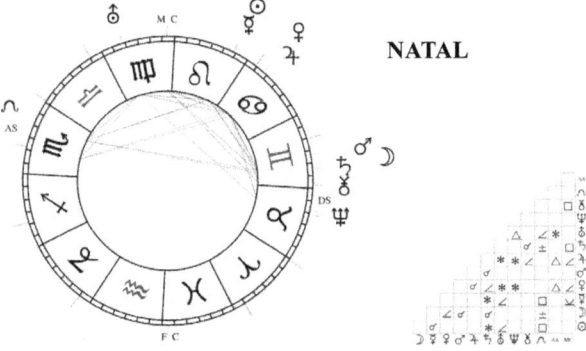

126 LUNAR RETURNS

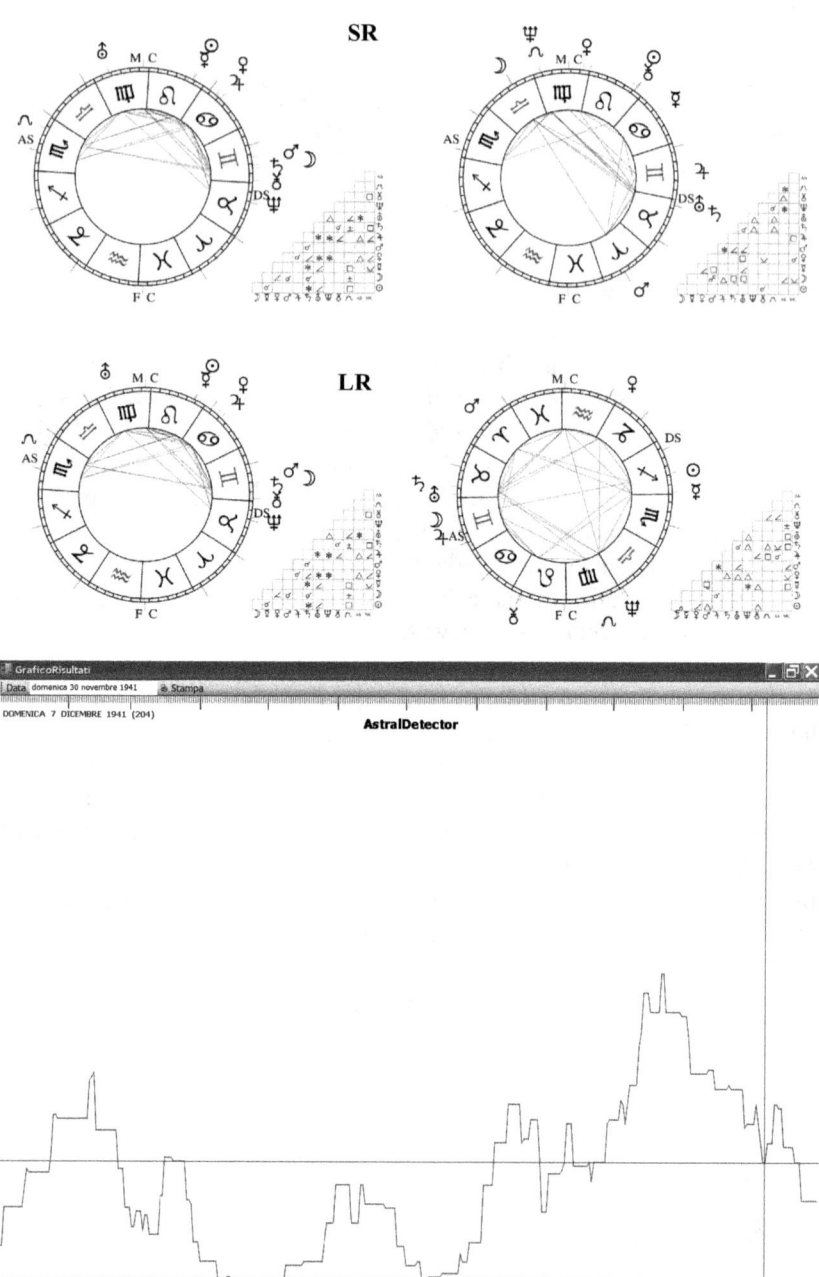

# 15.
# Lunar Return on airliners

Several times, with practical examples both in my books and in my magazine *Ricerca '90*, I have shown how to aim a Solar Return and/or a Lunar Return 'on the fly' – or better said: 'on the flight' – in order to reach places that one could not reach on the dry land.

Remember that in such events (which are the subject of one whole chapter of my book *I fondamenti dell'astrologia medica*, Armenia editore) you usually have two options: taking a taxi plane or hiring a private aircraft with a pilot from a flying club.

I would avoid the first because it would be quite expensive – although of course the notion of 'expensive' is a relative one, depending also from the subject's needs and financial situations. In fact, a rich man seeking desperately to save his own life would certainly choose this solution instead of the other, perhaps less expensive but unsure ways.

Usually it's easier to contact a flying club, where you'd certainly meet a keen flyer whose main dream is to be allowed to fly for free for hours: he'd be only glad if you refund the cost of fuel and give him an extra income of some Euros.

Now let me introduce a brand new method; something that – to my knowledge – nobody has ever tried before. Nonetheless it is something that, being pure mathematics, can be said to be self-proven.

Say that a David Smith wants to spend his Lunar Return in Milan, Italy, on the 21st of January 2008 at 1:02 pm GMT. As you can see from the relevant chart, it is a very bad Return. Say that David's current SR is detrimental too, so that he wants to aim (i.e.

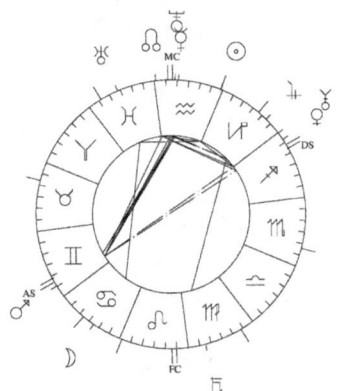

relocate according to the rules given in my books) this bad LR in order to avoid further risks for himself. The ideal place for such relocation would be an isle in the very middle of the Ocean between Senegal (on the West coast of Central Africa) and Brazil (to be more precise, the North-East point of Brazil). This is one of the emptiest portions of this planet. If Our Lord had been passionately fond of Aimed Solar Returns, he would have certainly filled up this void with at least one island in the middle.

Alas, there's no island in there. Yet, our brain often can be better than an island – so I made up my mind and invented the method that I'm going to expose. In my opinion, it's something that has very solid theoretical basis and can be applied without spending 50,000 Euros for a taxi plane, but only 1,000 Euros on an airliner.

It consists of tracing the route of an airliner, say flying Lisbon to Recife, provided that you know ALL the points touched by the route during the flight, and at what time you'll be flying over any of them.

It is not a 'mission impossible'! I'm going to show you how, and after the following single example, you'll be able to do the same for any area of the world and apply it to any Aimed SR and/or Aimed LR.

The most difficult point is getting the precise route of the flight. Forget about asking the airlines: they aren't going to tell you anything for security reasons because of the hazard posed by terrorism.

My friend Pino Valente was smart enough to find out, on the Internet, the webpage of the fans of flight simulation. As everybody knows, people like these can become really manic in their wish to create a perfect simulation of flights; therefore they get to know whatever may be needed to be known as far as routes are concerned. Also on 'normal' webpages devoted to travels, like for example www.opodo.it, you can get to know the kind of aircraft, the departure & arrival time, the time needed to reach there, and everything else that you need for the purposes that I'm explaining to you.

Now this is the URL of the webpage for flight simulators:
http://rfinder.asalink.net/
It is necessary to subscribe and login; you'll have access to this area:
http://rfinder.asalink.net/free/autoroute_rt.php

From www.opodo.it I got to know that there's a flight TAP TP151 Lisbon to Recife leaving Lisbon on the 21$^{st}$ January 2008 at 10:50; the flight takes 7 hours and 45 minutes. Hence you can get, from the Route Finder webpage, the following table containing really *all* the information that you need. We'll consider only the second part of the table, listing all the virtual points of the sky that are used by air traffic controllers to guide the aircrafts along very narrow skyways: Nakos, Barok, Bentu, Nevel, Mitla...

In the following map we have traced all these virtual nodes of the sky and we have connected them to form a line.

## RouteFinder
*Route generator for PC flight simulation use - **NOT FOR REAL WORLD NAVIGATION***
(C)2005-2007 ASA srl - Italy

Computed route from **LISBOA** (LPPT, LP) to **GUARARAPES GILBERTO FREYRE INTSB** (

```
Cruise altitude between FL330 and FL330
LPPT   (0.0nm)    -SID->  NAKOS  (47.8nm)   -UZ4->  BAROK  (174.3nm)  -UN873->
BENTU  (274.5nm)  -UN873-> NEVEL (395.5nm)  -UN873-> MITLA (519.8nm)  -UN873->
SAMAR  (549.7nm)  -UN873-> GDV   (727.2nm)  -UN729-> REMGI (787.1nm)  -UN729->
DEREV  (809.3nm)  -UN857-> BIPET (930.0nm)  -UN857-> ETIBA (1184.4nm) -UN857->
GUNET  (1304.7nm) -UN857-> ORABI (1555.9nm) -UN857-> BOTNO (1722.6nm) -UN857-:
DELAX  (2074.0nm) -UN857-> MAROA (2203.1nm) -UN857-> ERETU (2427.2nm) -UN857-:
NOISE  (2544.7nm) -UN857-> CLOVE (2564.9nm) -UN857-> NEURA (2702.3nm) -UN857-:
FNO    (2900.5nm) -UB623-> ESGUM (3091.8nm) -B623->  ISADO (3148.0nm) -DCT->
SBRF   (3196.2nm)
```

Details:

| ID    | FREQ  | TRK | DIST | Coords                        | Name/Remarks      |
|-------|-------|-----|------|-------------------------------|-------------------|
| LPPT  |       | 0   | 0    | N38°46'52.72" W009°08'09.31"  | LISBOA            |
| NAKOS |       | 198 | 48   | N38°00'00.00" W009°20'04.18"  | NAKOS             |
| BAROK |       | 202 | 126  | N35°58'00.00" W010°01'24.00"  | BAROK             |
| BENTU |       | 224 | 100  | N34°37'42.00" W011°14'37.00"  | BENTU             |
| NEVEL |       | 223 | 121  | N32°59'51.00" W012°40'18.00"  | NEVEL             |
| MITLA |       | 223 | 124  | N31°18'30.00" W014°04'56.00"  | MITLA             |
| SAMAR |       | 223 | 30   | N30°53'59.00" W014°24'56.00"  | SAMAR             |
| GDV   | 112.9 | 206 | 178  | N28°04'37.49" W015°25'44.35"  | GRAN CANARIA      |
| REMGI |       | 180 | 60   | N27°05'24.72" W015°16'10.57"  |                   |
| DEREV |       | 180 | 22   | N26°43'23.42" W015°12'39.79"  |                   |
| BIPET |       | 220 | 121  | N25°00'00.00" W016°21'31.67"  | BIPET             |
| ETIBA |       | 220 | 254  | N21°20'17.75" W018°40'43.63"  | ETIBA             |
| GUNET |       | 220 | 120  | N19°35'42.00" W019°44'06.00"  | GUNET             |
| ORABI |       | 221 | 251  | N15°56'18.00" W021°52'12.00"  | ORABI             |
| BOTNO |       | 222 | 167  | N13°30'00.00" W023°14'30.00"  | BOTNO             |
| DELAX |       | 223 | 351  | N08°20'12.00" W026°03'06.00"  | DELAX             |
| MAROA |       | 225 | 129  | N06°26'08.00" W027°03'44.00"  | MAROA             |
| ERETU |       | 225 | 224  | N03°07'42.00" W028°48'00.00"  | ERETU             |
| NOISE |       | 227 | 118  | N01°23'40.20" W029°42'33.00"  | NOISE             |
| CLOVE |       | 227 | 20   | N01°05'42.60" W029°51'39.00"  | CLOVE             |
| NEURA |       | 227 | 137  | S00°56'10.80" W030°54'51.00"  | NEURA             |
| FNO   | 113.7 | 228 | 198  | S03°52'12.72" W032°25'45.55"  | FERNANDO          |
| ESGUM |       | 231 | 191  | S06°37'33.00" W034°02'14.40"  | ESGUM             |
| ISADO |       | 232 | 56   | S07°26'03.60" W034°30'45.60"  | ISADO             |
| SBRF  |       | 233 | 48   | S08°07'36.46" W034°55'22.94"  | GUARARAPES GILBERTO |

On Giovanna Bianco & Pino Valente's website www.bianco-valente.com you can see their work of 2005 titled *Relational Domain* – it's a beautiful work of art resembling the world of synapses, the connections between the sky and human mind, the air traffic controllers' celestial nodes, the communication between our brain and the reality of universe...

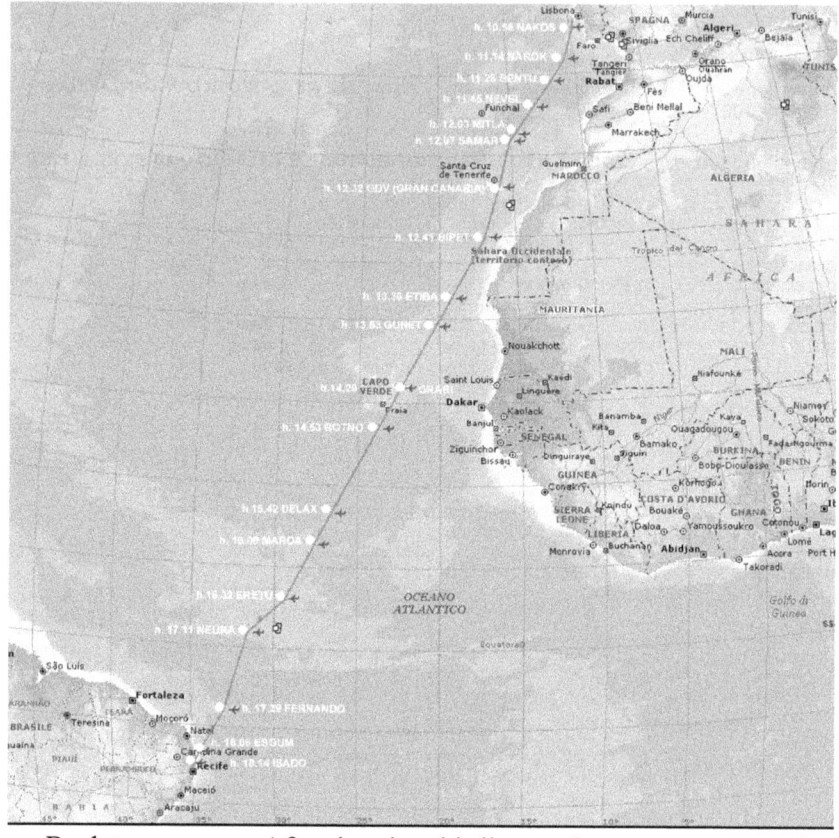

Back to our scope. After drawing this line on the map you proceed as follows. You open the astrological software that you use to calculate Solar returns and/or Lunar Returns. There you add new 'locations' in its database, say: Nakos Radar, longitude 9°20'W and latitude 38°00'N, Barok Radar longitude 10°01'W and latitude 35°58'N and so on.

As you already know, the time zone is not required while casting SRs and LRs, so when you're asked to input the Time Zone, you can simply digit '1'.

Now consider the following four maps of ALR that I have cast to explain this method.

Compare them with the already given map of BLR of Milan, Italy – a very bad one. Having added the additional locations to our software program, it is now able to cast a LR for Maroa. Taken for granted that the map of SR and the map of LR must have the domification of the place where the subject is there in that moment – neither the place of his birth nor the place of his usual residence – nobody can deny that the result is striking. It isn't important to know what time will it be there in their local time, because our software calculates the GMT of the LR and relocates the map of that moment on to Maroa. Those who still doubt about this method, may cast the Aimed LR for Cape Verde (for example, Sale) and they can see that the resulting map is almost identical to the map cast for Orabi Radar (in fact, the geographic coordinates of the two locations are very close).

With the tables given here you can calculate anything. We know that the aircraft, an Airbus A330-220, flying at an average cruise speed of 412 Mph (nautical miles per hour) takes 7 hours and 45 minutes to fly the whole route Lisbon to Recife, corresponding to 3,196 nautical miles. Knowing the distance between the single points of the line that we have traced on our map, we can also know at what time we'll be flying over each of those points.

The method's only drawback is that the aircraft may take off later than the scheduled time, but you can always recalculate the route by heart. In fact, consider our map with the dotted line. Say that you had reckoned to be over Maroa for your Aimed LR. Now being late, instead of flying over Maroa, you'll be flying over Delax in the very moment in which the LR takes place. An as you can see from the chart cast for Delax, it's good anyway.

If you wish to get a safe calculation, you can apply larger margins of tolerance and reckon that if the aircraft takes off with a delay of, say, less than 30 minutes, the pilots are able to make up time by flying a little more than the usual cruise speed.

I believe that you have now a new tool, and a very feasible one, to achieve the goals that you wish: moreover, spending no more than one hundred Euros instead of, say, fifty thousand Euros.

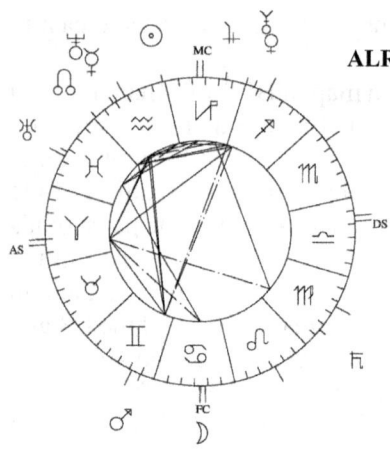

**ALR, Maroa**

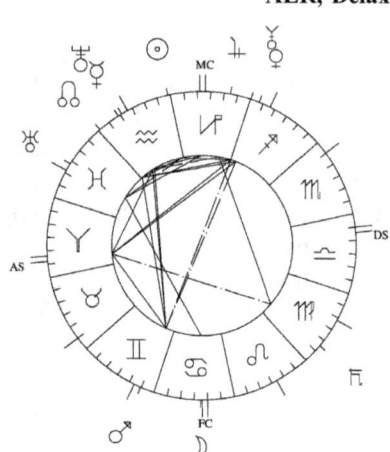

**ALR, Delax**

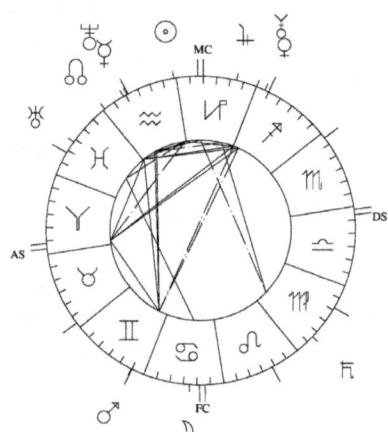

**ALR, Cape Verde**

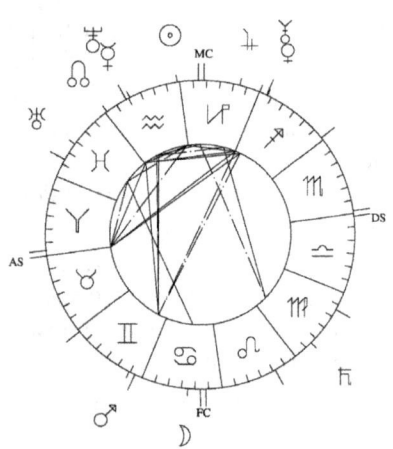

**ALR, Orabi**

# 16.
# Lunar Return in Flores

My LR of the 1st of February was quite difficult to aim. Or better said: while at a first sight its relocation appeared extremely simple to be planned and calculated, when I proceeded with the exercise I realized that it would be a kind of benchmark, or a sort of *summa*, of all my studies in astrology so far.

First of all, I'd like to make some preliminary remarks of personal character.

Some of you may perhaps be aware that I separated from my wife in spring 2006. We went on living together in separate rooms for a couple of years, deferring judicial separation because our daughter Luna, despite having already grown up to be a little woman (at the end of august 1984) strongly opposed our decision by means of a series of self-injuring actions that prevented me from proceeding effectively.

It is my opinion that a parting is never a positive event, but in certain cases it is the lesser of two evils when two partners become convinced that the daily micro conflicts overpass the positivity of living as a couple.

Considering that I got engaged at the age of twenty and I separated judicially with official signatures at the age of sixty, at the end of my marital path I can say that very few subjects born – like me – with the conjunction of Venus and Uranus in their 12th Natal House would have been able to carry on one relationship for more than forty years.

Most of my male and female friends offered me their condolences on this event, but my answer to them was that I have considered this situation not as a mourning but as an opportunity that life has offered to me.

I don't know to whom I should be more grateful for the life that I've received as a present and that I have lived in a winning way in almost all its fields. I have no regrets; I believe that I've been lucky beyond reason.

Yet one cannot forget that separation from a lawyer is not the same as separation from a steelworker – I know hundreds of people whom have been tortured and flayed alive in separation suits that have lasted up to six or seven years.

In my case, from the day in which I charged a lawyer to start this procedure for me, I have finished with it in about one month. Many people were surprised, saying that I hadn't even to go and sleep under a bridge!

Well, if I wasn't able to improve my own life and to achieve particularly positive results using my AA (Active Astrology), how could I pretend to try and improve the others' life with the same tools?

I am not claiming that I achieved my goal for free – I am saying that obviously I have paid a fee for it, especially as far as stress, time, money, and battles are concerned: but it has been a much lower toll than what life would have collected from me.

So back to my Aimed LR of the beginning of February 2006. By that time I had a couple of meetings with the lawyer, whom I hadn't charged yet to act for me. There were two LRs left to relocate and I felt that I must not make a mistake.

This is why I first considered the possibility of aiming my LR in Bordeaux, France. There I would have placed a marvellous, very strict conjunction of Venus and Jupiter on the cusp between the $5^{th}$ and the $6^{th}$ House of LR. One should not expect more from life... especially if in that moment what you care for most is your own health, your daughters' health, the chance of meeting the right partner, a little help in your activity and in your working relationships, and so on. Yet I had another completely different goal, namely: closing as soon as possible a situation that prevented me from putting all my energies into something more constructive.

Now, from this point of view the ALR of Bordeaux was the worst one could imagine, for how could I have reached separation by mutual consent with a stellium in the $7^{th}$ House and Mars in the $11^{th}$ House? Even considering that the Ascendant of the LR falling in my natal $1^{st}$ House – for the reasons that I've explained in several points of this volume – didn't worry me at all, I couldn't have stood the least chance of achieving such goal.

So I started scanning the whole surface of the globe in search of a suitable location where I could have aimed my LR, but I wasn't able to find one. I felt that a radical change in my approach was required, in order to reach a brand new dimension even if, at a first sight, it might appear to be absurd. And in fact, in part, it was absurd: it was the island of Flores, in the Azores (Portugal). I would have obtained the greatest celestial protection there concerning a possible legal agreement that nobody – lawyers included – believed possible.

On the other hand, the sky over Flores might have represented the sum of the worst meanings of the 6$^{th}$ House; and I also had the Ascendant falling in the 12$^{th}$ House, and Mars in the 12$^{th}$ House of LR. Perhaps Flores could have been the worst Aimed LR ever: I wouldn't have suggested it even to my worst enemy. Some of you would claim that, with the protection of a previous good SR, for the reasons explained in other sections of this volume I shouldn't have feared from anything terrible. Well, terrible perhaps not, mortal perhaps not – but something detrimental, perhaps a little bit less dangerous than mortal, yes! Do not forget the fact that in my SR, which I had aimed to Río Gallego, there was Uranus in the 9$^{th}$ House, and above all the Ascendant and Mars in the 12$^{th}$ House. This might have caused even a stroke to me, keeping in mind that I am sixty years old now and that I have always been very active all my life.

So I was uncertain about this decision. This is quite unusual of me, for I usually take even important decisions in less than a minute.

Eventually I resolved to leave and to reach there. I took five flights to reach there and five more on my way back (still spending a paltry amount: 700 Euros altogether). I remained there many days because it's necessary to be there several days in advance: in fact, due to strong winds, sometimes the flights are also suspended for two-three days. I stayed at a bed & breakfast hotel (I think it's the only one open on the island): it was so chilly that I had to sleep without taking my clothes off. Food – you had better forget about it: I ate only the bread and jam that they served for breakfast. I don't mean to offend the Portuguese, but that was the only edible thing in the middle of the Atlantic Ocean.

As soon as my LR took place, troubles arrived as forecast. I resolved to try and leave by an earlier flight than the one I had booked. Twice they registered me into a waiting list and only at the very last minute they would tell me whether I could fly or not. So I had to run for hundreds of metres in Flores and for kilometres in Lisbon in a sea of sweat with my only one, extremely heavy (due to my heavy clothes) hand luggage and I could not drink a drop of water for a long while. In Lisbon I literally got very close to having a heart attack. Once back home I started preparations for the legal 'battle' that perhaps would not be a real battle – for I virtually accepted all the conditions that the opposite lawyer imposed upon me – but when the time arrived to reach a written agreement, promises were broken and new claims arrived. To make a long story short, few days before my new Return, after a sequel of events in which I was forced to take part in actions of great tensions, I charged my lawyer to proceed and during my transit in Heathrow (London) I phoned him. He told me that my brother had intervened – and I wish to express here my gratefulness to him for his brotherly and affectionate mediation – and this would eventually lead to an agreement (Venus and Jupiter on the Descendant of the RL, i.e. within a distance of 2.5 degrees from the Descendant).

I am not certain about my willingness to repeat such an experience. I also had the flu, which I haven't had in the last twenty years, as well as strong pain in my arms all along during that lunar month. You can be sure that I would reflect very much before repeating such an experience. And if I met those who claim that an Ascendant of Return in the natal 12th House and Mars of Return in the 12th House of Return make you grow – well I think that I'd imitate Hannibal Lecter and eat them up, on the spot and without cooking them.

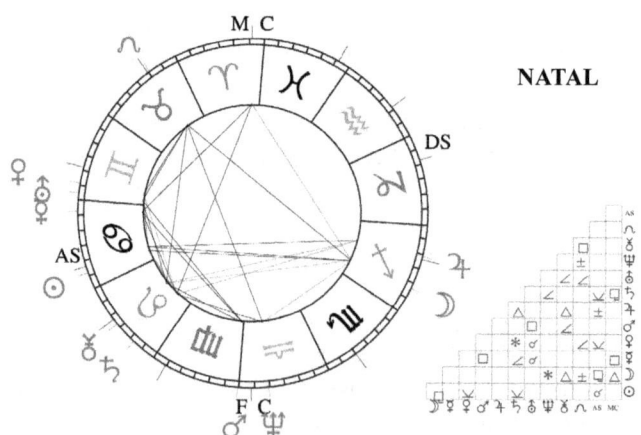

**NATAL**

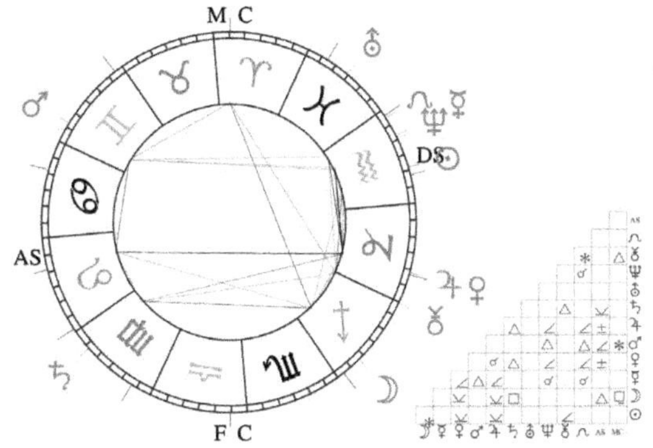

**ALR, Bordeaux**

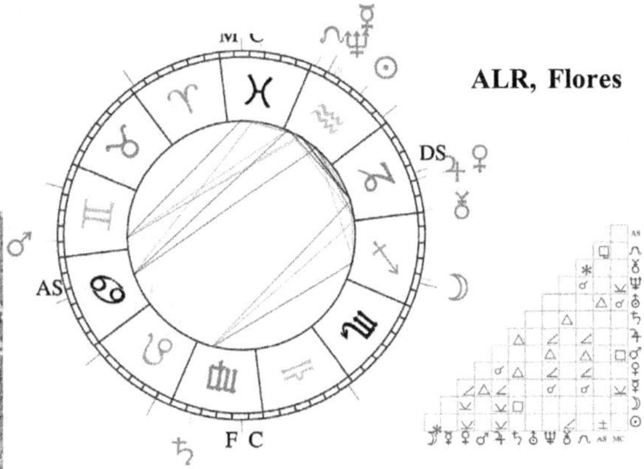

**ALR, Flores**

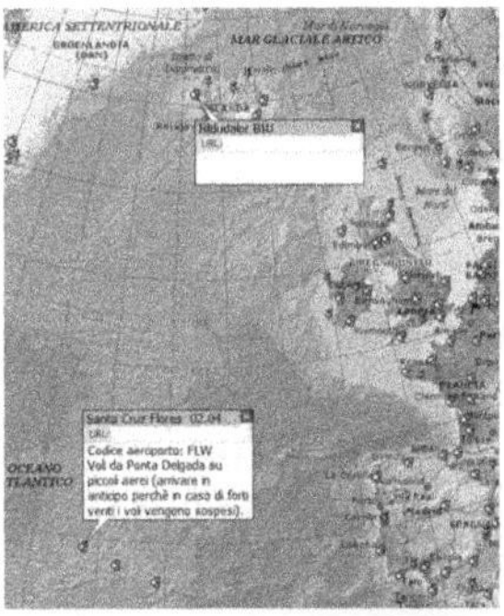

Icelanders claim to possess a small western portion of European land, somewhere close to Bildudalur. Portuguese claim the same in connection with the island of Flores, in the Azores. I've been personally to both places and if I say that the Portuguese are right, it's because the geographic map proves so, as you can see here.

# 17.
# Lunar Return in Peterhead

This Aimed Lunar Return followed the one of Flores, and it was intended to seal up the result of the ALR of Flores. My friend Pino Valente was there as I thought about it – he actually knew and knows everything about me and my astrological plans: one day he could become my official biographer. So this is how I was reasoning: Placing several celestials in the 2$^{nd}$ and in the 8$^{th}$ House of LR, meant that there will be a significant flow of outgoing money. Considering that my financial possibilities are not really huge, a 'significant flow' can only mean that I'll reach an agreement for separation by mutual consent – what else if not that?

Once again it seemed to be a quite an easy thing to be put into practice, but in reality it turned out to be extremely difficult to find out the proper place I believe that I couldn't have succeeded without help from *Aladino*.

The place I chose for this ALR was Peterhead, Scotland. It's an approximately 45-minute drive from Dyce where Aberdeen airport is. Beside the already mentioned goal, in this ALR I would also have Venus on the cusp of the 2$^{nd}$-3$^{rd}$ House, which would relieve me from certain expenses and would help me spread my books abroad, where in fact I am attaining very important results. On the other hand I would prevent Mars from even getting close (within the range of 2.5 degrees) from the cusp of the 7$^{th}$-8$^{th}$ House of the LR – for I was aiming an agreement, not a battle.

Keep in mind that I can swear on the precision of my time of birth, as well as on a wonderful piece of software that is able to calculate the cusps of the Houses with a precision of ten thousandths of seconds, although I am satisfied to reach a precision to the minutes of degrees. Thus, assisted by that wonderful tool called *Google Earth*) I selected a specific road in Peterhead in which I could attain that astounding result, which also let me prove once again the correctness of my time of birth. While all the protagonists of this story forecast 6 or 7 years of harsh legal battles, on Wednesday the 17th of March at 12:57 I signed all the papers related with my legal separation.

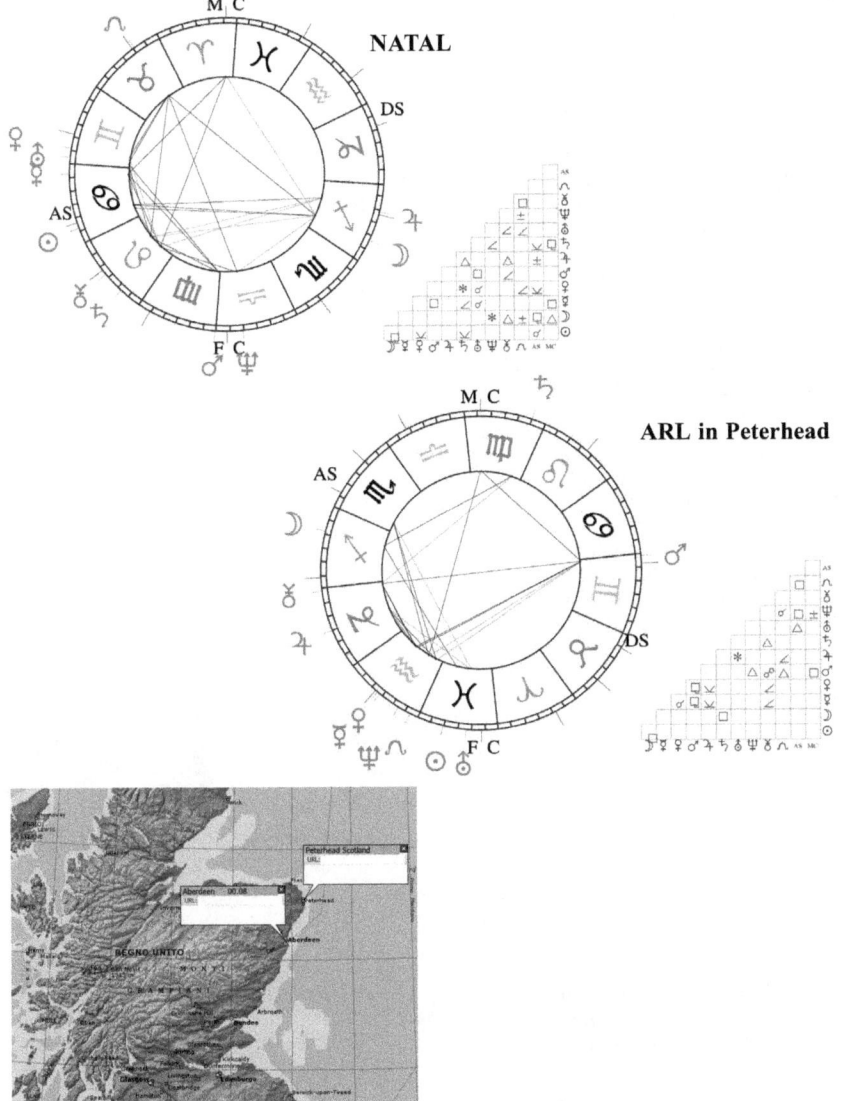

Tema natale per 2 29  Nato a Seaview Hotel Peterhead (00) (GB) il 29/02/02008 ore: 01.10

Sole :in Pesci 09°49'30,3722
Luna :in Sagittario 09°18'32,7389
Mercurio :in Aquario 12°57'28,1330
Venere :in Aquario 14°02'40,5650
Marte :in Gemelli 28°40'45,2434
Giove :in Capricorno 15°25'47,6642
Saturno :in Vergine 04°47'14,0445  Retrogrado
Urano :in Pesci 18°08'24,0756
Nettuno :in Aquario 22°23'28,5678
Plutone :in Capricorno 00°51'03,9673
Nodo Medio :in Aquario 27°12'57,6428  Retrogrado
Nodo Vero :in Aquario 27°38'20,6285
Lilith(Apogeo Medio) :in Scorpione 25°23'32,2720
Apogeo Osculante :in Scorpione 26°28'54,2498  Retrogrado
Chirone :in Aquario 17°35'10,2343
Pholus :in Sagittario 10°16'23,4081
Ceres :in Toro 20°13'56,0746
Pallas :in Pesci 28°32'17,7328
Juno :in Sagittario 23°55'01,1651
Vesta :in Pesci 05°35'08,3763
Casa 1 :in Scorpione 24°05'02,2154
Casa 2 :in Sagittario 25°52'57,0279
Casa 3 :in Aquario 11°46'56,6985
Casa 4 :in Pesci 23°25'08,2824
Casa 5 :in Ariete 21°10'49,0746
Casa 6 :in Toro 10°01'27,7247
Casa 7 :in Toro 24°05'02,2154
Casa 8 :in Gemelli 25°52'57,0279
Casa 9 :in Leone 11°46'56,6985
Casa 10 :in Vergine 23°25'08,2824
Casa 11 :in Bilancia 21°10'49,0746
Casa 12 :in Scorpione 10°01'27,7247

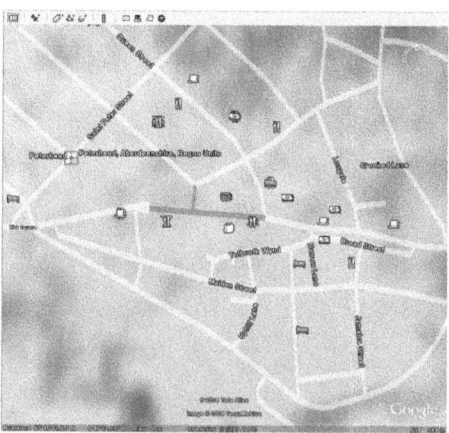

**This is the area of my hotel in Peterhead, which I was able to select thanks to the extremely high level of precision of Google Earth.**

# 18.
# The atrocious saga of death in Gandhi's "family"

A cursed family, a deathly saga that maybe hasn't come to an end yet. Until now the cruel scythe of fate has struck them four times in three generations: I refer to Gandhi's family (I'll explain later why I call it a 'family' even if it can not be regarded as a strictly nuclear family). As you know, immediately after its independence from Britain – an independence conquered through decades of non–violent struggle – India broke in two. The Muslim population settled down in Pakistan, while the predominantly Hindu population occupied the other area, properly corresponding to the actual borders of India. But both West and East of Karachi other minorities remained active, some of them were fundamentalists and proved to be very aggressive against other ethnic groups. So the Mahatma ('Great Soul') Gandhi, while on his way to evening prayers, was assassinated by Nathuram Godse, a young Hindu fanatic, on the 30th of January 1948 at 5:41 pm (source: *Encyclopedia Britannica*, and Grazia Bordoni). This closed a very important page of (almost) contemporary history, which had seen this little big man challenging the huge British Empire and winning, thanks to the ultimate determination of his own fortitude – and without any guns. But that day also inaugurated a bad serial that we would have never wanted to watch: the killing of the 'descendants' of Mohandas Karamchand Gandhi.

On the 23rd of June 1980, his 'grand-nephew' (as we are going to see later, Indira was not a daughter of the Mahatma, but this does not lessen the astrological relevance of what follows) Sanjay crashed and died in a plane during a drill.

Only four years later, on the 31st of October 1984 at 2:00 pm in the garden of his residence in New Delhi, Indira Gandhi fell struck by the shots of two of her own Sikh bodyguards, who wanted to avenge a massacre of 450 of their brothers in faith. The massacre had been provoked a few months earlier by an attack, ordered by Indira herself, against the Golden Temple in Amritsar.

Last (but will it really be the end of this bloody trail of events?) another son of Indira, Rajiv – who had taken over the reins of politics after the death of his brother and his mother – was also assassinated in revenge for the intervention of Indian troops in Sri Lanka against the separatist Tamils.

It's a long stream of blood that has accompanied (striking not only its summits) the history of this modern democracy conveying a culture of many thousand years. We are talking of one of the fundamental cultures of the human race, and also the cradle of an extremely erudite astrology that millions of people around the world still study and practice today.

In the section of this book devoted to the dating of events that take place between one birthday and the next, I propose you to consider these four tragic episodes as seen through the stars of their protagonists and also through the birth chart of Sonia Maino, Rajiv's Italian wife. Consider it an exercise just like others, having the aim to show you how astrology can be verified both by 'listening' to a single-voice-song and through a chorus of many voices. There is no doubt that this is an extraordinary game of apparent coincidences where the stars interweave the movement of the hands and of the gears of a giant clockwork mechanism, in which each individual movement must necessarily obey the mechanical work of the entire machinery.

Of course, according to the rules of *Active Astrology*, we *can* intervene in the operation of these gears – but that's another story that would take us far from the scope of this section.

Let us begin, then, starting from that exceptional little big man, wonderfully personified on the screen by Ben Kingsley in 1982 film *Gandhi*, which was directed by Richard Attenborough and was awarded many Academy Awards.

Mohandas Karamchand Gandhi was born in Porbandar on the 2nd of October 1869, at 7:08 am. These (including the following birth data of the other members of Gandhi 'family') are extremely reliable data: we can be almost 100% sure of the accuracy of every single time of birth, given the great astrological tradition that has been surviving for thousands of years there. Thanks to that, we can say that every newborn has its birth chart immediately cast and drawn in India.

The first extraordinary thing to note is that the Mahatma, Indira, and her son Rajiv: all of them were murdered and all of them had Mars in the first House of the natal chart. Indira's other son, Sanjay, also died of a violent death, but in an air exercise. He was not killed, but he had Mars in the twelfth natal House, opposite Uranus (the fatal plane crash).

Let us focus back to the Mahatma. I would like to display the biography of this exceptional man, trying to highlight the many significant passages of his life in relation to the planetary transits and the numerous Solar Returns that characterized his journey on this planet. But by doing so, we would get out the scope of this chapter. I will therefore go directly to the transits and to the SRs covering those four dramatic deadly events.

This is what happened the day of his death, on the 30$^{th}$ of January 1948, at 5:41 pm in New Delhi. Pluto trine Saturn (two degrees of orb), **Pluto square Venus** (two degrees of orb), Neptune sextile Saturn (one degree of orb), **Saturn square Pluto** (two degrees of orb), Saturn trine Neptune (one degree of orb), Saturn square Jupiter (one degree of orb), **Saturn square Mars** (two degrees of orb and we are referring to that dangerous radix Mars in the first House!), **Saturn conjunct Moon** (*zero degrees of orb!*), Jupiter trine Neptune (two degrees of orb), Jupiter semisquare Neptune (two degrees of orb), Jupiter trine Moon (one degree of orb), Mars sesquisquare Neptune (one degree of orb), Mars sextile Mercury (one degree of orb), Venus sextile Pluto (three degrees of orb), Venus trine Uranus (three degrees of orb), Venus square Saturn (two degrees of orb), Venus trine Venus (two degrees of orb), Mercury trine the Ascendant (zero degrees of orb), Mercury sesquisquare Sun (two degrees of orb), Moon sesquisquare Jupiter (three degrees of orb), Moon conjunct Sun (zero degrees of orb), Sun sextile Saturn (three degrees of orb), and Sun trine Sun (zero degrees of orb).

His Solar Return of 1947 – 1948 has the Ascendant in the eleventh natal House, a stellium in the first House of SR, the Sun also in the first House of SR, and a terrible cluster of celestials in the eleventh House of SR: I really think that it could not be more eloquent.

His Lunar Return covering the day of the murder has the Ascendant in the natal seventh House (the declared enemies and also the attacks) as well as a good number of celestials in the eighth and the eleventh House of LR.

With regard to the Houses we can note that Saturn and Pluto were passing through the tenth House of birth, while transiting Neptune was in the twelfth House, Uranus in the eighth House, and Mars in the eleventh.

## Comparative Aspects
## Death transits of Mahatma /Mahatma Gandhi

**Sun:**
   **Trine with Sun 120 Degrees**
   Square with Mercury 95 Degrees
   **Sexstile with Saturn 57 Degrees**
   Opposite with Node 185 Degrees

**Moon:**
   **Joined with Sun 0 Degrees**
   **Sesquiquad with Jupiter    137 Degrees**
   Sexstile with Node 63 Degrees

**Mercury:**
   **Sesquiquad with Sun 137 Degrees**
   Opposite with Moon 186 Degrees
   **Trine with Ascendant 120 Degrees**

**Venus:**
   **Trine with Venus 118 Degrees**
   Trine with Mars 116 Degrees
   **Square with Saturn 92 Degrees**
   **Trine with Uranus 127 Degrees**
   **Sexstile with Pluto 63 Degrees**

**Mars:**
   **Sexstile with Mercury 59 Degrees**
   Semi-sex with Node 30 Degrees
   **Sesquiquad with Neptune 136 Degrees**

**Ascendant:**
   Sexstile with Sun 62 Degrees
   Square with Mercury 86 Degrees
   Trine with Saturn 125 Degrees
   Joined with Node 2 Degrees

**Mid Heaven:**
  Opposit with Mercury 183 Degrees
  Opposit with Ascendant 174 Degrees
  Square with Mid Heaven 85 Degrees
  Square with Node 93 Degrees

**Jupiter:**
  **Trine with Moon 121 Degrees**
  **Semi-squ with Mercury 47 Degrees**
  Semi-sex with Mars 32 Degrees
  Joined with Saturn 8 Degrees
  Sesquiquad with Node 136 Degrees
  **Trine with Neptune 118 Degrees**

**Saturn:**
  **Joined with Moon 0 Degrees**
  Square with Venus 86 Degrees
  **Square with Mars 88 Degrees**
  **Square with Jupiter 89 Degrees**
  Semi-sex with Uranus 28 Degrees
  **Trine with Neptune 121 Degrees**
  **Square with Pluto 92 Degrees**

**Uranus:**
  Sexstile with Moon 57 Degrees
  Trine with Ascendant 123 Degrees
  Semi-sex with Jupiter 32 Degrees
  Semi-sex with Uranus 29 Degrees

**Node:**
  Square with Moon 90 Degrees
  Opposit with Venus 177 Degrees
  Opposit with Mars 179 Degrees
  Joined with Jupiter 0 Degrees
  Sexstile with Uranus 62 Degrees
  Semi-sex with Neptune 30 Degrees
  Joined with Pluto 1 Degrees

**Neptune:**
  Joined with Sun 3 Degrees
  **Sexstile with Saturn 59 Degrees**
  Opposit with Neptune 174 Degrees

**Pluto:**
  Joined with Moon 6 Degrees
  **Square with Venus 92 Degrees**
  Square with Mars 94 Degrees
  **Trine with Saturn 118 Degrees**
  Trine with Neptune 115 Degrees
  Square with Pluto 86 Degrees

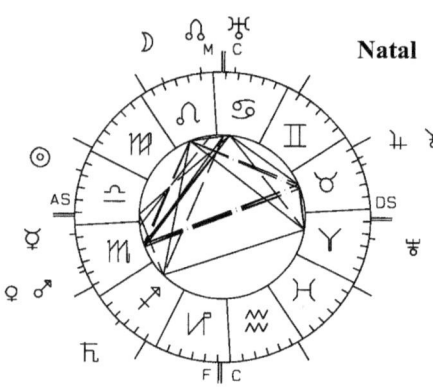

**Natal**

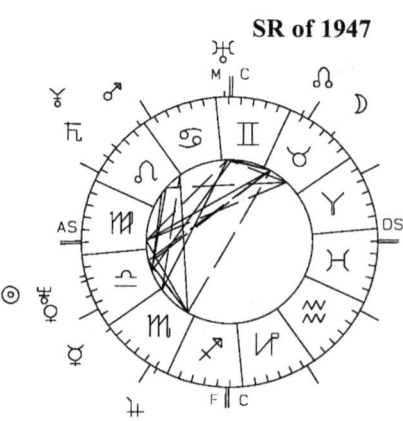

**SR of 1947**

**Relevant LR**

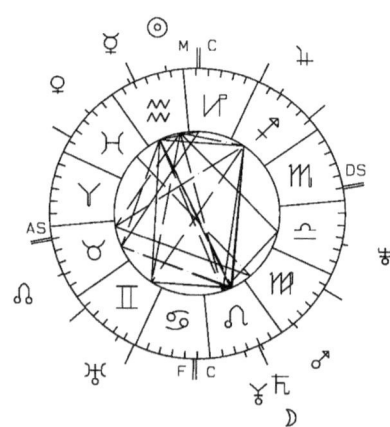

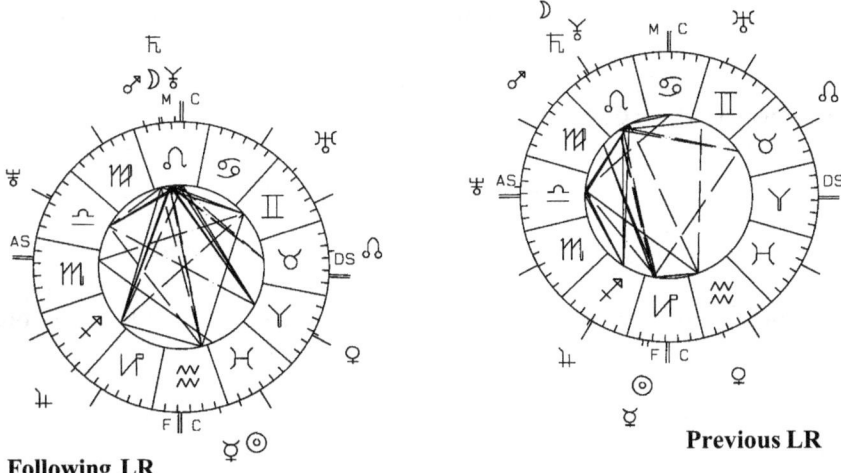

**Following LR**                                     **Previous LR**

Let us consider now the transits of Sanjay Gandhi's death, which took place on the 23rd of June 1980, in New Delhi. Transits have been calculated for noon, since the precise time of the event is unknown, or at least it does not appear either in Grazia Bordoni's archive (www.graziabordoni.it) or in the *Encyclopedia Britannica*. Sanjay Gandhi died in a plane crash. He was born in New Delhi on the 14th of December 1946, at 9:27 am. Here are the transits of the event, always taken from the perspective of the Mahatma's natal chart: **Pluto opposite Neptune** (*zero degrees of orb!*), Pluto sextile Moon (one degree of orb), Neptune trine Neptune (two degrees of orb), Neptune semisquare Mercury (two degrees of orb), Neptune trine Moon (one degree of orb), Uranus trine Uranus (zero degrees of orb), Uranus opposite Jupiter (one degree of orb), **Uranus square Moon** (two degrees of orb; at this point I would have found it very convenient to take into consideration also the transit of Uranus conjunct Mars, but there are three degrees of orb in between them, so we had better neglect it), **Uranus semisquare Sun** (two degrees of orb), Saturn trine Pluto (three degrees of orb), Saturn sextile Uranus (one degree of orb), Saturn trine Jupiter (zero degrees of orb), Jupiter sesquisquare Neptune (one degree of orb), Jupiter semisquare Uranus (two degrees of orb), Jupiter sextile Mercury (two degrees of orb), Mars trine Pluto (two degrees of orb), Mars sextile Uranus (two degrees of orb), Mars trine Jupiter (two degrees of orb), Mars sextile Mars (three degrees of orb), Mars semisquare Mercury (two degrees of orb), Venus sextile Neptune (one degree of orb), Venus sesquisquare Mercury (one degree of orb), Venus sextile Moon (zero degrees of orb), Mercury conjunct Uranus (two degrees of orb), Mercury sextile Jupiter (three degrees of orb), Mercury conjunct Medium Coeli (one degree of orb), Mercury square the Ascendant (one degree of orb), Moon conjunct Mercury (one degree of orb), Sun semisquare Pluto (one degree of orb), Sun sesquisquare Mars and Venus (one degree of orb), and Sun trine Mercury.

The Solar Return of that year has the Ascendant falling in the ninth natal House (accidents), Saturn of SR in the third House of SR (still, accidents) and Uranus of SR in the fifth House of SR (sudden and / or incidental event happening to 'son' or to a 'nephew').

The Lunar Return is 'marked' by the Ascendant in the eleventh House of radix, by Mars of LR at the Ascendant of LR, by a stellium of LR over the twelfth and the first House pf LR, by Mercury of LR in the eleventh House of LR, and by Uranus of LR in the third House of LR (accidents).

With regard to the Houses we can note a transit Pluto in the Mahatma's twelfth natal House, Uranus in his first natal House (very close to his radix Mars), and Saturn and Mars in the eleventh House.

**Comparative Aspects**
**Death transits of Sanjay /Mahatma Gandhi**

**Sun:**
 **Trine with Mercury 121 Degrees**
 **Sesquiquad with Venus 134 Degrees**
 **Sesquiquad with Mars 136 Degrees**
 Trine with Ascendant 113 Degrees
 Semi-sex with Node 32 Degrees
 **Semi-squ with Pluto 44 Degrees**

**Moon:**
 **Joined with Mercury 1 Degrees**
 Joined with Ascendant 6 Degrees
 Square with Node 87 Degrees

**Mercury:**
 Trine with Mars 114 Degrees
 **Square with Ascendant 91 Degrees**

**Joined with Mid Heaven 1 Degrees**
**Sexstile with Jupiter 63 Degrees**
**Joined with Uranus 2 Degrees**
Square with Neptune 95 Degrees

**Venus:**
**Sexstile with Moon 60 Degrees**
**Sesquiquad with Mercury 134 Degrees**
Trine with Ascendant 126 Degrees
Semi-sex with Jupiter 29 Degrees
Opposit with Saturn 172 Degrees
Semi-sex with Uranus 32 Degrees
Semi-squ with Node 44 Degrees
**Sexstile with Neptune 61 Degrees**
Semi-sex with Pluto 32 Degrees

**Mars:**
Semi-sex with Moon 30 Degrees
**Semi-squ with Mercury 43 Degrees**
**Sexstile with Mars 57 Degrees**
**Trine with Jupiter 120 Degrees**
**Sexstile with Uranus 58 Degrees**
Semi-squ with Node 46 Degrees
**Trine with Pluto 122 Degrees**

**Ascendant:**
Semi-sex with Ascendant 28 Degrees
Sexstile with Mid Heaven 60 Degrees
Trine with Jupiter 126 Degrees

**Mid Heaven:**
Trine with Mercury 127 Degrees
Trine with Ascendant 119 Degrees
Semi-sex with Mid Heaven 29 Degrees

**Jupiter:**
**Sexstile with Mercury 58 Degrees**
**Semi-squ with Uranus 43 Degrees**

Semi-sex with Node 30 Degrees
**Sesquiquad with Neptune 136 Degrees**

**Saturn:**
Semi-sex with Moon 31 Degrees
**Sexstile with Mars 57 Degrees**
**Trine with Jupiter 120 Degrees**
**Sexstile with Uranus 59 Degrees**
Semi-squ with Node 46 Degrees
**Trine with Pluto 123 Degrees**

**Uranus:**
**Semi-squ with Sun 43 Degrees**
**Square with Moon 92 Degrees**
Joined with Venus 5 Degrees
Joined with Mars 3 Degrees
Trine with Mid Heaven 116 Degrees
**Opposit with Jupiter 181 Degrees**
**Trine with Uranus 120 Degrees**
Opposit with Pluto 184 Degrees

**Node:**
Semi-squ with Sun 46 Degrees
Joined with Moon 2 Degrees
Square with Mars 85 Degrees
Sexstile with Ascendant 63 Degrees
Square with Jupiter 92 Degrees
Semi-sex with Uranus 30 Degrees
Trine with Neptune 124 Degrees
Square with Pluto 95 Degrees

**Neptune:**
**Trine with Moon 121 Degrees**
**Semi-squ with Mercury 47 Degrees**
Semi-sex with Mars 32 Degrees
Joined with Saturn 8 Degrees
Sesquiquad with Node 136 Degrees
**Trine with Neptune 118 Degrees**

## Pluto:
**Sexstile with Moon 59 Degrees**
Semi-sex with Mars 29 Degrees
Joined with Ascendant 6 Degrees
Square with Uranus 87 Degrees
**Opposit with Neptune 180 Degrees**

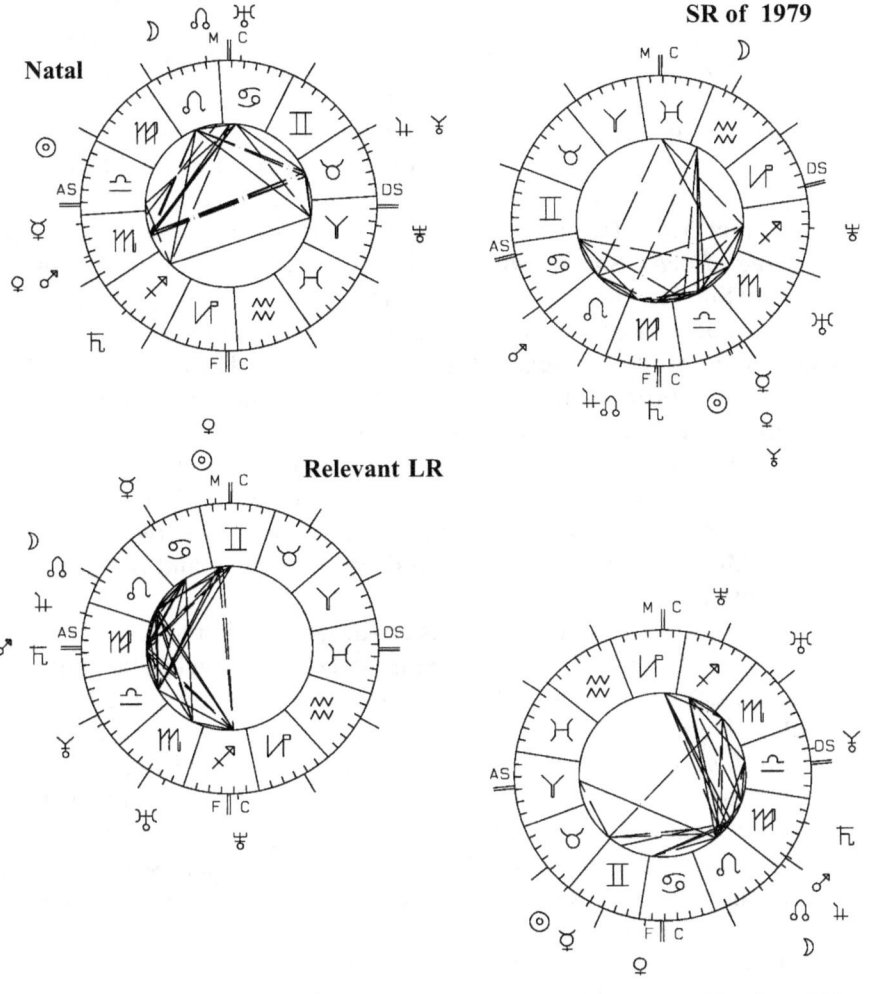

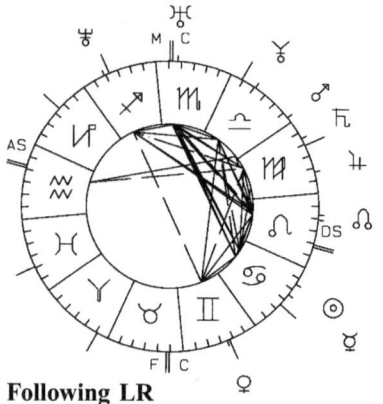

**Following LR**

Let us now consider the assassination of Indira Gandhi, that took place in New Delhi on the 31st of October 1984, at 2:00 pm. Here are the transits on the Mahatma's birth chart: **Pluto conjunct Mercury** (*one degree of orb*), **Uranus conjunct Saturn** (*zero degrees of orb!*), **Uranus sesquisquare Medium Coeli** (*zero degrees of orb!*), **Uranus semisquare Ascendant** (*zero degrees of orb!*), Uranus sextile sun (two degrees of orb), **Saturn opposite Pluto** (*zero degrees of orb!*), Saturn opposite Jupiter (three degrees of orb), **Saturn conjunct Mars** (*zero degrees of orb!*), **Saturn conjunct Venus** (*one degree of orb*), **Saturn square Moon** (three degrees of orb), Jupiter square Sun (one degree of orb), Mars trine Pluto (*zero degrees of orb!*), Mars square Neptune (*zero degrees of orb!*), Mars trine Jupiter (two degrees of orb), Mars sextile Mars (zero degrees of orb) and Venus (two degrees of orb), Venus conjunct Saturn (one degree of orb), Venus sesquisquare Medium Coeli (two degrees of orb), Venus semisquare Ascendant (two degrees of orb), Mercury opposite Pluto (three degrees of orb), Mercury trine Uranus (one degree of orb), Mercury opposite Jupiter (zero degrees of orb), Mercury conjunct Mars (two degrees of orb), Mercury square Moon (zero degrees of orb), and Moon square Mercury (two degrees of orb).

In his Solar Return the Sun lies on the cusp of first to second House, while the Ascendant is in his eleventh natal House: exactly sticking to the point... Let us pause to reflect for a moment and look at the bar chart below. It contains the fundamental rules which, in my school, feature an *annus horribilis*, namely: Mars or the Sun or the Ascendant or a stellium in the first or sixth or twelfth House, a stellium spread over the first and twelfth House, and a stellium in the eighth House. The tiny bars show the degree of 'negativity' produced by each element on a scale from 1 to 100; and as you can see, the value of each of them reaches a theoretical value of 100 points in the chart. This does not mean that if the Mahatma had had simultaneously, say, seven of those positions in his Solar Return of 1984, he would have scored 700 points! For the maximum, the worst of all (let us define it 'hell', the mother of all disasters, or whatever you wish to call it), always corresponds to 100 points. So the final result does not change even if in a Solar Return you find *only* the Sun of SR in the first House of SR – the negative score of the year is still: 100 over 100 points! This is what marks the year and defines it negative intensity. The specificity of that negativity is shown by the Ascendant of the Return falling on the eleventh natal House: a probable death.

**Comparative Aspects**
**Death transits of Indira /Mahatma Gandhi**

**Sun:**
Semi-sex with Sun 29 Degrees
Joined with Mercury 4 Degrees
Joined with Venus 8 Degrees
Square with Node 93 Degrees

**Moon:**
Trine with Sun 116 Degrees
**Square with Mercury 92 Degrees**
Opposit with Node 181 Degrees

**Mercury:**
**Square with Moon 90 Degrees**
Joined with Venus 4 Degrees
**Joined with Mars 2 Degrees**
Trine with Mid Heaven 114 Degrees
**Opposit with Jupiter 180 Degrees**
**Trine with Uranus 119 Degrees**
**Opposit with Pluto 183 Degrees**

**Venus:**
Trine with Moon 113 Degrees
**Semi-squ with Ascendant 47 Degrees**
**Sesquiquad with Mid Heaven 137 Degrees**
**Joined with Saturn 1 Degrees**
Trine with Neptune 125 Degrees

**Mars:**
   **Sexstile with Venus 62 Degrees**
   **Sexstile with Mars 60 Degrees**
   Opposit with Mid Heaven 172 Degrees
   **Trine with Jupiter 122 Degrees**
   Opposit with Uranus 176 Degrees
   **Square with Neptune 90 Degrees**
   **Trine with Pluto 120 Degrees**

**Ascendant:**
   Sesquiquad with Sun 136 Degrees
   Opposit with Moon 184 Degrees
   Trine with Ascendant 119 Degrees
   Square with Jupiter 86 Degrees

**Mid Heaven:**
   Sexstile with Sun 57 Degrees
   Semi-sex with Mercury 32 Degrees
   Joined with Saturn 5 Degrees
   Sesquiquad with Uranus 134 Degrees
   Trine with Node 122 Degrees

**Jupiter:**
   **Square with Sun 89 Degrees**

**Saturn:**
   **Square with Moon 87 Degrees**
   **Joined with Venus 1 Degrees**
   **Joined with Mars 0 Degrees**
   **Opposit with Jupiter 177 Degrees**
   Trine with Uranus 116 Degrees
   **Opposit with Pluto 180 Degrees**

**Uranus:**
   **Sexstile with Sun 62 Degrees**
   **Semi-squ with Ascendant 45 Degrees**
   **Sesquiquad with Mid Heaven 135 Degrees**
   **Joined with Saturn 0 Degrees**

Trine with Node 127 Degrees
Trine with Neptune 127 Degrees

**Node:**
Sexstile with Mid Heaven 57 Degrees
Joined with Jupiter 8 Degrees

**Neptune:**
Sexstile with Ascendant 63 Degrees

**Pluto:**
**Joined with Mercury 1 Degrees**
Joined with Ascendant 6 Degrees
Square with Node 88 Degrees

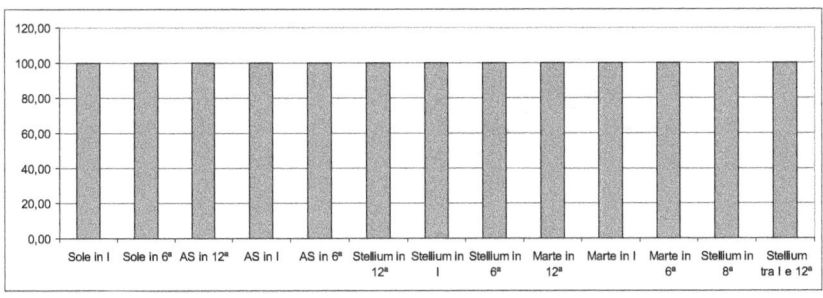

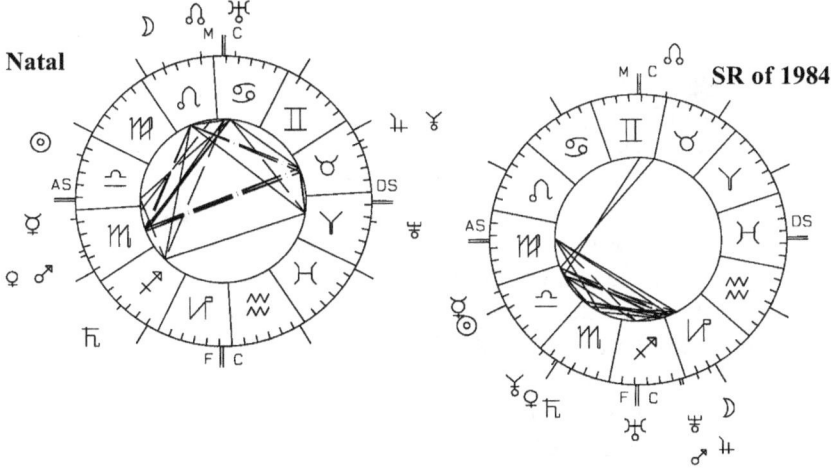

Natal            SR of 1984

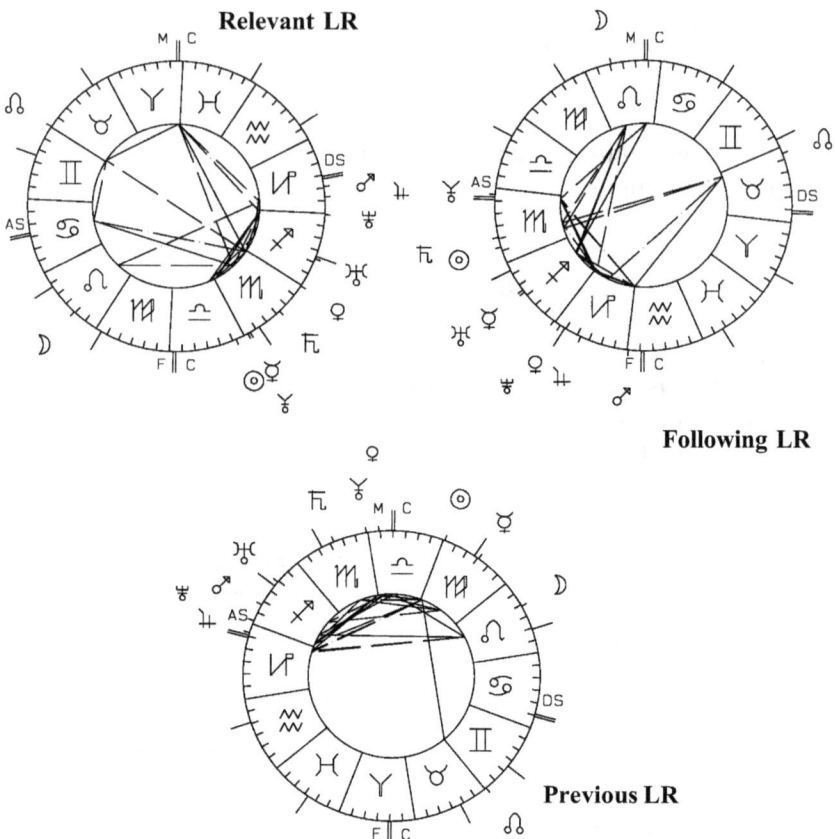

The Lunar Return covering the event has Mars of LR in the sixth House of LR (which in other words, tells us the same as what described a few lines above), a stellium of LR in the sixth House of LR, and Saturn and Uranus of LR in the fifth House of LR.

With regard to the Houses we can note that Saturn was transiting the first House radix, **almost exactly conjunct Venus and Mars**.

Furthermore we can not but stress that the assassination took place within the range of 20 days before Indira Gandhi's birthday, and less than one month before the Mahatma's birthday.

Let us consider, now, the transits over the birth chart of the '*Great Soul*' on the day of young Rajiv's death. **Pluto opposite Pluto** (one degree of orb), Pluto opposite Jupiter (two degrees of orb), **Pluto conjunct**

Mars (*zero degrees of orb!*), **Pluto conjunct Venus** (two degrees of orb), **Pluto square Moon** (two degrees of orb), Neptune trine Pluto (two degrees of orb), Neptune square Neptune (two degrees of orb), Neptune sextile Mars (two degrees of orb) and Venus (zero degrees of orb), **Saturn square Mercury** (three degrees of orb), Saturn trine Sun (three degrees of orb), Jupiter sextile Sun (one degree of orb), **Mars sesquisquare Saturn** (*zero degrees of orb!*), **Mars conjunct Medium Coeli** (*one degree of orb*), **Mars square Ascendant** (two degrees of orb, please note that the latter three transits form a really fatal series!), Venus trine Venus (two degrees of orb), Mercury opposite Mercury (three degrees of orb), Moon square Saturn, Moon semisquare Medium Coeli (zero degrees of orb) and semisquare Ascendant (one degree of orb).

His Solar Revolution of 1990–1991 points the finger at the Sun of SR in the eighth House of SR, a stellium of SR in the eighth House of SR, Uranus of SR in the eleventh House of SR, and a stellium of SR spread over the first and the twelfth house of SR.

The Lunar Return is also didactic in its image of death: Mars in the first House, the Sun in the eleventh House, Venus in the twelfth House, and Saturn in the seventh House.

With regard to the Houses we can see **Pluto in the first House, almost exactly conjunct Mars and Venus**, and Mars standing out at the Midheaven.


**Comparative Aspects**
**Death transits of Rajiv /Mahatma Gandhi**

**Sun:**

**Moon:**
 **Semi-squ with Ascendant 44 Degrees**
 **Semi-squ with Mid Heaven 45 Degrees**
 **Square with Saturn 91 Degrees**
 Trine with Pluto 113 Degrees

**Mercury:**
 **Opposit with Mercury 177 Degrees**
 Square with Node 88 Degrees

**Venus:**
   **Trine with Venus 122 Degrees**
   Trine with Mars 124 Degrees
   Joined with Uranus 7 Degrees
   Square with Neptune 85 Degrees

**Mars:**
   **Square with Ascendant 88 Degrees**
   **Joined with Mid Heaven 1 Degrees**
   **Sesquiquad with Saturn 135 Degrees**
   Joined with Uranus 5 Degrees
   Joined with Node 6 Degrees

**Ascendant:**
   Square with Ascendant 88 Degrees
   Opposit with Mid Heaven 178 Degrees
   Trine with Jupiter 116 Degrees
   Opposit with Uranus 182 Degrees
   Square with Neptune 85 Degrees
   Trine with Pluto 114 Degrees

**Mid Heaven:**
   Joined with Mercury 0 Degrees
   Joined with Ascendant 7 Degrees
   Square with Node 89 Degrees

**Jupiter:**
   **Sexstile with Sun 61 Degrees**
   Square with Mercury 86 Degrees
   Trine with Saturn 124 Degrees
   Joined with Node 3 Degrees

**Saturn:**
   **Trine with Sun 117 Degrees**
   **Square with Mercury 93 Degrees**
   Opposit with Node 182 Degrees

**Uranus:**
Square with Sun 94 Degrees
Trine with Jupiter 127 Degrees
Semi-sex with Saturn 30 Degrees
Trine with Pluto 125 Degrees

**Node:**
Sexstile with Mars 63 Degrees
Square with Ascendant 85 Degrees
Opposit with Mid Heaven 175 Degrees
Trine with Jupiter 119 Degrees
Opposit with Uranus 179 Degrees
Square with Neptune 87 Degrees
Trine with Pluto 116 Degrees

**Neptune:**
**Sexstile with Venus 60 Degrees**
**Sexstile with Mars 58 Degrees**
Trine with Jupiter 124 Degrees
Opposit with Uranus 174 Degrees
**Square with Neptune 92 Degrees**
**Trine with Pluto 122 Degrees**

**Pluto:**
**Square with Moon 88 Degrees**
**Joined with Venus 2 Degrees**
**Joined with Mars 0 Degrees**
**Opposit with Jupiter 178 Degrees**
Trine with Uranus 116 Degrees
Opposit with Pluto 181 Degrees

160 LUNAR RETURNS

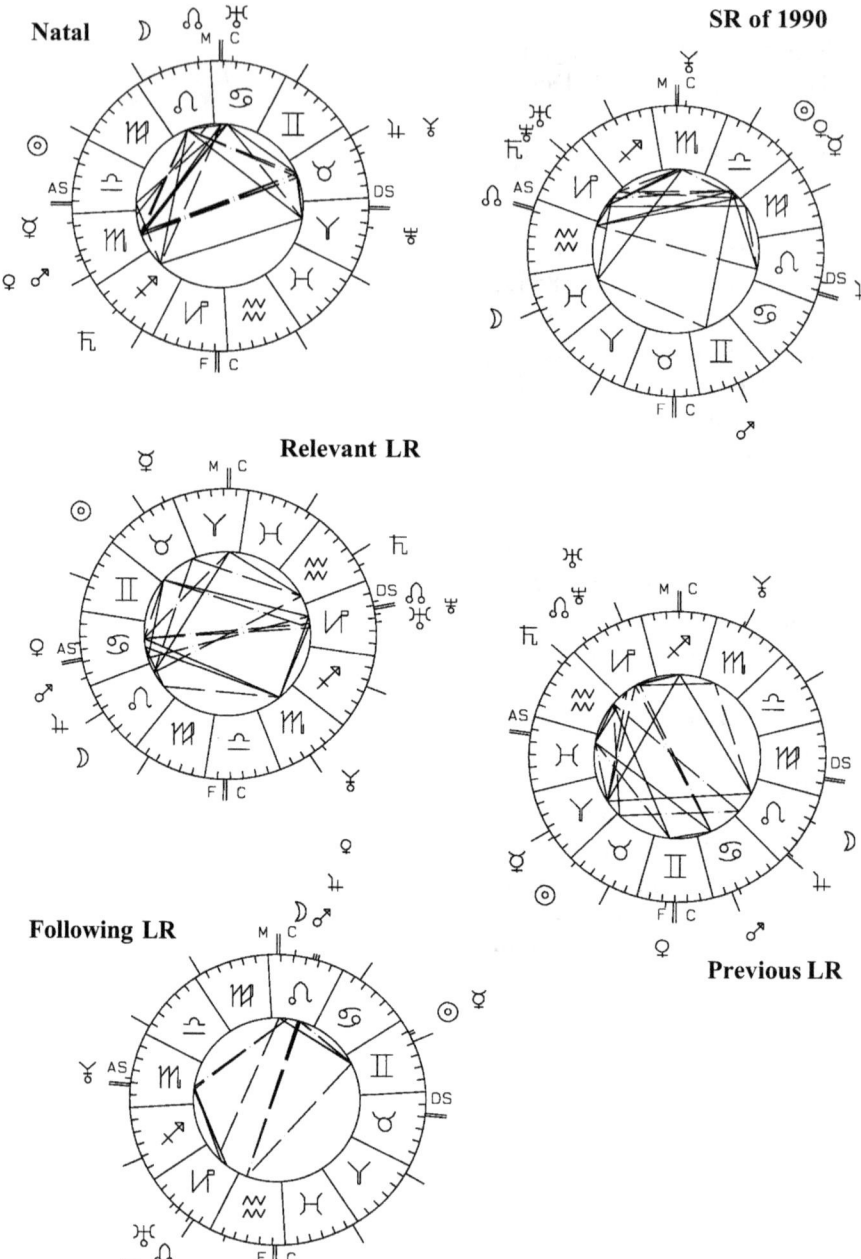

# THE ATROCIOUS SAGA OF DEATH IN GANDHI'S "FAMILY"

**Now let us consider Indira Priyadarshini Gandhi, the only daughter of Prime Minister Jawaharlal Nehru.** She studied at the University of Visva–Bharati in West Bengal, and then in Oxford, England. In 1960 she married Feroze Gandhi, a fellow party member of the National Congress. Few people know that Feroze Gandhi was not a relative of the Mahatma.

However, the political–spiritual connection – which is also somehow engraved in their common surname – acting as a binding force to the recent history of the period immediately following the independence of India – allows us to consider those birth charts as inextricably bound together. In the same way, I am sure that a foster son's celestials are very similar to those of the foster parent. Indira Gandhi was born in Allahabad on the 19$^{th}$ of November 1917 at 11:11 pm, and she was killed in Delhi on the 31$^{st}$ of October 1984 at 2:00 pm.

Here are her stars at the moment of the murder of the Mahatma: **Pluto conjunct Saturn** (*zero degrees of orb!*), Neptune sextile Saturn (two degrees of orb), **Neptune square Venus** (*zero degrees of orb!*), **Neptune semisquare Sun** (two degrees of orb), Uranus semisquare Neptune (one degree of orb), Saturn semisquare Pluto (one degree of orb), **Saturn opposite Uranus** (*one degree of orb*), **Saturn square Medium Coeli** (two degrees of orb), **Saturn conjunct Ascendant** (*zero degrees of orb!*), Jupiter sesquisquare Neptune (two degrees of orb), Jupiter sextile Uranus (two degrees of orb), Jupiter trine Ascendant (one degree of orb), Mars sextile Pluto (one degree of orb), Mars square Mercury (one degree of orb), Venus sextile Medium Coeli (three degrees of orb) and sextile Venus (one degree of orb), Venus semisquare Moon (one degree of orb), Mercury square Sun (one degree of orb), Moon square Pluto (two degrees of orb), Moon sextile Neptune (two degrees of orb), Moon trine Jupiter (zero degrees of orb), Moon sextile Mercury (three degrees of orb), Sun opposite Neptune (two degrees of orb), Sun trine Jupiter (one degree of orb), and Sun sextile Mercury (three degrees of orb).

The Solar Return (the same applies to transits), had the Mahatma been the genetic father of Indira, could not be more eloquent in this regard: the Ascendant of SR is on the cusp of the fourth natal House, the Sun of SR is in the first House of SR, there is a stellium spread over the first and the twelfth House of SR, Uranus in the eighth House, and the tremendous conjunction Mars–Saturn at the Medium

Coeli of the SR! (If my severe proofreader let me do so, at this point I would certainly write three exclamation points in a row).

The Lunar Return is just as spectacular: the Sun of LR is in the first House of LR, there is a stellium spread over the first and the twelfth House of LR, as well as a terrible accumulation of celestials in the eighth House.

With regard to the Houses we can note that, on that day, transiting Pluto and Saturn where clutching the future Prime Minister's Ascendant while Mars was just a little ahead, still in her first House, and very close to her natal Mars. Neptune had just entered his eleventh natal House.

**Comparative Aspects**
**Death transits of Mahatma /Indira Gandhi**

**Sun:**
    **Sexstile with Mercury 63 Degrees**
    **Trine with Jupiter 119 Degrees**
    Opposit with Saturn 175 Degrees
    **Opposit with Neptune 182 Degrees**

**Moon:**
    **Sexstile with Mercury 57 Degrees**
    Square with Venus 95 Degrees
    Semi-sex with Mars 29 Degrees
    **Trine with Jupiter 120 Degrees**
    Square with Node 85 Degrees
    **Sexstile with Neptune 61 Degrees**
    **Square with Pluto 92 Degrees**

**Mercury:**
    **Square with Sun 89 Degrees**
    Semi-sex with Moon 28 Degrees
    Opposit with Ascendant 186 Degrees
    Joined with Uranus 6 Degrees

**Venus:**
   **Semi-squ with Moon 46 Degrees**
   **Sexstile with Venus 61 Degrees**
   Opposit with Mars 186 Degrees
   **Sexstile with Mid Heaven 63 Degrees**

**Mars:**
   **Square with Mercury 91 Degrees**
   Joined with Mars 4 Degrees
   Square with Jupiter 86 Degrees
   Trine with Node 118 Degrees
   **Sexstile with Pluto 59 Degrees**

**Ascendant:**
   Trine with Mercury 119 Degrees
   Semi-sex with Mars 32 Degrees
   Sexstile with Jupiter 59 Degrees
   Joined with Saturn 7 Degrees
   Joined with Neptune 0 Degrees
   Semi-sex with Pluto 31 Degrees

**Mid Heaven:**
   Square with Moon 93 Degrees
   Trine with Node 118 Degrees

**Jupiter:**
   **Trine with Ascendant 121 Degrees**
   Trine with Saturn 126 Degrees
   **Sexstile with Uranus 58 Degrees**
   **Sesquiquad with Neptune 133 Degrees**

**Saturn:**
   **Joined with Ascendant 0 Degrees**
   **Square with Mid Heaven 92 Degrees**
   Joined with Saturn 5 Degrees
   **Opposit with Uranus 179 Degrees**
   Sesquiquad with Node 133 Degrees
   **Semi-squ with Pluto 44 Degrees**

**Uranus:**
Sexstile with Ascendant 57 Degrees
Trine with Uranus 123 Degrees
**Semi-squ with Neptune 44 Degrees**

**Node:**
Opposit with Sun 187 Degrees
Trine with Venus 126 Degrees
Square with Ascendant 90 Degrees
Joined with Mid Heaven 1 Degrees
Square with Saturn 85 Degrees
Square with Uranus 90 Degrees
Sesquiquad with Node 136 Degrees
Semi-squ with Pluto 45 Degrees

**Neptune:**
**Semi-squ with Sun 43 Degrees**
**Square with Venus 90 Degrees**
Trine with Jupiter 125 Degrees
**Sexstile with Saturn 58 Degrees**
Trine with Uranus 127 Degrees

**Pluto:**
Joined with Ascendant 6 Degrees
Square with Mid Heaven 86 Degrees
**Joined with Saturn 0 Degrees**
Opposit with Uranus 186 Degrees
Joined with Neptune 6 Degrees

# THE ATROCIOUS SAGA OF DEATH IN GANDHI'S "FAMILY"

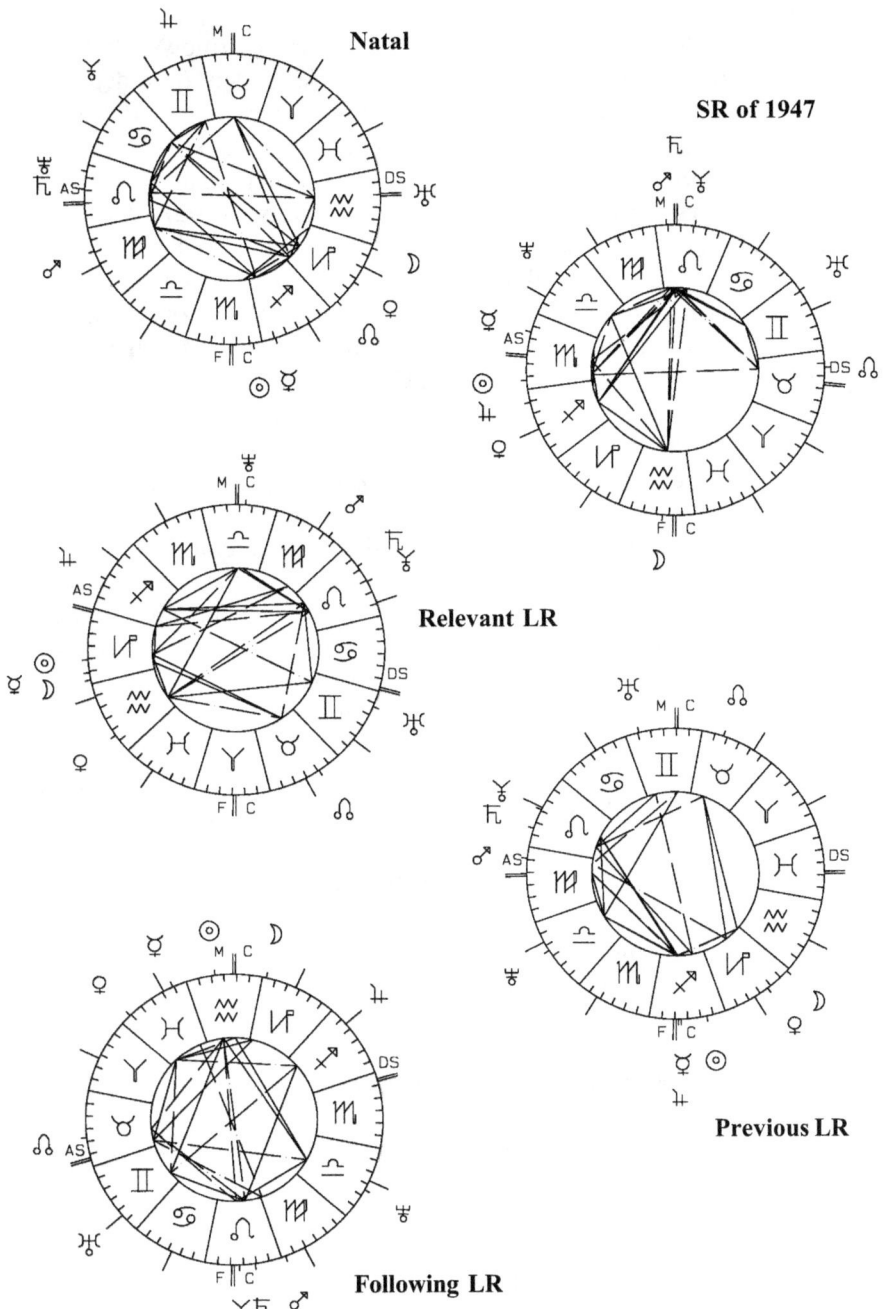

Transits for the death of her son Sanjay are as follows: Pluto trine Uranus (zero degrees of orb), Pluto sextile Ascendant (two degrees of orb), **Pluto semisquare Mercury** (*one degree of orb*), Neptune sesquisquare Neptune (two degrees of orb), Neptune sextile Uranus (two degrees of orb), Neptune trine Ascendant (one degree of orb), **Uranus sesquisquare Pluto** (*one degree of orb*), **Uranus square Ascendant** (two degrees of orb), Saturn semisquare Neptune (two degrees of orb), Saturn trine Medium Coeli (three degrees of orb), Jupiter sextile Pluto (one degree of orb), Jupiter square Jupiter (three degrees of orb), **Jupiter square Mercury** (*one degree of orb*), **Mars semisquare Mercury** (two degrees of orb), Mars trine Medium Coeli (three degrees of orb), Venus semisquare Neptune (two degrees of orb), Venus trine Uranus (zero degrees of orb), Venus sextile Ascendant (zero degrees of orb), Mercury semisquare Jupiter (one degree of orb) and Mars (zero degrees of orb), Mercury trine Sun (two degrees of orb), Sun conjunct Pluto (three degrees of orb), and Sun semisquare Medium Coeli (one degree of orb).

The Solar Return 'maps' the Ascending falling in the first natal House, Mars in the twelfth House, a stellium spread over the first and the twelfth House, and another stellium (with Uranus) in the third House (the third and the ninth House are related with accidents).

The Lunar Return is at least as clear and terrible at the same time: Ascendant in the sixth House, the Sun in the fifth (!) House, a quite detrimental stellium in the eighth House, and Pluto in the ninth House.

With regard to the Houses we can note that Pluto was passing through the third House (remember, the third and the ninth House are related with accidents) while Neptune had just entered the fifth House radix.

**Comparative Aspects**
**Death transits of Sanjay /Indira Gandhi**

**Sun:**
**Semi-squ with Mid Heaven 44 Degrees**
Opposit with Node 181 Degrees
**Joined with Pluto 3 Degrees**

**Moon:**
Square with Moon 86 Degrees
Sexstile with Node 61 Degrees

Trine with Pluto 116 Degrees

**Mercury:**
**Trine with Sun 122 Degrees**
Opposit with Moon 184 Degrees
**Semi-squ with Mars 45 Degrees**
**Semi-squ with Jupiter 46 Degrees**

**Venus:**
**Sexstile with Ascendant 60 Degrees**
Semi-sex with Mid Heaven 32 Degrees
**Trine with Uranus 120 Degrees**
**Semi-squ with Neptune 47 Degrees**

**Mars:**
Trine with Moon 127 Degrees
Trine with Venus 113 Degrees
Semi-sex with Ascendant 30 Degrees
**Trine with Mid Heaven 123 Degrees**
**Semi-squ with Neptune 43 Degrees**

**Ascendant:**
Sexstile with Sun 60 Degrees
Trine with Moon 121 Degrees

**Mid Heaven:**
Semi-squ with Saturn 47 Degrees
Trine with Uranus 127 Degrees
Opposit with Node 186 Degrees
Joined with Pluto 8 Degrees

**Jupiter:**
**Square with Mercury 91 Degrees**
Joined with Mars 4 Degrees
**Square with Jupiter 87 Degrees**
Trine with Node 118 Degrees
**Sexstile with Pluto 59 Degrees**

**Saturn:**
    Trine with Moon 127 Degrees
    Semi-sex with Ascendant 31 Degrees
    **Trine with Mid Heaven 123 Degrees**
    **Semi-squ with Neptune 43 Degrees**

**Uranus:**
    Joined with Sun 4 Degrees
    **Square with Ascendant 92 Degrees**
    Opposit with Mid Heaven 184 Degrees
    Square with Uranus 87 Degrees
    **Sesquiquad with Pluto 136 Degrees**

**Node:**
    Square with Sun 94 Degrees
    Joined with Ascendant 2 Degrees
    Square with Mid Heaven 95 Degrees
    Joined with Saturn 8 Degrees
    Opposit with Uranus 177 Degrees
    Semi-squ with Pluto 47 Degrees

**Neptune:**
    **Trine with Ascendant 121 Degrees**
    Trine with Saturn 126 Degrees
    **Sexstile with Uranus 58 Degrees**
    **Sesquiquad with Neptune 133 Degrees**

**Pluto:**
    **Semi-squ with Mercury 46 Degrees**
    **Sexstile with Ascendant 58 Degrees**
    Trine with Uranus 120 Degrees

# THE ATROCIOUS SAGA OF DEATH IN GANDHI'S "FAMILY"    169

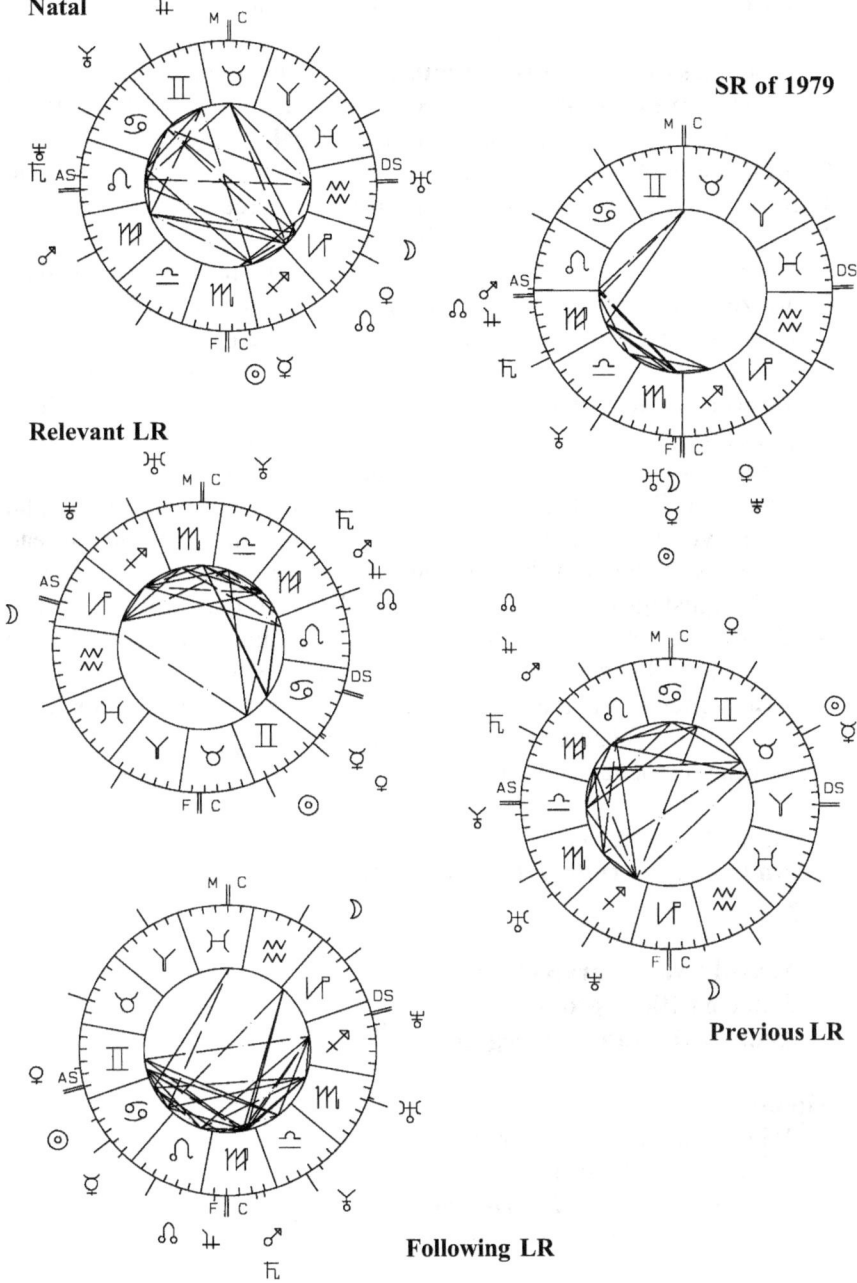

By contrast, here are the transits of Indira relating to her own death: Neptune sesquisquare Saturn (one degree of orb), **Uranus square Mars** (two degrees of orb), **Uranus semisquare Moon** (*one degree of orb*), **Saturn square Uranus** (two degrees of orb) **and square Saturn** (three degrees of orb), **Saturn opposite Medium Coeli** (*zero degrees of orb!*), **Saturn square Ascendant** (three degrees of orb), Jupiter opposite Pluto (three degrees of orb), Jupiter trine Mars (one degree of orb), Mars trine Medium Coeli (zero degrees of orb), Venus trine Saturn (one degree of orb), Venus semisquare Moon (one degree of orb), Mercury sesquisquare Pluto (zero degrees of orb), Mercury square Uranus (one degree of orb) and Ascendant (zero degrees of orb), Mercury opposite Medium Coeli (three degrees of orb), Moon opposite Neptune (two degrees of orb), Moon trine Jupiter (two degrees of orb), Moon sextile Mercury (one degree of orb), Sun trine Pluto (two degrees of orb), Sun square Neptune (one degree of orb), and Sun sextile Mars (one degree of orb).

The Solar Return basically displays an Ascendant in the first natal House (if you find that it is not enough to depict the event, please read what I've written about the bar chart above). The Lunar Return, which took place just the day before his death, has the Ascendant in the twelfth natal House, Mars in the sixth House and a stellium in the sixth House (as well as another stellium in the fourth House: change of home).

Also remember that at the time of her assassination, Indira's Mars was just entering her own sixth House radix. Once again, please note that the murder happened about twenty days before the victim's birthday.

**Comparative Aspects**
**Death transits of Indira /Indira Gandhi**

**Sun:**
    **Sexstile with Mars 59 Degrees**
    **Square with Neptune 91 Degrees**
    **Trine with Pluto 122 Degrees**

**Moon:**
    Joined with Moon 7 Degrees
    **Sexstile with Mercury 59 Degrees**
    **Trine with Jupiter 122 Degrees**
    Semi-sex with Node 32 Degrees

**Opposit with Neptune 178 Degrees**

Mercury:
   Joined with Sun 6 Degrees
   **Square with Ascendant 90 Degrees**
   **Opposit with Mid Heaven 183 Degrees**
   **Square with Uranus 89 Degrees**
   **Sesquiquad with Pluto 135 Degrees**

Venus:
   **Semi-squ with Moon 44 Degrees**
   Joined with Mercury 7 Degrees
   Semi-sex with Venus 30 Degrees
   Square with Mars 94 Degrees
   Trine with Ascendant 113 Degrees
   Opposit with Jupiter 185 Degrees
   Trine with Saturn 119 Degrees
   Trine with Neptune 126 Degrees

Mars:
   Joined with Venus 4 Degrees
   **Trine with Mid Heaven 120 Degrees**
   Semi-sex with Uranus 31 Degrees

Ascendant:
   Square with Sun 88 Degrees
   Opposit with Ascendant 184 Degrees
   Joined with Uranus 4 Degrees

Mid Heaven:
   Joined with Mercury 0 Degrees
   Square with Mars 87 Degrees
   Opposit with Jupiter 178 Degrees
   Trine with Neptune 119 Degrees

Jupiter:
   Semi-sex with Mercury 32 Degrees
   Joined with Venus 4 Degrees

**Trine with Mars 119 Degrees**
Joined with Node 5 Degrees
**Opposit with Pluto 183 Degrees**

**Saturn:**
  **Square with Ascendant 87 Degrees**
  **Opposit with Mid Heaven 180 Degrees**
  **Square with Saturn 93 Degrees**
  **Square with Uranus 92 Degrees**
  Semi-squ with Node 45 Degrees

**Uranus:**
  **Semi-squ with Moon 46 Degrees**
  Joined with Mercury 5 Degrees
  Semi-sex with Venus 32 Degrees
  **Square with Mars 92 Degrees**
  Opposit with Jupiter 184 Degrees
  Trine with Saturn 117 Degrees
  Trine with Neptune 124 Degrees

**Node:**
  Opposit with Sun 178 Degrees
  Trine with Moon 121 Degrees
  Opposit with Mercury 187 Degrees
  Sesquiquad with Venus 135 Degrees

**Neptune:**
  Semi-sex with Sun 32 Degrees
  Semi-sex with Moon 28 Degrees
  **Sesquiquad with Saturn 134 Degrees**
  Joined with Node 3 Degrees
  Opposit with Pluto 174 Degrees

**Pluto:**
  Square with Moon 85 Degrees
  Sexstile with Node 60 Degrees
  Square with Neptune 85 Degrees
  Trine with Pluto 117 Degrees

# THE ATROCIOUS SAGA OF DEATH IN GANDHI'S "FAMILY" 173

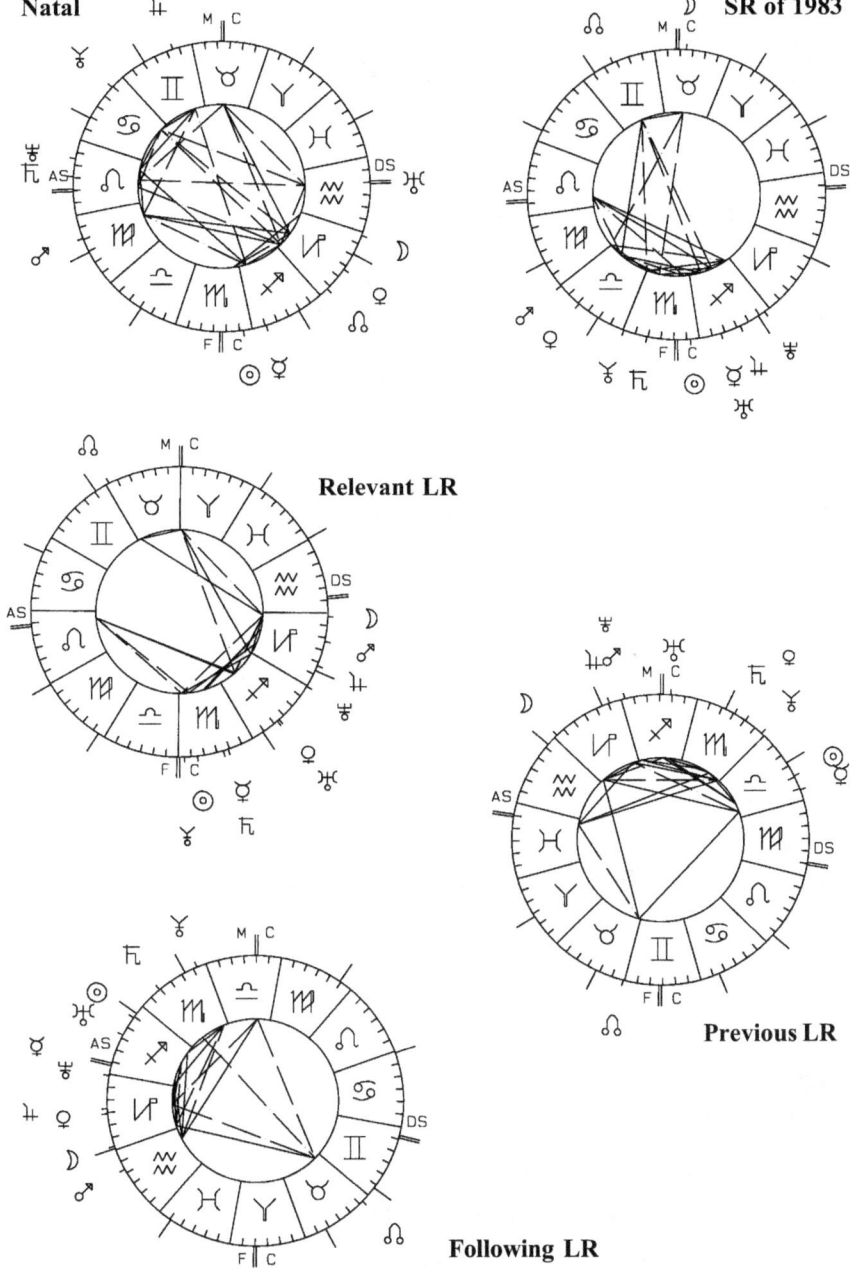

Natal

SR of 1983

Relevant LR

Previous LR

Following LR

Here are the transits of the Prime Minister the day of the death of her son Rajiv: Pluto sesquisquare natal Pluto (two degrees of orb), **Pluto square Uranus** (*one degree of orb*), **Pluto opposite Medium Coeli** (*one degree of orb*), **Pluto square Ascendant** (two degrees of orb), Neptune trine Medium Coeli (two degrees of orb), **Neptune conjunct Venus** (two degrees of orb), **Uranus conjunct Venus** (*zero degrees of orb!*), **Uranus semisquare Sun** (*one degree of orb*), Saturn opposite Neptune (one degree of orb), Saturn trine Jupiter (one degree of orb), Saturn trine Mercury (zero degrees of orb), Jupiter conjunct Neptune (zero degrees of orb), Jupiter sextile Jupiter (one degree of orb), Jupiter trine Mercury (two degrees of orb), **Mars opposite the Moon** (*one degree of orb*), Mars trine the Sun (one degree of orb), Venus opposite Venus (one degree of orb), Mercury sextile Pluto (one degree of orb), Mercury square Neptune (one degree of orb), Mercury trine Mars (three degrees of orb), Moon square Jupiter (three degrees of orb), Moon conjunct Mars (two degrees of orb), Moon trine Venus (two degrees of orb), Moon sesquisquare Moon (two degrees of orb), Sun sesquisquare Venus (two degrees of orb), and Sun trine the Moon (two degrees of orb).

The Solar Return stresses Mars on the cusp of the first House, a stellium in the seventh House (this House is also connected with violence, attacks), and Saturn at the Midheaven.

The Lunar Return has the Sun on the very cusp of the sixth / seventh House, and Venus in the eighth House.

With regard to the Houses we can observe that Uranus and Neptune were transiting in the fifth House just over the radix Venus, while Mars had just entered the twelfth House to oppose the subject's natal Moon.


**Comparative Aspects
Death transits of Rajiv /Indira Gandhi**

**Sun:**
 Opposit with Sun 176 Degrees
 **Trine with Moon 122 Degrees**
 Opposit with Mercury 185 Degrees
 **Sesquiquad with Venus 137 Degrees**
 Joined with Jupiter 7 Degrees

**Moon:**
   **Sesquiquad with Moon 137 Degrees**
   **Trine with Venus 122 Degrees**
   **Joined with Mars 2 Degrees**
   Trine with Mid Heaven 113 Degrees
   **Square with Jupiter 93 Degrees**

**Mercury:**
   Trine with Venus 113 Degrees
   **Trine with Mars 123 Degrees**
   Semi-sex with Jupiter 31 Degrees
   Trine with Node 123 Degrees
   **Square with Neptune 91 Degrees**
   **Sexstile with Pluto 59 Degrees**

**Venus:**
   **Opposit with Venus 179 Degrees**
   Semi-sex with Saturn 30 Degrees
   Joined with Pluto 8 Degrees

**Mars:**
   **Trine with Sun 119 Degrees**
   **Opposit with Moon 181 Degrees**

**Ascendant:**
   Sexstile with Sun 57 Degrees
   Joined with Moon 4 Degrees
   Sesquiquad with Mars 134 Degrees
   Trine with Mid Heaven 114 Degrees
   Sesquiquad with Jupiter 134 Degrees

**Mid Heaven:**
   Semi-sex with Mercury 32 Degrees
   Sexstile with Node 59 Degrees
   Square with Neptune 86 Degrees
   Trine with Pluto 118 Degrees

**Jupiter:**
  **Trine with Mercury 118 Degrees**
  Semi-sex with Mars 31 Degrees
  **Sexstile with Jupiter 59 Degrees**
  Joined with Saturn 7 Degrees
  **Joined with Neptune 0 Degrees**
  Semi-sex with Pluto 32 Degrees

**Saturn:**
  Joined with Moon 8 Degrees
  **Sexstile with Mercury 60 Degrees**
  **Trine with Jupiter 121 Degrees**
  Opposit with Saturn 172 Degrees
  **Opposit with Neptune 179 Degrees**

**Uranus:**
  **Semi-squ with Sun 46 Degrees**
  **Joined with Venus 0 Degrees**
  Trine with Mars 124 Degrees
  Trine with Mid Heaven 125 Degrees
  Opposit with Pluto 188 Degrees

**Node:**
  Joined with Moon 6 Degrees
  Semi-squ with Mercury 45 Degrees
  Joined with Venus 7 Degrees
  Trine with Mid Heaven 116 Degrees
  Sesquiquad with Jupiter 137 Degrees
  Semi-sex with Uranus 28 Degrees

**Neptune:**
  **Joined with Venus 2 Degrees**
  Trine with Mars 127 Degrees
  **Trine with Mid Heaven 122 Degrees**

**Pluto:**
  Joined with Sun 8 Degrees
  **Square with Ascendant 88 Degrees**

## THE ATROCIOUS SAGA OF DEATH IN GANDHI'S "FAMILY"

**Opposit with Mid Heaven 181 Degrees**
Square with Saturn 94 Degrees
Square with Uranus 91 Degrees
Semi-squ with Node 44 Degrees
Sesquiquad with Pluto 133 Degrees

**Natal**

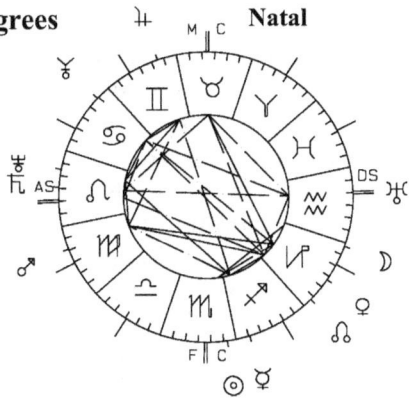

**SR of 1990**

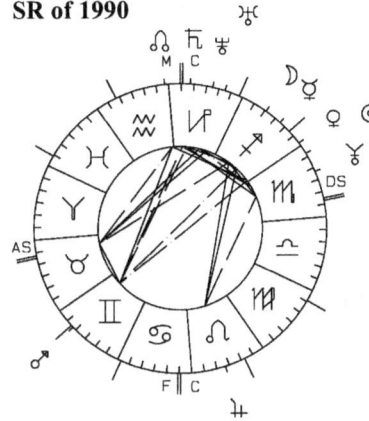

**Relevant LR**

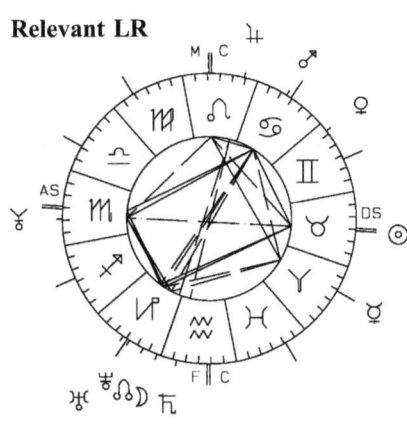

**Previous LR**

**Following LR**

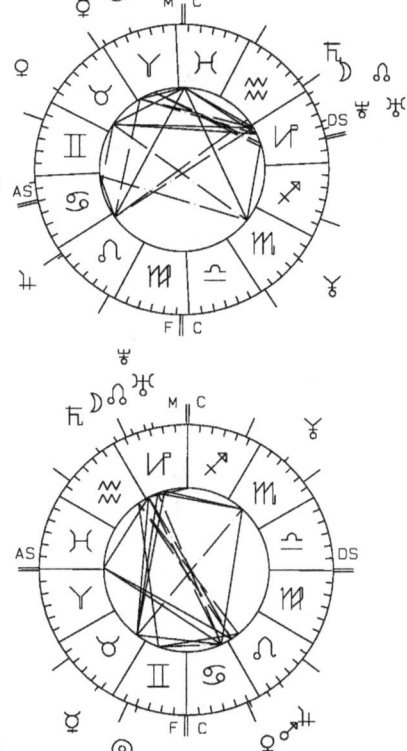

Let us consider now the astral situation of Sanjay Gandhi (born in New Delhi on the 14th of December 1946, at 9:27 am, died on the 23rd of June 23 1980). We can note his transit in relation to the killing of the Mahatma: **Pluto conjunct Pluto** (*zero degrees of orb!*), **Pluto sesquisquare Mars** (two degrees of orb), Neptune sextile Pluto (one degree of orb), Neptune conjunct Neptune (two degrees of orb), **Uranus conjunct Uranus** (two degrees of orb), **Uranus semisquare Saturn** (*zero degrees of orb!*), **Uranus opposite the Sun** (*one degree of orb*), Saturn sextile Uranus (zero degrees of orb), Saturn trine Sun (one degree of orb), Jupiter opposite Uranus (*one degree of orb*), **Jupiter conjunct the Sun** (*zero degrees of orb!*), **Mars conjunct Moon** (*one degree of orb*), Venus trine Jupiter (two degrees of orb) and Venus (three degrees of orb), Mercury sesquisquare Neptune (zero degrees of orb), Mercury sextile Mars (one degree of orb), Moon conjunct Neptune (two degrees of orb), Moon sextile Saturn (one degree of orb), Sun trine Neptune (two degrees of orb), Sun opposite Saturn (one degree of orb), Sun square Medium Coeli (two degrees of orb), and Sun semisquare Sun (two degrees of orb).

The Solar Return that embraces that span of time had the Ascendant falling on the fourth natal House (the 'father', the 'grandfather'), the Sun in the eighth House of SR, while Pluto, Saturn, and Mars in the fourth House (the latter on the cusp).

The Lunar Return – in turn – seems a photocopy of the previous chart: it has the same Ascendant and the same stellium in the fourth House, to which you can add Venus in the eleventh House.

As for transits in the Houses, Pluto and Saturn were crossing the seventh House radix (external aggressions) while Mars had just entered the eighth natal House and was closely conjunct to Sanjay's radix Moon.

**Comparative Aspects**
**Death transits of Mahatma /Sanjay Gandhi**

**Sun:**
   **Semi-squ with Sun 47 Degrees**
   **Square with Mid Heaven 88 Degrees**
   **Opposit with Saturn 181 Degrees**
   Trine with Node 122 Degrees
   **Trine with Neptune 118 Degrees**

Opposit with Pluto 176 Degrees

**Moon:**
Semi-sex with Moon 32 Degrees
**Sexstile with Saturn 59 Degrees**
Trine with Node 117 Degrees
**Joined with Neptune 2 Degrees**

**Mercury:**
Square with Mercury 85 Degrees
**Sexstile with Mars 59 Degrees**
Semi-sex with Ascendant 31 Degrees
Trine with Uranus 114 Degrees
**Sesquiquad with Neptune 135 Degrees**

**Venus:**
**Trine with Venus 117 Degrees**
Trine with Mid Heaven 124 Degrees
**Trine with Jupiter 118 Degrees**
Square with Uranus 95 Degrees
Square with Node 86 Degrees

**Mars:**
**Joined with Moon 1 Degrees**
Square with Mercury 86 Degrees
Trine with Mars 113 Degrees

**Ascendant:**
Sesquiquad with Sun 134 Degrees
Semi-sex with Moon 28 Degrees
Trine with Mercury 114 Degrees
Square with Mid Heaven 94 Degrees
Joined with Saturn 1 Degrees
Semi-squ with Uranus 47 Degrees
Sexstile with Neptune 63 Degrees
Joined with Pluto 6 Degrees

**Mid Heaven:**
Trine with Moon 124 Degrees

Trine with Mars 124 Degrees

**Jupiter:**
  **Joined with Sun 0 Degrees**
  Joined with Mars 6 Degrees
  **Opposit with Uranus 181 Degrees**
  Trine with Pluto 127 Degrees

**Saturn:**
  **Trine with Sun 121 Degrees**
  Square with Venus 87 Degrees
  Trine with Mars 127 Degrees
  Square with Jupiter 86 Degrees
  **Sexstile with Uranus 60 Degrees**
  Joined with Pluto 6 Degrees

**Uranus:**
  **Opposit with Sun 179 Degrees**
  Opposit with Mars 185 Degrees
  **Semi-squ with Saturn 45 Degrees**
  **Joined with Uranus 2 Degrees**

**Node:**
  Opposit with Venus 178 Degrees
  Trine with Ascendant 115 Degrees
  Opposit with Jupiter 177 Degrees
  Semi-sex with Uranus 30 Degrees

**Neptune:**
  Semi-sex with Mid Heaven 28 Degrees
  Trine with Uranus 113 Degrees
  Trine with Node 121 Degrees
  **Joined with Neptune 2 Degrees**
  **Sexstile with Pluto 59 Degrees**

**Pluto:**
  Trine with Sun 127 Degrees
  Square with Venus 93 Degrees
  **Sesquiquad with Mars 133 Degrees**

# THE ATROCIOUS SAGA OF DEATH IN GANDHI'S "FAMILY" 181

Square with Mid Heaven 87 Degrees
Square with Jupiter 93 Degrees
Joined with Saturn 5 Degrees
Sexstile with Node 62 Degrees
**Joined with Pluto 0 Degrees**

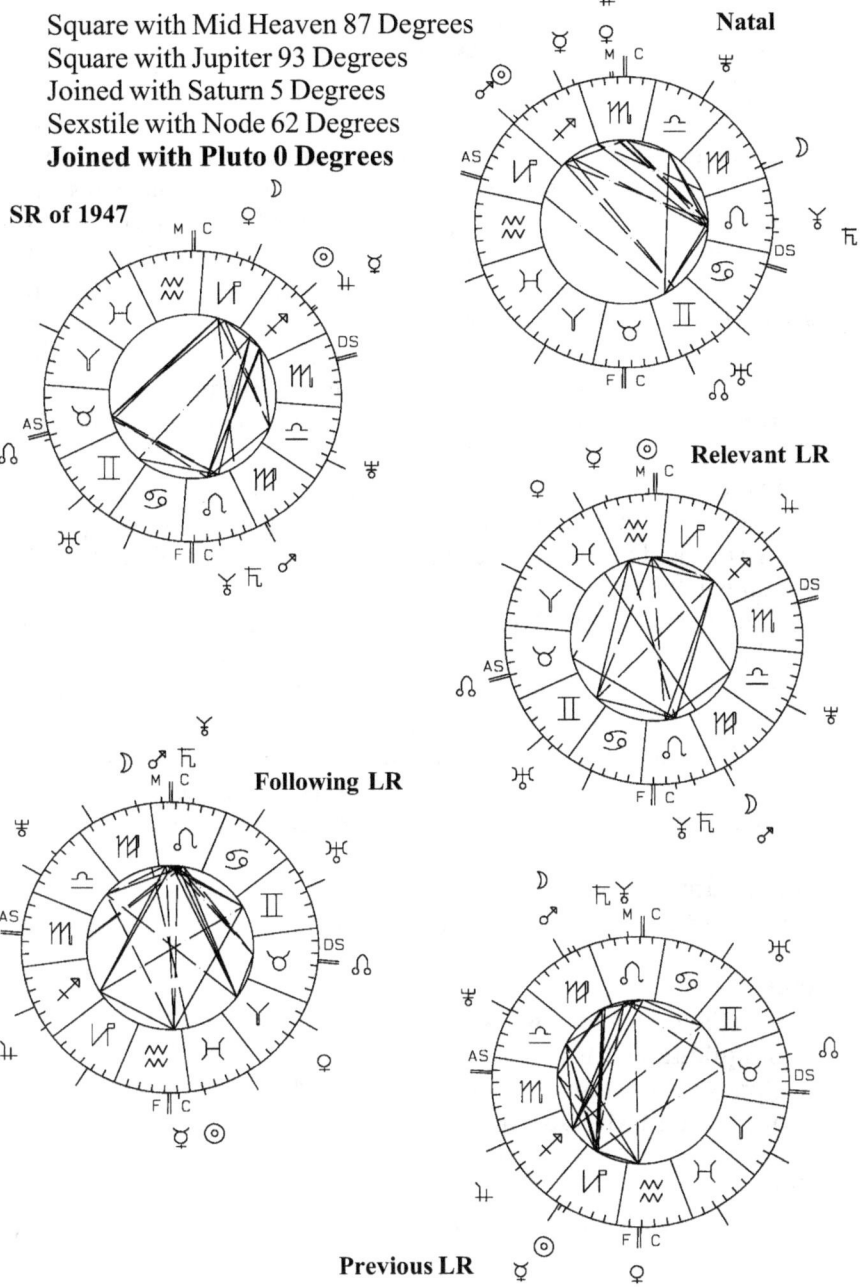

Here are the transits at his own death: Pluto trine Uranus (one degree of orb), **Pluto semisquare Moon** (two degrees of orb), Sun sextile Pluto (two degrees of orb), Neptune opposite Uranus (one degree of orb), **Neptune conjunct Sun** (*zero degrees of orb!*), Uranus sextile Ascendant (two degrees of orb), **Saturn square Uranus** (*one degree of orb*), Saturn trine Ascendant (three degrees of orb), **Saturn square Sun** (*zero degrees of orb!*), **Jupiter conjunct Moon** (*zero degrees of orb!*), **Mars square Uranus** (*zero degrees of orb!*), Mars trine Ascendant (three degrees of orb), Mars sextile Venus (three degrees of orb), **Mars square Sun** (*zero degrees of orb!*), Venus conjunct Uranus (zero degrees of orb), Venus opposite the Sun (one degree of orb), Mercury opposite the Ascendant (zero degrees of orb), Sun sesquisquare Jupiter (zero degrees of orb) and Venus (zero degrees of orb), and Sun sextile Moon (three degrees of orb).

In the Solar Return of 1979–1980 we meet an old acquaintance (the Ascendant of Return in the first natal House) along with a bad stellium (with Mars and Saturn) in the eighth House, and the conjunction Sun–Neptune in the eleventh House.

The relevant Lunar Return has a stellium (with Mars and Saturn) in the ninth House (accidents), the Ascendant in the eleventh natal House, Uranus and Neptune in the eleventh House, and Neptune on the Ascendant (a blunder? Perhaps a mistake?).

As for transits in the Houses, we see Pluto in the ninth House (accidents), Neptune in the eleventh House (conjunct to the Sun: a blunder?), and the close conjunction Mars–Saturn in the eighth House.

**Comparative Aspects**
**Death transits of Sanjay /Sanjay Gandhi**

**Sun:**
   **Sexstile with Moon 63 Degrees**
   **Sesquiquad with Venus 135 Degrees**
   Opposit with Mars 175 Degrees
   **Sesquiquad with Jupiter 135 Degrees**

**Moon:**
   Semi-sex with Mercury 29 Degrees

**Mercury:**
   Trine with Mercury 127 Degrees
   Trine with Venus 113 Degrees
   **Opposit with Ascendant 180 Degrees**

**Venus:**
   **Opposit with Sun 181 Degrees**
   Opposit with Mars 187 Degrees
   **Joined with Uranus 0 Degrees**
   Joined with Node 8 Degrees

**Mars:**
   **Square with Sun 90 Degrees**
   **Sexstile with Venus 57 Degrees**
   **Trine with Ascendant 123 Degrees**
   **Square with Uranus 90 Degrees**

**Ascendant:**
   Square with Mars 90 Degrees
   Trine with Ascendant 117 Degrees
   Semi-squ with Mid Heaven 44 Degrees
   Semi-squ with Pluto 43 Degrees

**Mid Heaven:**
   Opposit with Sun 174 Degrees
   Opposit with Mars 180 Degrees
   Sesquiquad with Mid Heaven 134 Degrees
   Joined with Uranus 6 Degrees
   Semi-squ with Pluto 46 Degrees

**Jupiter:**
   **Joined with Moon 0 Degrees**
   Square with Mercury 86 Degrees

**Saturn:**
   **Square with Sun 90 Degrees**
   **Trine with Ascendant 123 Degrees**
   **Square with Uranus 91 Degrees**

**Uranus:**
   Semi-sex with Sun 29 Degrees
   Joined with Venus 4 Degrees
   **Sexstile with Ascendant 62 Degrees**
   Joined with Jupiter 5 Degrees

**Node:**
   Trine with Sun 118 Degrees
   Square with Venus 85 Degrees
   Trine with Mars 124 Degrees
   Sexstile with Uranus 62 Degrees
   Semi-squ with Neptune 47 Degrees

**Neptune:**
   **Joined with Sun 0 Degrees**
   Joined with Mars 6 Degrees
   **Opposit with Uranus 181 Degrees**
   Trine with Pluto 127 Degrees

**Pluto:**
   **Sexstile with Sun 62 Degrees**
   **Semi-squ with Moon 43 Degrees**
   Semi-sex with Venus 28 Degrees
   Square with Ascendant 95 Degrees
   Semi-sex with Jupiter 28 Degrees
   **Trine with Uranus 119 Degrees**
   Trine with Node 127 Degrees
   Joined with Neptune 8 Degrees

# THE ATROCIOUS SAGA OF DEATH IN GANDHI'S "FAMILY"

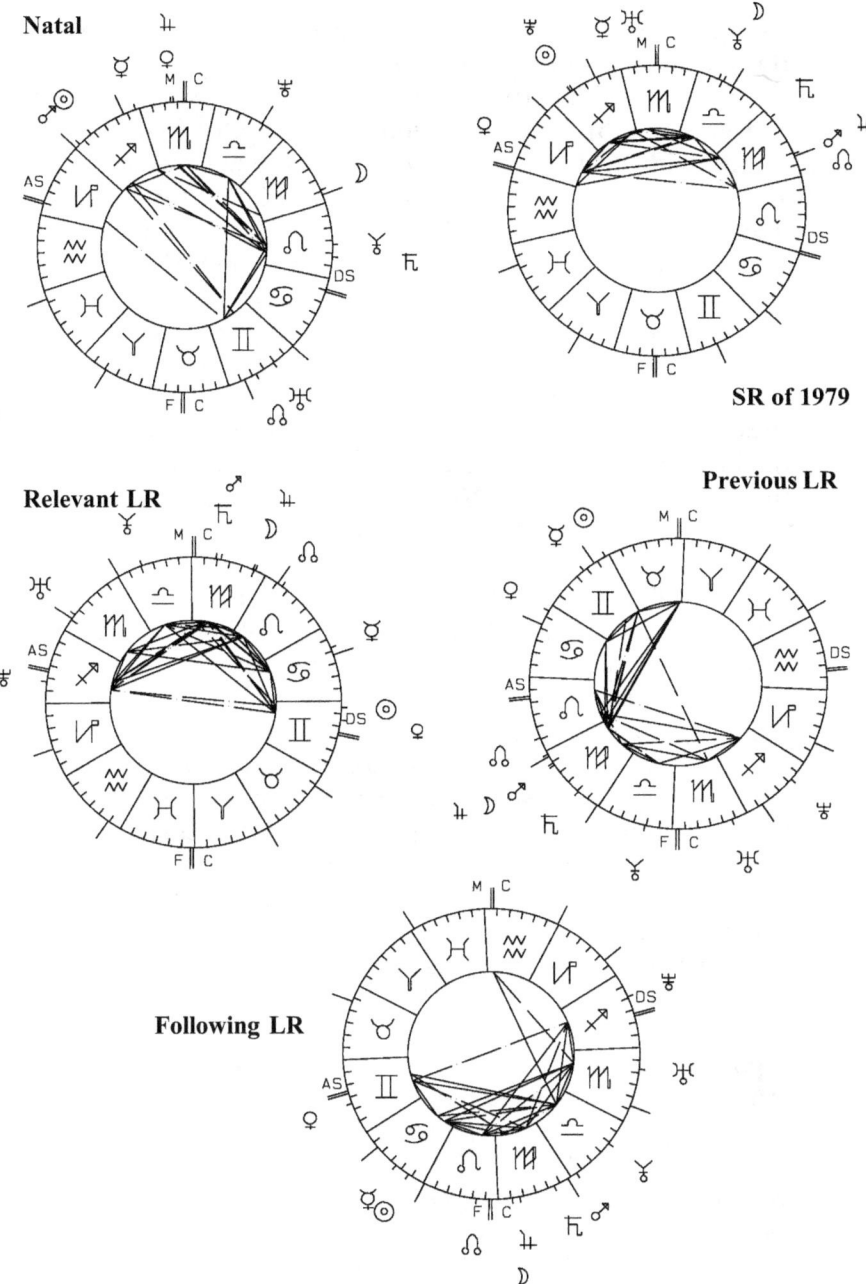

Transits of the day of his mother's death: **Neptune sesquisquare Pluto** (*one degree of orb*), **Neptune conjunct Mars** (*one degree of orb*), Uranus trine Pluto (two degrees of orb), Uranus sextile Neptune (one degree of orb), **Saturn conjunct with Jupiter** (*zero degrees of orb!*) **and with Venus** (*zero degrees of orb!*), Jupiter square Neptune (two degrees of orb), Jupiter sextile Medium Coeli (three degrees of orb), Jupiter trine Moon (three degrees of orb), Mars sextile Jupiter (one degree of orb), Mars sextile Venus (zero degrees of orb), Mars semisquare Mercury (two degrees of orb), Venus trine Pluto (zero degrees of orb), Venus sextile Neptune (two degrees of orb), Mercury conjunct Jupiter (three degrees of orb), Mercury sextile Ascendant (three degrees of orb), Mercury conjunct Venus (three degrees of orb), Moon sesquisquare Uranus (one degree of orb), Moon opposite Saturn (three degrees of orb), Moon semisquare Sun (one degree of orb), Sun square Saturn (one degree of orb), Sun conjunct Medium Coeli (three degrees of orb), Sun sextile Moon (two degrees of orb), and Sun semisquare Sun (two degrees of orb).

The Solar Return highlights an Ascendant in the twelfth natal House, the Sun of SR on the cusp of the twelfth House of SR, a stellium in the eleventh House, and the Medium Coeli (the mother) just in between Saturn and Pluto.

While the Lunar Return suggests that we observe its Ascendant in the seventh natal House (this House also refers to attacks), Mars on the cusp between the fifth and the sixth House, and a stellium (with Saturn) in the fourth House (this House refers to parents: both mother and father).

As for transits in the natal Houses, Neptune was on the cusp of the eleventh–twelfth House just over the radix Mars, Uranus was also in the eleventh House, Saturn was in the tenth House (the mother) conjunct Venus (the mother), and Mars was transiting the twelfth House.

**Comparative Aspects**
**Death transits of Indira /Sanjay Gandhi**

**Sun:**
 **Semi-squ with Sun 43 Degrees**
 **Sexstile with Moon 62 Degrees**
 **Joined with Mid Heaven 3 Degrees**

Joined with Jupiter 8 Degrees
**Square with Saturn 89 Degrees**

**Moon:**
    **Semi-squ with Sun 44 Degrees**
    **Opposit with Saturn 177 Degrees**
    **Sesquiquad with Uranus 134 Degrees**
    Trine with Node 126 Degrees
    Trine with Neptune 115 Degrees
    Opposit with Pluto 172 Degrees

**Mercury:**
    Semi-sex with Sun 30 Degrees
    **Joined with Venus 3 Degrees**
    **Sexstile with Ascendant 63 Degrees**
    **Joined with Jupiter 3 Degrees**

**Venus:**
    Joined with Sun 8 Degrees
    Semi-sex with Mid Heaven 32 Degrees
    Trine with Saturn 125 Degrees
    Opposit with Uranus 173 Degrees
    Opposit with Node 182 Degrees
    **Sexstile with Neptune 62 Degrees**
    **Trine with Pluto 120 Degrees**

**Mars:**
    **Semi-squ with Mercury 47 Degrees**
    **Sexstile with Venus 60 Degrees**
    Joined with Ascendant 6 Degrees
    **Sexstile with Jupiter 61 Degrees**

**Ascendant:**
    Sexstile with Sun 63 Degrees
    Sexstile with Mars 57 Degrees
    Semi-sex with Ascendant 30 Degrees
    Trine with Uranus 115 Degrees
    Sesquiquad with Neptune 134 Degrees

**Mid Heaven:**
    Square with Moon 90 Degrees
    Joined with Mercury 5 Degrees
    Trine with Saturn 118 Degrees
    Opposit with Node 175 Degrees
    Trine with Pluto 113 Degrees

**Jupiter:**
    **Trine with Moon 123 Degrees**
    **Sexstile with Mid Heaven 57 Degrees**
    **Square with Neptune 88 Degrees**

**Saturn:**
    **Joined with Venus 0 Degrees**
    Joined with Mid Heaven 6 Degrees
    **Joined with Jupiter 0 Degrees**
    Square with Pluto 94 Degrees

**Uranus:**
    Semi-sex with Mid Heaven 30 Degrees
    Trine with Saturn 123 Degrees
    Opposit with Uranus 172 Degrees
    Opposit with Node 180 Degrees
    Sexstile with Neptune 61 Degrees
    **Trine with Pluto 118 Degrees**

**Node:**
    Opposit with Mercury 183 Degrees
    Trine with Ascendant 124 Degrees

**Neptune:**
    Joined with Sun 7 Degrees
    Trine with Moon 113 Degrees
    **Joined with Mars 1 Degrees**
    **Sesquiquad with Pluto 136 Degrees**

**Pluto:**
    Semi-sex with Mercury 29 Degrees
    Joined with Mid Heaven 8 Degrees

# THE ATROCIOUS SAGA OF DEATH IN GANDHI'S "FAMILY"

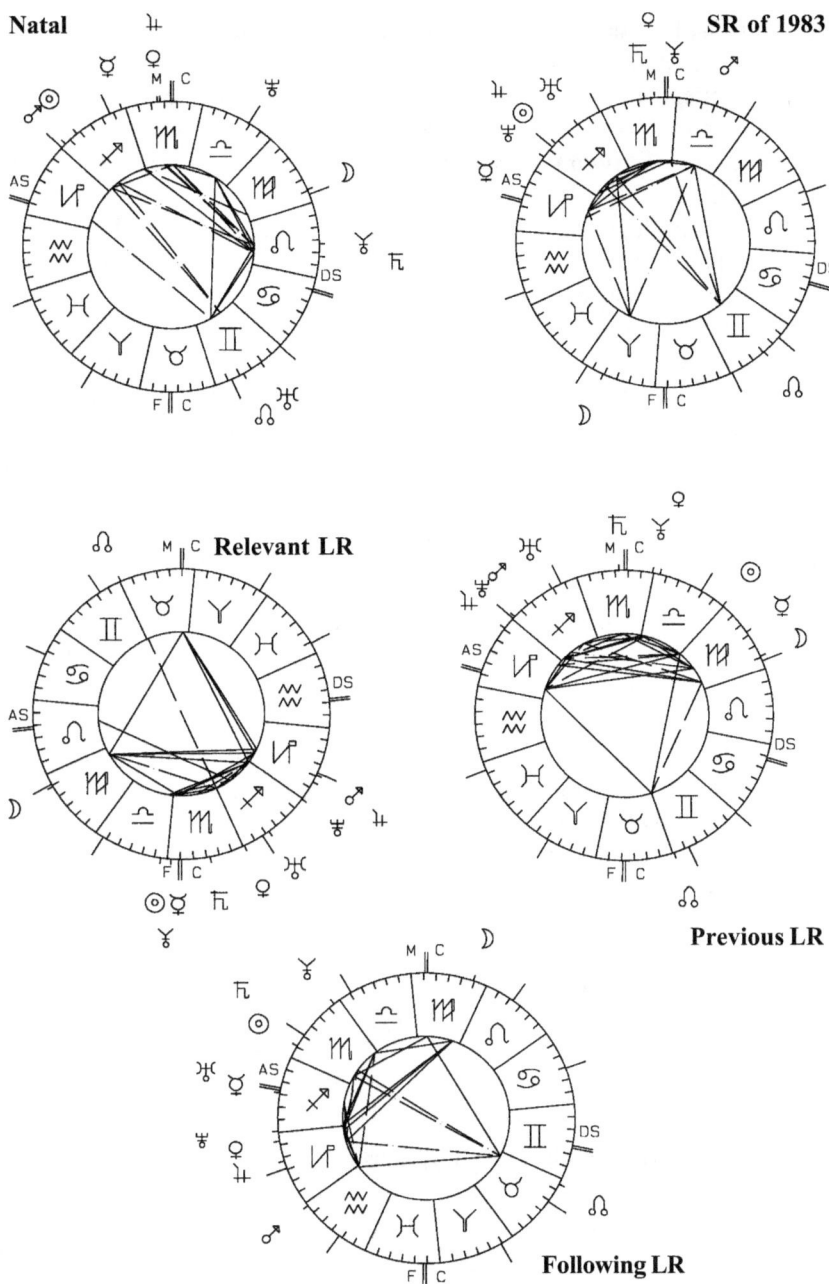

Transits of the death of his brother Rajiv: **Pluto conjunct with Jupiter** (one degree of orb) **and with Venus** (*zero degrees of orb!*), Neptune sextile Jupiter (one degree of orb) and Venus (two degrees of orb), Uranus square Neptune (two degrees of orb), Uranus sextile Medium Coeli (two degrees of orb), **Saturn sesquisquare Uranus** (two degrees of orb), Saturn opposite Saturn (two degrees of orb), **Saturn semisquare the Sun** (*zero degrees of orb!*), Jupiter sextile Neptune (three degrees of orb), Jupiter semisquare Uranus (two degrees of orb), Jupiter conjunct Saturn (zero degrees of orb), **Jupiter square Medium Coeli** (three degrees of orb), **Jupiter sesquisquare Sun** (one degree of orb), **Mars Opposite the Ascendant** (three degrees of orb), Venus trine to Jupiter (three degrees of orb), to the Medium Coeli (three degrees of orb), and to natal Venus (three degrees of orb); Venus sesquisquare Mercury (two degrees of orb), Mercury semisquare Uranus (two degrees of orb), Mercury square Saturn (two degrees of orb), Mercury trine the Moon (one degree of orb), Mercury sesquisquare Sun (zero degrees of orb), Moon sextile Medium Coeli (zero degrees of orb), Moon sesquisquare the Ascendant (two degrees of orb), and Sun opposite Mercury (one degree of orb).

The Solar Return has the Ascendant in the eighth natal House, Mars in the eighth House, and a strong stellium in the third House (brothers).

The Lunar Return relevant to the event in question took place exactly on the day of the murder, at 6:59 London time, therefore at 3:34 pm Delhi time, a few hours before the fatal attack. It 'prints' out the image of a clear Ascendant in the eighth natal House, as well as Pluto in the third House, and Mars in the eleventh House.

Concerning the transits in the Houses, we can note Uranus and Neptune in the twelfth House of birth, Saturn in the first House, while Mars just entered the seventh House.

**Comparative Aspects**
**Death transits of Rajiv/Sanjay Gandhi**

**Sun:**
Square with Moon 95 Degrees
**Opposit with Mercury 181 Degrees**
Trine with Ascendant 126 Degrees

**Moon:**
Joined with Moon 5 Degrees

Sesquiquad with Ascendant 133 Degrees
**Sexstile with Mid Heaven 60 Degrees**
Semi-sex with Saturn 32 Degrees
Square with Node 90 Degrees
Semi-sex with Neptune 29 Degrees

**Mercury:**
**Sesquiquad with Sun 135 Degrees**
**Trine with Moon 119 Degrees**
Opposit with Mid Heaven 185 Degrees
**Square with Saturn 92 Degrees**
**Semi-squ with Uranus 43 Degrees**

**Venus:**
**Sesquiquad with Mercury 137 Degrees**
**Trine with Venus 123 Degrees**
**Trine with Mid Heaven 117 Degrees**
**Trine with Jupiter 123 Degrees**
Semi-sex with Node 32 Degrees
Square with Neptune 86 Degrees
Semi-sex with Pluto 29 Degrees

**Mars:**
Trine with Mercury 124 Degrees
**Opposit with Ascendant 177 Degrees**
Semi-squ with Node 46 Degrees

**Ascendant:**
Semi-sex with Sun 32 Degrees
Joined with Ascendant 0 Degrees

**Mid Heaven:**
Sexstile with Moon 57 Degrees
Semi-sex with Mercury 28 Degrees
Joined with Mid Heaven 7 Degrees
Sesquiquad with Uranus 133 Degrees

**Jupiter:**
**Sesquiquad with Sun 134 Degrees**

Semi-sex with Moon 28 Degrees
Trine with Mercury 113 Degrees
**Square with Mid Heaven 93 Degrees**
**Joined with Saturn 0 Degrees**
**Semi-squ with Uranus 47 Degrees**
**Sexstile with Neptune 63 Degrees**
Joined with Pluto 5 Degrees

**Saturn:**
**Semi-squ with Sun 45 Degrees**
Square with Mid Heaven 85 Degrees
**Opposit with Saturn 178 Degrees**
**Sesquiquad with Uranus 133 Degrees**
Trine with Node 125 Degrees
Trine with Neptune 116 Degrees
Opposit with Pluto 173 Degrees

**Uranus:**
Trine with Moon 127 Degrees
**Sexstile with Mid Heaven 62 Degrees**
**Square with Neptune 92 Degrees**

**Node:**
Semi-sex with Sun 30 Degrees
Sesquiquad with Moon 136 Degrees
Sexstile with Venus 63 Degrees
Joined with Ascendant 2 Degrees

**Neptune:**
**Semi-squ with Mercury 45 Degrees**
**Sexstile with Venus 58 Degrees**
Joined with Ascendant 8 Degrees
**Sexstile with Jupiter 59 Degrees**
Square with Neptune 95 Degrees

**Pluto:**
Semi-sex with Sun 32 Degrees
**Joined with Venus 0 Degrees**
Joined with Mid Heaven 7 Degrees

# THE ATROCIOUS SAGA OF DEATH IN GANDHI'S "FAMILY"    193

**Joined with Jupiter 1 Degrees**
Square with Pluto 95 Degrees

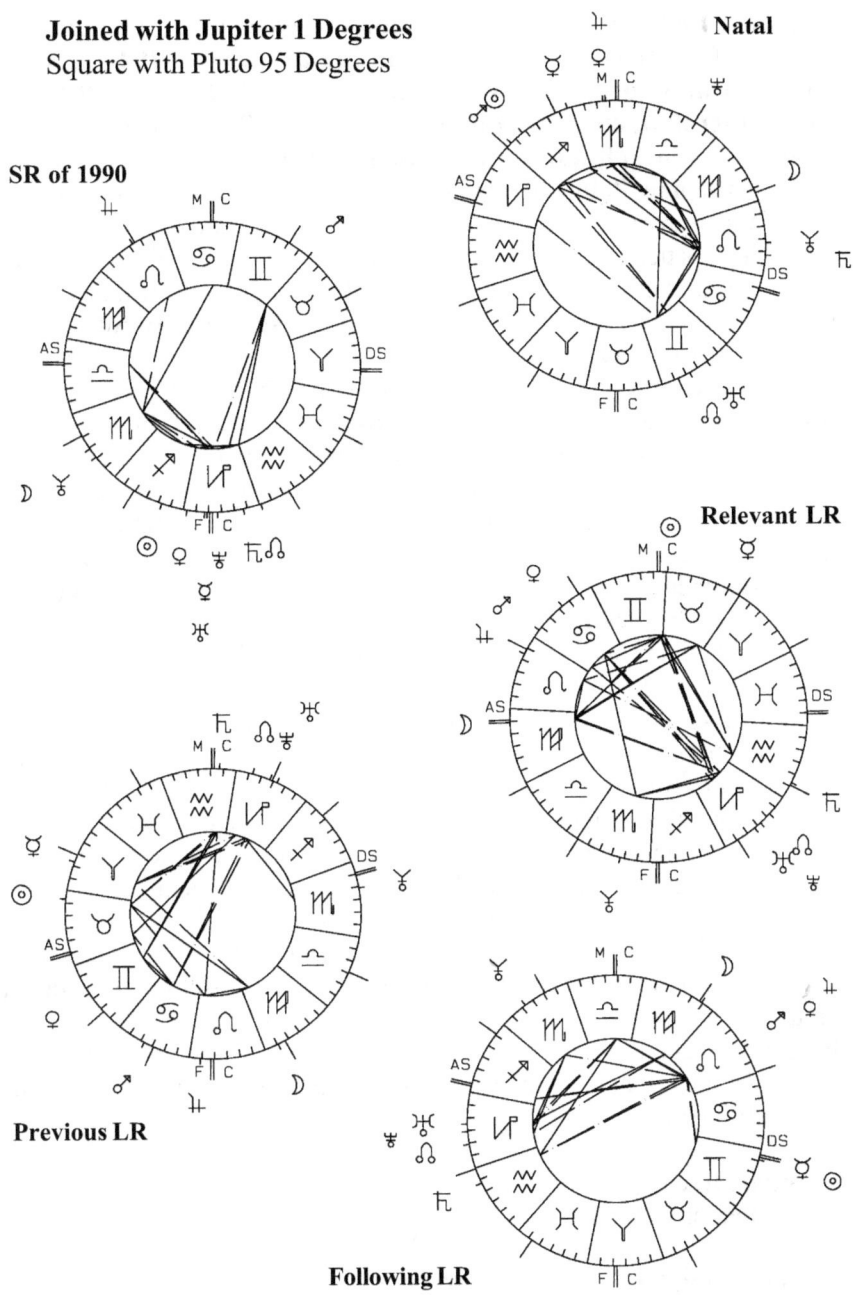

**SR of 1990**

**Natal**

**Previous LR**

**Relevant LR**

**Following LR**

Now let us examine the same four tragedies from the point of view of Rajiv (born in New Delhi on the 20th August 1944 at 8:11 am, died in Sriperumbudur on the 21st May 1991 at 10:20 pm). Remember that, until his brother Sanjay lived, Rajiv didn't want to be involved in politics, but after Sanjay and his mother died, He became the new Prime Minister of India. Here are his transits on the day of the murder of who might be called his 'spiritual grandfather', to whom he was tied by irrefutable huge bonds of political, social, religious, historical kind etc.: Pluto sextile Uranus (one degree of orb), Neptune trine Uranus (zero degrees of orb), **Neptune semisquare Sun** (*zero degrees of orb!*), **Uranus semisquare Pluto** (*one degree of orb*), **Uranus conjunct Medium Coeli** (*zero degrees of orb!*), **Uranus square Ascendant** (*one degree of orb*), **Uranus square Mars** (*one degree of orb*), Uranus square Mercury (one degree of orb), Saturn sextile Medium Coeli (three degrees of orb), **Jupiter opposite Medium Coeli** (*one degree of orb*), **Jupiter square Ascendant** (*one degree of orb*), Jupiter square Mercury (one degree of orb), Mars sextile Saturn (three degrees of orb), Mars conjunct Jupiter (zero degrees of orb), Venus square Uranus (two degrees of orb), Venus opposite Venus (three degrees of orb), Mercury opposite the Sun (one degree of orb), Moon sextile Pluto (one degree of orb), Moon square Saturn (zero degrees of orb), Sun opposite Pluto (zero degrees of orb); and Sun sesquisquare the Midheaven (two degrees of orb), the Ascendant (two degrees of orb), Mars (zero degrees of orb), and Mercury (two degrees of orb).

The Solar Return highlights the spectacular conjunction Mars–Uranus on the Ascendant, and the Ascendant itself falling on the tenth natal House (remember that if the tenth House – in the SR – is linked to other bad positions, it carries detrimental meanings).

The Lunar Return is no less heavy and meaningful: Ascendant in the twelfth natal House, Mars in the twelfth House, and a stellium in twelfth House. Concerning the transit of the celestials in the natal House, we have Saturn and Pluto crossing the eleventh House, Neptune in the first House, Uranus 'standing out' at the Midheaven, and Mars passing through the twelfth House.

**Comparative Aspects**
**Death transits of Mahatma /Rajiv Gandhi**
**Sun:**
    **Sesquiquad with Mercury 137 Degrees**

**Sesquiquad with Mars 135 Degrees**
**Sesquiquad with Ascendant 137 Degrees**
**Sesquiquad with Mid Heaven 133 Degrees**
Trine with Uranus 124 Degrees
Trine with Neptune 126 Degrees
**Opposit with Pluto 180 Degrees**

## Moon:
Semi-sex with Jupiter 32 Degrees
**Square with Saturn 90 Degrees**
Trine with Uranus 115 Degrees
Joined with Neptune 5 Degrees
**Sexstile with Pluto 59 Degrees**

## Mercury:
**Opposit with Sun 179 Degrees**
Trine with Mid Heaven 116 Degrees

## Venus:
Opposit with Moon 184 Degrees
Opposit with Mercury 173 Degrees
**Opposit with Venus 183 Degrees**
Opposit with Ascendant 173 Degrees
Trine with Saturn 113 Degrees
**Square with Uranus 88 Degrees**

## Mars:
Joined with Sun 7 Degrees
Joined with Moon 6 Degrees
Joined with Venus 7 Degrees
**Joined with Jupiter 0 Degrees**
**Sexstile with Saturn 57 Degrees**
Semi-sex with Neptune 28 Degrees

## Ascendant:
Semi-squ with Mercury 44 Degrees
Semi-squ with Mars 47 Degrees
Semi-squ with Ascendant 44 Degrees
Semi-squ with Mid Heaven 44 Degrees

Semi-sex with Jupiter 28 Degrees
Semi-sex with Saturn 29 Degrees
Joined with Pluto 2 Degrees

**Mid Heaven:**
Trine with Sun 116 Degrees
Trine with Jupiter 124 Degrees
Square with Node 85 Degrees

**Jupiter:**
Trine with Sun 114 Degrees
**Square with Mercury 89 Degrees**
Square with Mars 86 Degrees
**Square with Ascendant 89 Degrees**
**Opposit with Mid Heaven 179 Degrees**
Opposit with Uranus 188 Degrees

**Saturn:**
Joined with Sun 6 Degrees
Semi-sex with Mercury 31 Degrees
Semi-sex with Ascendant 31 Degrees
**Sexstile with Mid Heaven 57 Degrees**

**Uranus:**
**Square with Mercury 89 Degrees**
**Square with Mars 91 Degrees**
**Square with Ascendant 89 Degrees**
**Joined with Mid Heaven 0 Degrees**
**Semi-squ with Pluto 46 Degrees**

**Node:**
Trine with Mercury 122 Degrees
Trine with Mars 125 Degrees
Trine with Ascendant 122 Degrees
Semi-sex with Mid Heaven 32 Degrees
Sesquiquad with Neptune 133 Degrees

**Neptune:**
**Semi-squ with Sun 45 Degrees**

## THE ATROCIOUS SAGA OF DEATH IN GANDHI'S "FAMILY"   197

Semi-sex with Moon 32 Degrees
Semi-sex with Venus 31 Degrees
Square with Saturn 95 Degrees
**Trine with Uranus 120 Degrees**

**Pluto:**
   **Sexstile with Uranus 61 Degrees**
   Joined with Pluto 4 Degrees

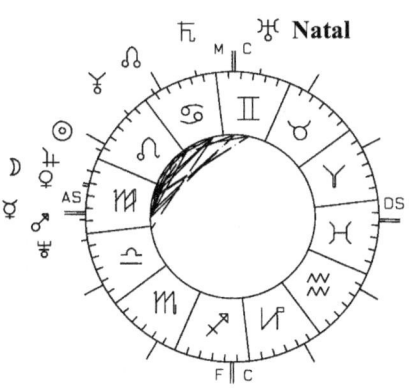
Natal

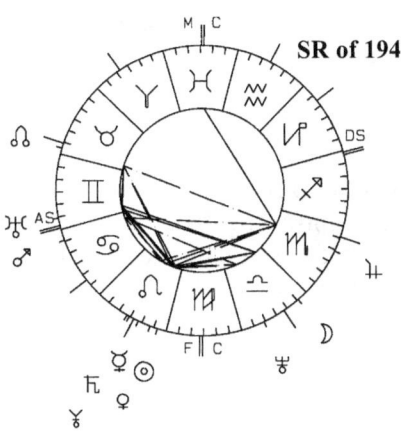
SR of 1947

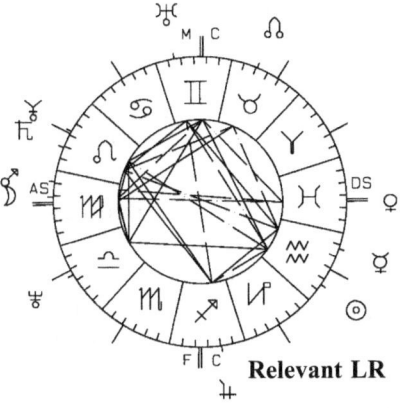
Relevant LR

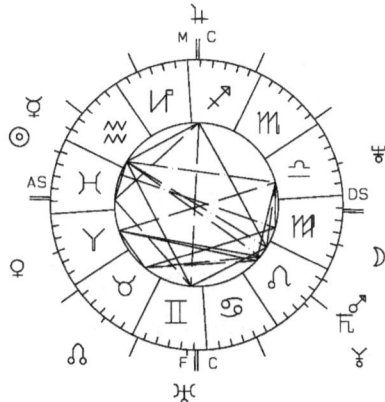
Following LR

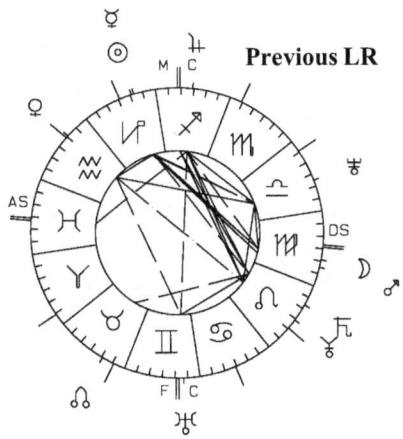
Previous LR

His transits on the day of his brother Sanjay's death were as follows: Pluto semisquare Jupiter (two degrees of orb), **Neptune opposite Medium Coeli** (two degrees of orb), **Neptune square Ascendant** (*one degree of orb*), **Neptune square Mercury** (*one degree of orb*), **Uranus sesquisquare Saturn** (one degree of orb), Uranus sextile the Ascendant (zero degrees of orb) and sextile Mercury (zero degrees of orb), **Saturn square Medium Coeli** (*one degree of orb*); **Saturn conjunct Ascendant** (*zero degrees of orb!*), **Mars** (three degrees of orb), **and Mercury** (*zero degrees of orb!*); Jupiter sextile Saturn (three degrees of orb), **Jupiter conjunct Jupiter** (*zero degrees of orb!*), **Mars square Medium Coeli** (two degrees of orb); **Mars conjunct Ascendant** (*one degree of orb*), **Mars** (three degrees of orb) **and Mercury** (*one degree of orb*); Venus conjunct Medium Coeli (two degrees of orb), Venus square Ascendant (two degrees of orb) and Mercury (one degree of orb): Mercury sextile the Ascendant (three degrees of orb), Mars (zero degrees of orb), and Mercury (three degrees of orb); Mercury semisquare Venus (two degrees of orb) and the Moon (one degree of orb); Sun square Neptune (zero degrees of orb) and sextile to Jupiter (three degrees of orb). An impressive combination of many important transits, very significant ones and with very close orbs.

The Solar Return is characterized by the Sun in the sixth House, a stellium in the sixth House, the Ascendant of SR falling on the natal sixth, Pluto in the eighth House, and Uranus in the ninth House (the air crash). I think that those who criticize Solar Returns could not really ask for more from this chart.

The Moon Revolution is no less clear: Ascendant of LR in the ninth House (accidents) and the Sun in the first House (100 out of 100 points of negativity!).

As for the transits in the natal Houses, we can see Neptune in the third radix House, Uranus on the cusp of the second–third House, and the close conjunction Mars–Saturn literally laid down on the Ascendant. I think, to put it mildly, that this picture deserves to represent, perhaps, the whole theory of transits read together with the Solar and the Lunar Returns as a magnificent instrument of forecasting within the frame of an astrology aiming to highlight concrete facts rather than to build abstract ideas.

**Comparative Aspects**
**Death transits of Sanjay /Rajiv Gandhi**

**Sun:**
  **Sexstile with Jupiter 63 Degrees**
  Joined with Saturn 5 Degrees
  **Square with Neptune 90 Degrees**

**Moon:**
  Trine with Saturn 114 Degrees
  Semi-sex with Neptune 29 Degrees

**Mercury:**
  Semi-sex with Sun 32 Degrees
  **Semi-squ with Moon 46 Degrees**
  **Sexstile with Mercury 57 Degrees**
  **Semi-squ with Venus 47 Degrees**
  **Sexstile with Mars 60 Degrees**
  **Sexstile with Ascendant 57 Degrees**
  Semi-sex with Mid Heaven 32 Degrees
  Joined with Node 1 Degrees

**Venus:**
  **Square with Mercury 91 Degrees**
  Square with Mars 94 Degrees
  **Square with Ascendant 92 Degrees**
  **Joined with Mid Heaven 2 Degrees**
  Joined with Uranus 6 Degrees

**Mars:**
  **Joined with Mercury 1 Degrees**
  Joined with Venus 8 Degrees
  **Joined with Mars 3 Degrees**
  **Joined with Ascendant 1 Degrees**
  **Square with Mid Heaven 88 Degrees**

**Ascendant:**
  Semi-sex with Sun 29 Degrees

    Joined with Mercury 5 Degrees
    Joined with Mars 2 Degrees
    Joined with Ascendant 4 Degrees
    Square with Mid Heaven 94 Degrees
    Sexstile with Node 60 Degrees
    Joined with Neptune 5 Degrees
    Semi-squ with Pluto 47 Degrees

**Mid Heaven:**
    Sexstile with Sun 60 Degrees
    Square with Mercury 85 Degrees
    Square with Mars 87 Degrees
    Square with Ascendant 85 Degrees
    Joined with Mid Heaven 4 Degrees
    Semi-sex with Node 29 Degrees

**Jupiter:**
    Joined with Sun 7 Degrees
    Joined with Moon 5 Degrees
    Joined with Venus 6 Degrees
    **Joined with Jupiter 0 Degrees**
    **Sexstile with Saturn 57 Degrees**

**Saturn:**
    **Joined with Mercury 0 Degrees**
    **Joined with Mars 3 Degrees**
    **Joined with Ascendant 0 Degrees**
    **Square with Mid Heaven 89 Degrees**

**Uranus:**
    Square with Sun 85 Degrees
    **Sexstile with Mercury 60 Degrees**
    Sexstile with Mars 57 Degrees
    **Sexstile with Ascendant 60 Degrees**
    **Sesquiquad with Saturn 134 Degrees**
    Trine with Node 116 Degrees

**Node:**
- Joined with Sun 4 Degrees
- Semi-sex with Mercury 29 Degrees
- Semi-sex with Mars 31 Degrees
- Semi-sex with Ascendant 29 Degrees
- Sexstile with Mid Heaven 60 Degrees
- Semi-squ with Saturn 45 Degrees

**Neptune:**
- Trine with Sun 114 Degrees
- **Square with Mercury 89 Degrees**
- Square with Mars 86 Degrees
- **Square with Ascendant 89 Degrees**
- **Opposit with Mid Heaven 178 Degrees**
- Opposit with Uranus 188 Degrees

**Pluto:**
- Trine with Mid Heaven 116 Degrees
- **Semi-squ with Jupiter 43 Degrees**
- Trine with Uranus 126 Degrees

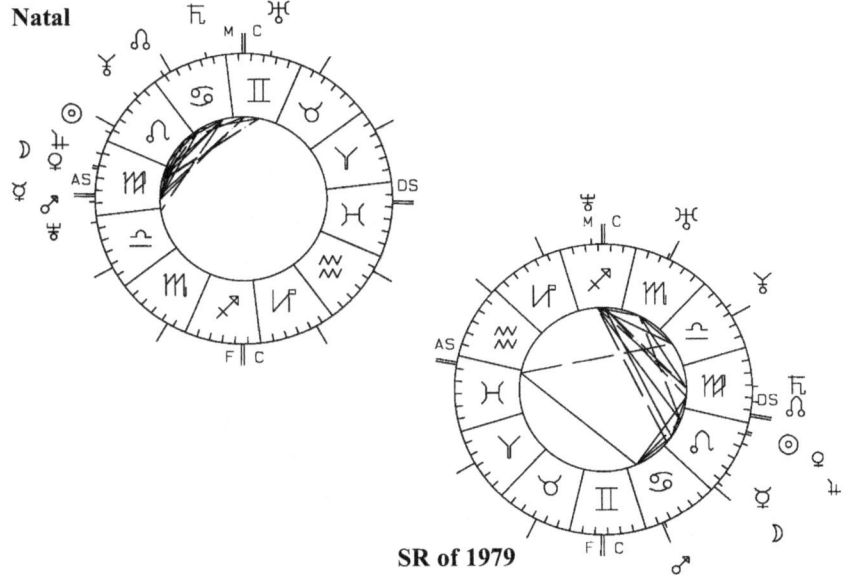

Natal

SR of 1979

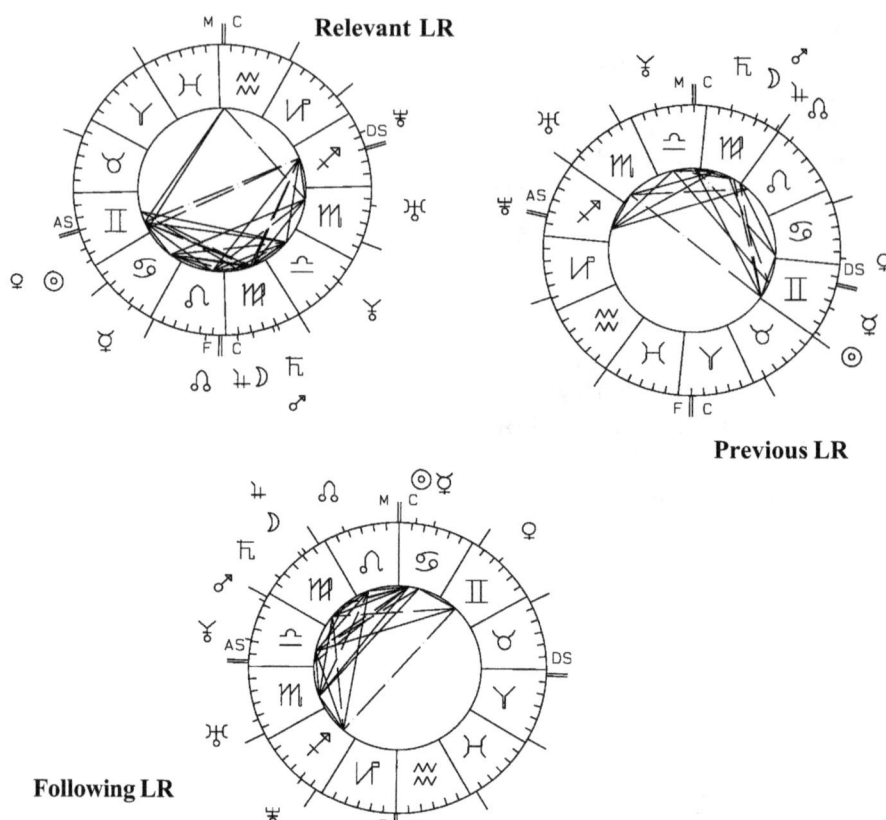

**Relevant LR**

**Previous LR**

**Following LR**

Let's see, now, the transits on the death of his mother Indira. Neptune trine the Sun (two degrees of orb), Uranus trine Pluto (two degrees of orb), **Uranus opposite Uranus** (two degrees of orb), **Uranus square Venus** (*one degree of orb*) **and Moon** (*zero degrees of orb!*), **Saturn semisquare Neptune** (*zero degrees of orb!*), **Jupiter opposite Saturn** (*one degree of orb*), Jupiter trine Jupiter (three degrees of orb) and the Moon (two degrees of orb); Mars sesquisquare Jupiter (two degrees of orb), Venus opposite Uranus (zero degrees of orb), Venus square Venus (one degree of orb) and the Moon (two degrees of orb); Mercury sesquisquare Saturn (two degrees of orb), Mercury sextile the Ascendant (one degree of orb) and Mercury (one degree of orb); Moon trine Neptune (three degrees of orb), Moon sesquisquare the Midheaven (two degrees of orb), the Ascendant (one degree of orb), and Mercury (one degree of orb); Sun square Pluto (one degree of orb), Sun trine Saturn (zero degrees of orb), Sun sextile Jupiter (two degrees of orb) and the Moon (three degrees of orb); and the Sun semisquare the Ascendant (one degree of orb), Mars (two degrees of orb), and Mercury (one degree of orb).

The Solar Return 'glosses' as follows: Mars in the sixth House, a stellium sixth House, the Sun in the fourth House, a stellium in the fourth House, and the Moon in the twelfth House.

These are the references of the Lunar Return: stellium spread over the first and the twelfth House, Sun in the eleventh House, and stellium in the eleventh House.

As for the Houses, we find Neptune transiting the fourth House, and Mars on the cusp between the fourth and fifth House.

**Comparative Aspects**
**Death transits of Indira /Rajiv Gandhi**

**Sun:**
    **Sexstile with Moon 57 Degrees**
    **Semi-squ with Mercury 46 Degrees**
    **Semi-squ with Mars 43 Degrees**
    **Semi-squ with Ascendant 46 Degrees**
    **Sesquiquad with Mid Heaven 136 Degrees**
    **Sexstile with Jupiter 62 Degrees**
    **Trine with Saturn 120 Degrees**
    **Square with Pluto 89 Degrees**

**Moon:**
    **Sesquiquad with Mercury 134 Degrees**
    **Sesquiquad with Ascendant 134 Degrees**
    **Sesquiquad with Mid Heaven 137 Degrees**
    Trine with Uranus 127 Degrees
    **Trine with Neptune 123 Degrees**
    Opposit with Pluto 176 Degrees

**Mercury:**
    **Sexstile with Mercury 59 Degrees**
    **Sexstile with Ascendant 59 Degrees**

**Sesquiquad with Saturn 133 Degrees**
Trine with Node 114 Degrees

**Venus:**
**Square with Moon 92 Degrees**
**Square with Venus 91 Degrees**
**Opposit with Uranus 180 Degrees**
Sesquiquad with Node 137 Degrees
Trine with Pluto 124 Degrees

**Mars:**
Trine with Moon 127 Degrees
Trine with Mercury 116 Degrees
Trine with Venus 126 Degrees
Trine with Mars 114 Degrees
Trine with Ascendant 116 Degrees
**Sesquiquad with Jupiter 133 Degrees**
Opposit with Node 172 Degrees

**Ascendant:**
Opposit with Sun 177 Degrees
Trine with Mid Heaven 118 Degrees
Sesquiquad with Saturn 133 Degrees

**Mid Heaven:**
Square with Moon 85 Degrees
Square with Jupiter 91 Degrees
Opposit with Uranus 173 Degrees
Sexstile with Neptune 63 Degrees
Trine with Pluto 117 Degrees

**Jupiter:**
**Trine with Moon 118 Degrees**
Trine with Venus 116 Degrees
**Trine with Jupiter 123 Degrees**
**Opposit with Saturn 181 Degrees**

**Saturn:**
   **Semi-squ with Neptune 45 Degrees**

**Uranus:**
   **Square with Moon 90 Degrees**
   **Square with Venus 89 Degrees**
   **Opposit with Uranus 178 Degrees**
   Sesquiquad with Node 135 Degrees
   **Trine with Pluto 122 Degrees**

**Node:**
   Square with Sun 88 Degrees
   Trine with Mercury 113 Degrees
   Trine with Mars 115 Degrees
   Trine with Ascendant 113 Degrees
   Sexstile with Node 57 Degrees
   Trine with Neptune 124 Degrees

**Neptune:**
   **Trine with Sun 122 Degrees**
   Square with Mars 95 Degrees
   Opposit with Mid Heaven 187 Degrees
   Trine with Jupiter 114 Degrees
   Opposit with Saturn 172 Degrees
   Square with Neptune 86 Degrees

**Pluto:**
   Sexstile with Jupiter 57 Degrees
   Trine with Saturn 115 Degrees
   Semi-sex with Neptune 29 Degrees

# LUNAR RETURNS

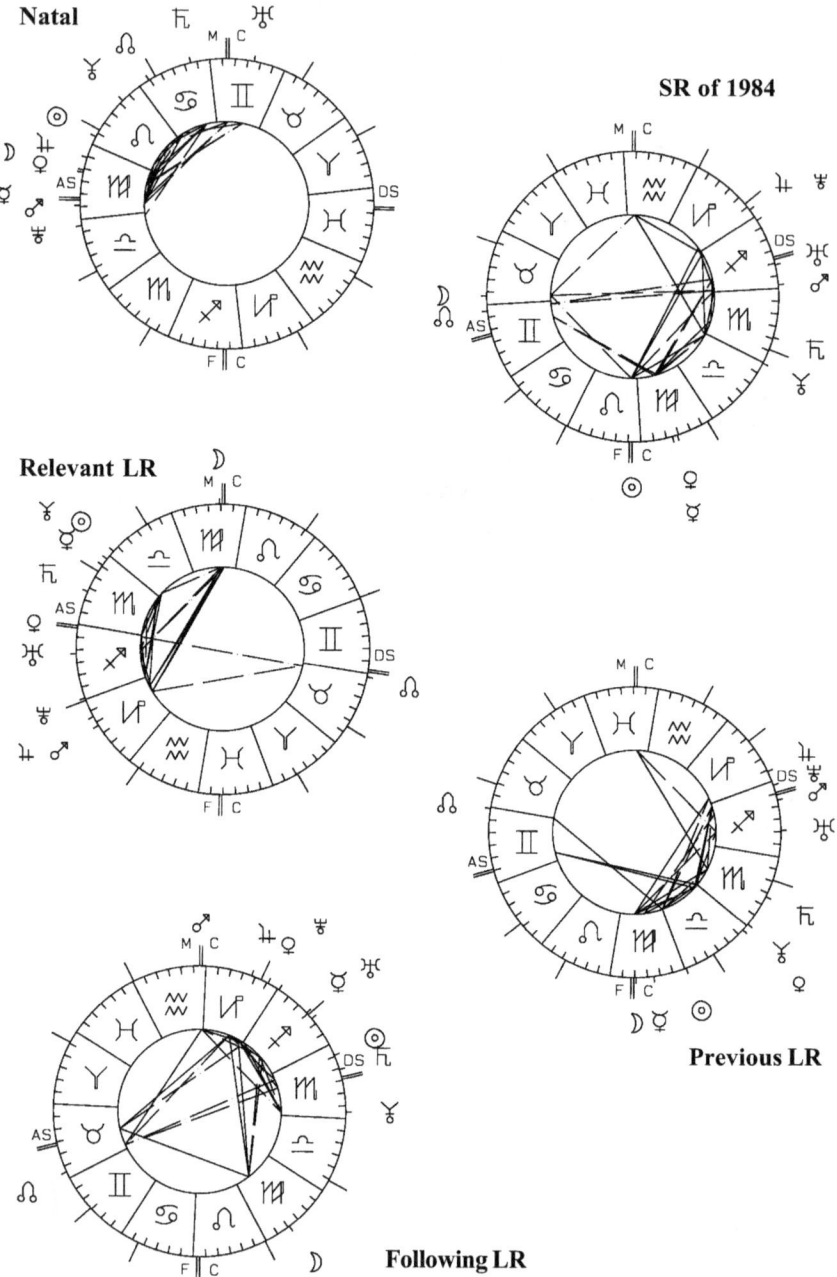

Finally, here are the transits in relation to his own murder: Pluto semisquare Neptune (one degree of orb), Uranus trine Venus (one degree of orb) and the Moon (two degrees of orb), **Uranus sesquisquare Sun** (*one degree of orb*), **Saturn opposite Pluto** (three degrees of orb), **Saturn sesquisquare the Midheaven** (*one degree of orb*), **the Ascendant** (*zero degrees of orb!*) **and Mercury** (*zero degrees of orb!*); **Jupiter conjunct Pluto** (*one degree of orb*), **Jupiter semisquare to the Midheaven** (*zero degrees of orb!*), **the Ascendant** (one *degree of orb*), **Mars** (*one degree of orb*), **and Mercury** (*one degree of orb*); **Mars semisquare to Uranus** (*one degree of orb*), **to Venus** (*one degree of orb*), **and to the Moon** (two degrees of orb); Mars sextile Mars (three degrees of orb), Venus sextile Venus (three degrees of orb), Venus semisquare the Sun (two degrees of orb), Mercury square Pluto (two degrees of orb), Mercury sextile Saturn (one degree of orb), Mercury trine Jupiter (one degree of orb), Mercury semisquare Medium Coeli (zero degrees of orb), Mercury sesquisquare with the Ascendant (zero degrees of orb) and with natal Mercury (zero degrees of orb); Moon square Uranus (two degrees of orb), Moon sextile Saturn (three degrees of orb), Moon conjunct to Venus (zero degrees of orb) and to the natal Moon (zero degrees of orb); and Sun trine Neptune (two degrees of orb).

Basically, in his Solar return we only find Mars in the seventh House but I certainly believe it is sufficient. Obviously also that Jupiter standing out at the Medium Coeli, if you read it together with the previous impressive sequence of dissonant transits (including those of Jupiter itself), could and should attract the attention of every student on the dangers of this announced, unfortunate headline that marked the native's year.

We should do some attention when considering his Lunar Return, because it took place at 4:07 pm London time (hence at 9:37 pm Delhi time) of the 21st of May 1991, exactly on the same day of Rajiv Gandhi's death in Sriperumbudur. But the latter happened at 10:20 pm, so *this* is the right Lunar Return to be considered, for it began less than an hour before his death. It basically shows a stellium in the first House, and Mars in the seventh House.

With regard to the Houses we can note a particularly interesting detail: Mars had just entered the eleventh House radix of the subject.

## Comparative Aspects
## Death transits of Rajiv /Rajiv Gandhi

**Sun:**
    Square with Sun 86 Degrees
    Trine with Mars 114 Degrees
    Square with Jupiter 95 Degrees
    **Trine with Neptune 122 Degrees**

**Moon:**
    **Joined with Moon 0 Degrees**
    **Joined with Venus 0 Degrees**
    Joined with Jupiter 5 Degrees
    **Sexstile with Saturn 63 Degrees**
    **Square with Uranus 88 Degrees**
    Semi-squ with Node 45 Degrees
    Semi-sex with Pluto 32 Degrees

**Mercury:**
    Trine with Moon 124 Degrees
    **Sesquiquad with Mercury 135 Degrees**
    Trine with Venus 125 Degrees
    **Sesquiquad with Ascendant 135 Degrees**
    **Semi-squ with Mid Heaven 45 Degrees**
    **Trine with Jupiter 119 Degrees**
    **Sexstile with Saturn 61 Degrees**
    **Square with Pluto 92 Degrees**

**Venus:**
    **Semi-squ with Sun 43 Degrees**
    **Sexstile with Venus 57 Degrees**
    Joined with Saturn 6 Degrees
    Semi-sex with Uranus 31 Degrees

**Mars:**
    Semi-sex with Sun 29 Degrees
    **Semi-squ with Moon 43 Degrees**
    **Semi-squ with Venus 44 Degrees**

**Sexstile with Mars 57 Degrees**
**Semi-squ with Uranus 44 Degrees**
Joined with Node 1 Degrees

**Ascendant:**
  Sesquiquad with Moon 133 Degrees
  Trine with Mercury 122 Degrees
  Trine with Mars 119 Degrees
  Trine with Ascendant 122 Degrees
  Opposit with Node 178 Degrees

**Mid Heaven:**
  Sexstile with Jupiter 58 Degrees
  Trine with Saturn 116 Degrees
  Semi-sex with Neptune 30 Degrees

**Jupiter:**
  **Semi-squ with Mercury 44 Degrees**
  **Semi-squ with Mars 46 Degrees**
  **Semi-squ with Ascendant 44 Degrees**
  **Semi-squ with Mid Heaven 45 Degrees**
  Semi-sex with Saturn 30 Degrees
  **Joined with Pluto 1 Degrees**

**Saturn:**
  **Sesquiquad with Mercury 135 Degrees**
  **Sesquiquad with Ascendant 135 Degrees**
  **Sesquiquad with Mid Heaven 136 Degrees**
  Trine with Uranus 126 Degrees
  Trine with Neptune 124 Degrees
  **Opposit with Pluto 177 Degrees**

**Uranus:**
  **Sesquiquad with Sun 136 Degrees**
  **Trine with Moon 122 Degrees**
  **Trine with Venus 121 Degrees**
  Opposit with Saturn 186 Degrees

**Node:**
   Trine with Mercury 120 Degrees
   Trine with Mars 117 Degrees
   Trine with Ascendant 119 Degrees
   Sesquiquad with Jupiter 136 Degrees
   Opposit with Node 175 Degrees

**Neptune:**
   Trine with Moon 125 Degrees
   Trine with Mercury 114 Degrees
   Trine with Venus 124 Degrees
   Trine with Ascendant 114 Degrees

**Pluto:**
   Sexstile with Mercury 57 Degrees
   **Semi-squ with Neptune 46 Degrees**

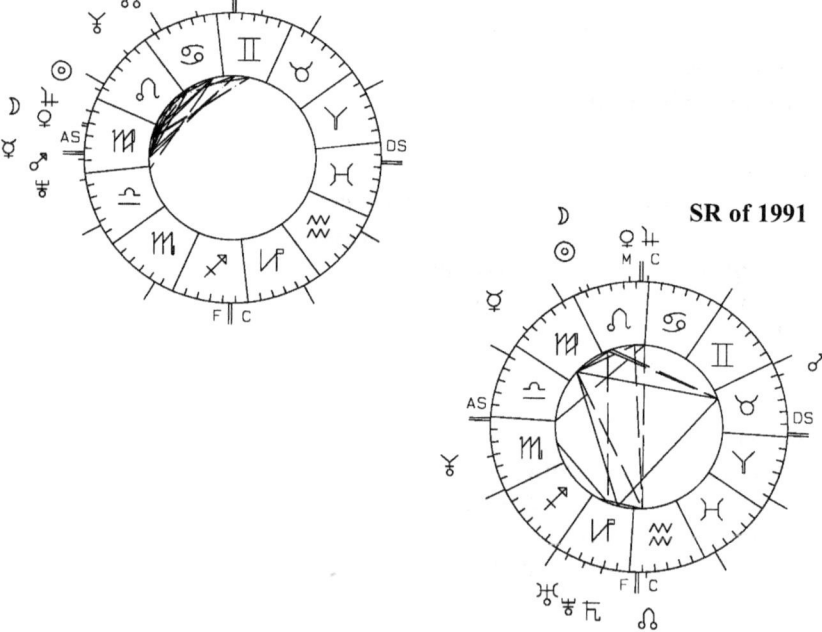

THE ATROCIOUS SAGA OF DEATH IN GANDHI'S "FAMILY"   211

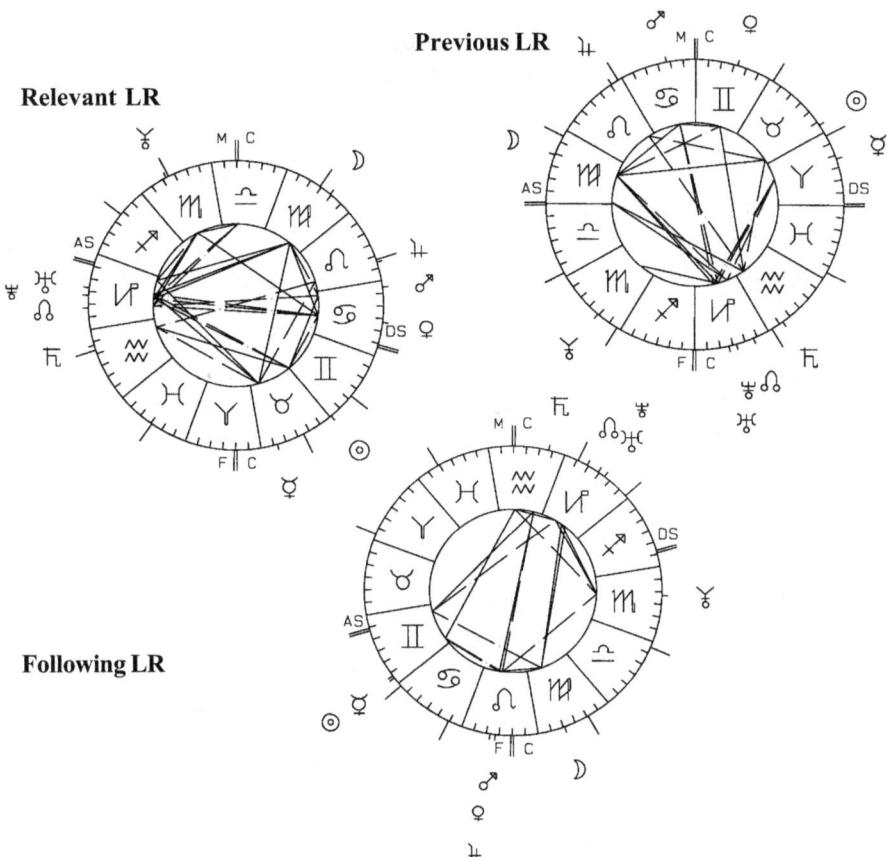

Now let us study the situation of Sonia Maino. She was born in a place called Lusiana, Italy on the 9th of December 1946. Lusiana is in the province of Vicenza, while Sonia used to spend most of her time in Turin. Sonia met Rajiv Gandhi while she was a student at university in England, and they married. Pluto conjunct Pluto (*zero degrees of orb!*), Pluto square Jupiter (two degrees of orb), Neptune sextile Pluto (one degree of orb), Neptune conjunct Neptune (two degrees of orb), Neptune semisquare Mercury (two degrees of orb), **Uranus conjunct Uranus** (two degrees of orb), **Uranus semisquare Saturn** (one degree of orb) **and the Medium Coeli** (two degrees of orb); **Uranus opposite Mars** (*one degree of orb*), Saturn sextile Uranus (zero degrees of orb), **Saturn conjunct Ascendant** (*zero degrees of orb!*), **Venus**

**square Saturn** (three degrees of orb), **Saturn semisquare Moon** (two degrees of orb), Saturn trine Sun (three degrees of orb), Jupiter opposite Uranus (*one degree of orb*), Jupiter trine Ascendant (zero degrees of orb), Jupiter conjunct to Mars (three degrees of orb) and to the Sun (three degrees of orb); Mars sextile the Moon (one degree of orb), Venus trine Jupiter (one degree of orb) and Venus (two degrees of orb); Venus square Sun (three degrees of orb), Mercury sesquisquare Neptune (one degree of orb), Mercury sextile Mars (two degrees of orb), Mercury square Mercury (zero degrees of orb), Moon conjunct Neptune (two degrees of orb), Moon sextile Saturn (one degree of orb), Moon semisquare the Ascendant (two degrees of orb), Sun trine Neptune (one degree of orb), Sun opposite Saturn (zero degrees of orb), Sun square Medium Coeli (zero degrees of orb), and Sun semisquare Mars (zero degrees of orb).

The Solar Return of 1947–1948 shows an ugly stellium (Mars, Saturn and Pluto) in the tenth House, as well as Mars on the cusp between the tenth and eleventh House.

The Lunar Return shows the same stellium, but placed in the eighth House. As for the transits in the natal Houses, we can see Saturn and Pluto crossing through the twelfth House, Uranus (obviously we are talking about a little girl – at the time the murder she was about two years and therefore her astral positions were very close to those of her birth chart) in the eleventh House, and mars in the first House.

**Comparative Aspects**
**Death transits of Mahatma /Sonia Maino**

**Sun:**
 **Semi-squ with Mars 45 Degrees**
 **Square with Mid Heaven 90 Degrees**
 **Opposit with Saturn 180 Degrees**
 Trine with Node 122 Degrees
 **Trine with Neptune 119 Degrees**
 Opposit with Pluto 176 Degrees

**Moon:**
 Square with Moon 95 Degrees
 **Semi-squ with Ascendant 47 Degrees**
 **Sexstile with Saturn 59 Degrees**

Trine with Node 116 Degrees
**Joined with Neptune 2 Degrees**

**Mercury:**
Trine with Moon 127 Degrees
**Square with Mercury 90 Degrees**
**Sexstile with Mars 62 Degrees**
Opposit with Ascendant 186 Degrees
Trine with Uranus 114 Degrees
**Sesquiquad with Neptune 136 Degrees**

**Venus:**
**Square with Sun 87 Degrees**
**Trine with Venus 118 Degrees**
**Trine with Jupiter 119 Degrees**
Square with Uranus 95 Degrees
Square with Node 87 Degrees

**Mars:**
**Sexstile with Moon 61 Degrees**
Trine with Mid Heaven 115 Degrees

**Ascendant:**
Sesquiquad with Mars 137 Degrees
Square with Mid Heaven 87 Degrees
Joined with Saturn 1 Degrees
Semi-squ with Uranus 46 Degrees
Sexstile with Neptune 63 Degrees
Joined with Pluto 6 Degrees

**Mid Heaven:**
Sesquiquad with Sun 134 Degrees
Sexstile with Moon 62 Degrees
Trine with Mars 127 Degrees
Joined with Mid Heaven 8 Degrees

**Jupiter:**
**Joined with Sun 3 Degrees**
**Joined with Mars 3 Degrees**

**Trine with Ascendant 120 Degrees**
**Opposit with Uranus 181 Degrees**
**Trine with Pluto 127 Degrees**

**Saturn:**
**Trine with Sun 117 Degrees**
**Semi-squ with Moon 47 Degrees**
**Square with Venus 87 Degrees**
Trine with Mars 124 Degrees
**Joined with Ascendant 0 Degrees**
Square with Jupiter 86 Degrees
**Sexstile with Uranus 60 Degrees**
Joined with Pluto 6 Degrees

**Uranus:**
Opposit with Sun 174 Degrees
**Opposit with Mars 181 Degrees**
Sexstile with Ascendant 57 Degrees
**Semi-squ with Mid Heaven 43 Degrees**
**Semi-squ with Saturn 46 Degrees**
**Joined with Uranus 2 Degrees**

**Node:**
Semi-squ with Moon 43 Degrees
Opposit with Mercury 187 Degrees
Opposit with Venus 177 Degrees
Square with Ascendant 90 Degrees
Opposit with Jupiter 176 Degrees
Semi-sex with Uranus 30 Degrees

**Neptune:**
**Semi-squ with Mercury 43 Degrees**
Trine with Uranus 113 Degrees
Trine with Node 121 Degrees
**Joined with Neptune 2 Degrees**
**Sexstile with Pluto 59 Degrees**

**Pluto:**
Trine with Sun 123 Degrees

## THE ATROCIOUS SAGA OF DEATH IN GANDHI'S "FAMILY"  215

Square with Venus 93 Degrees
Joined with Ascendant 6 Degrees
Square with Mid Heaven 94 Degrees
**Square with Jupiter 92 Degrees**
Joined with Saturn 5 Degrees
Sextile with Node 62 Degrees
**Joined with Pluto 0 Degrees**

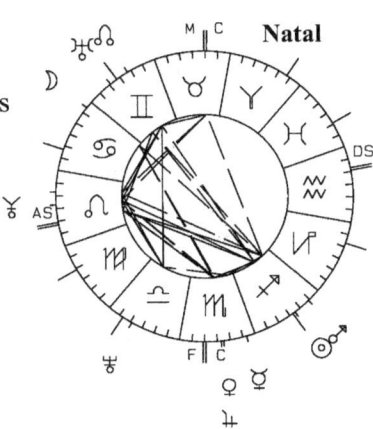
Natal

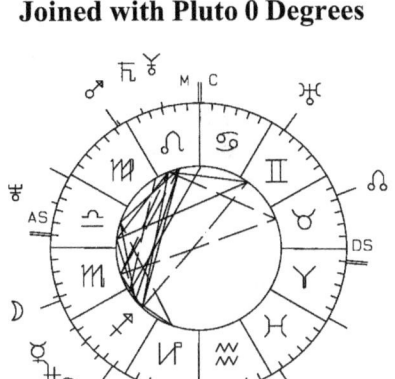
**SR of 1947**

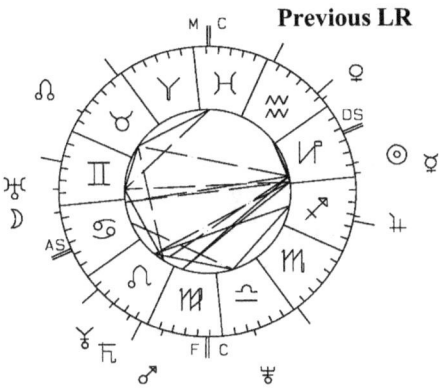
Previous LR

**Relevant LR**

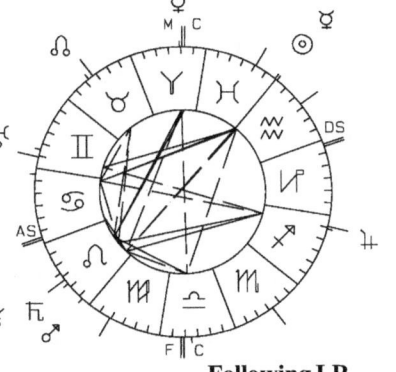
Following LR

Transits for the death of brother–in–law Sanjay: Pluto trine Uranus (one degree of orb), Pluto sextile the Ascendant (two degrees of orb) and the Sun (two degrees of orb); **Neptune opposite Uranus** (*zero degrees of orb!*), Neptune trine Ascendant (zero degrees of orb), **Uranus square Ascendant** (*one degree of orb*), **Saturn square Uranus** (*one degree of orb*), **Mars square Saturn** (three degrees of orb), **Mars square Uranus** (*zero degrees of orb!*) and square Mars (three degrees of orb); Venus conjunct Uranus (zero degrees of orb), Venus sextile Ascendant (zero degrees of orb), Venus opposite the Sun (one degree of orb), Mercury trine Mercury (two degrees of orb), Moon trine Moon (one degree of orb), Moon semisquare Sun (zero degrees of orb), Sun sesquisquare Jupiter (one degree of orb) and Venus (zero degrees of orb); and Sun conjunct Moon.

The Solar Return highlight the Ascendant in the third House (in–laws), a stellium with the Sun in the third House (in–laws), and a stellium – with Mars – in the eleventh House.

The Lunar Return depicts a stellium in the sixth House (Venus is on the cusp), another stellium in the eighth House (with Mars and Saturn), and Pluto in the ninth House (the air crash).

Concerning the transits of celestials in the Houses, Let us mention Pluto in the third House (in–laws).

## Comparative Aspects
## Death transits of Sanjay /Sonia Maino

**Sun:**
   **Joined with Moon 1 Degrees**
   **Sesquiquad with Venus 135 Degrees**
   Opposit with Mars 172 Degrees
   **Sesquiquad with Jupiter 134 Degrees**

**Moon:**
   **Semi-squ with Sun 45 Degrees**
   **Trine with Moon 119 Degrees**
   Opposit with Mid Heaven 172 Degrees

**Mercury:**
   **Trine with Mercury 122 Degrees**
   Trine with Venus 113 Degrees

**Venus:**
   **Opposit with Sun 177 Degrees**
   Opposit with Mars 184 Degrees
   **Sexstile with Ascendant 60 Degrees**
   **Joined with Uranus 0 Degrees**
   Joined with Node 8 Degrees

**Mars:**
   Square with Sun 86 Degrees
   **Square with Mars 93 Degrees**
   Semi-sex with Ascendant 30 Degrees
   **Square with Uranus 90 Degrees**

**Ascendant:**
   Sexstile with Mercury 59 Degrees
   Square with Mars 87 Degrees
   Sesquiquad with Mid Heaven 137 Degrees
   Semi-squ with Pluto 43 Degrees

**Mid Heaven:**
   Joined with Moon 6 Degrees
   Opposit with Mars 177 Degrees
   Semi-squ with Mid Heaven 47 Degrees
   Joined with Uranus 6 Degrees
   Semi-squ with Pluto 46 Degrees

**Jupiter:**
   Sexstile with Moon 61 Degrees
   Trine with Mid Heaven 115 Degrees

**Saturn:**
   Square with Sun 86 Degrees
   **Square with Mars 93 Degrees**
   Semi-sex with Ascendant 30 Degrees

**Square with Uranus 91 Degrees**

**Uranus:**
Joined with Mercury 4 Degrees
Joined with Venus 4 Degrees
Semi-sex with Mars 32 Degrees
**Square with Ascendant 91 Degrees**
Joined with Jupiter 5 Degrees

**Node:**
Trine with Sun 114 Degrees
Square with Mercury 93 Degrees
Trine with Mars 121 Degrees
Joined with Ascendant 2 Degrees
Sexstile with Uranus 62 Degrees
Semi-squ with Neptune 47 Degrees

**Neptune:**
Joined with Sun 3 Degrees
Joined with Mars 3 Degrees
**Trine with Ascendant 120 Degrees**
**Opposit with Uranus 181 Degrees**
Trine with Pluto 127 Degrees

**Pluto:**
**Sexstile with Sun 58 Degrees**
Semi-sex with Venus 28 Degrees
**Sexstile with Ascendant 58 Degrees**
**Trine with Uranus 119 Degrees**
Trine with Node 127 Degrees
Joined with Neptune 8 Degrees

# THE ATROCIOUS SAGA OF DEATH IN GANDHI'S "FAMILY"   219

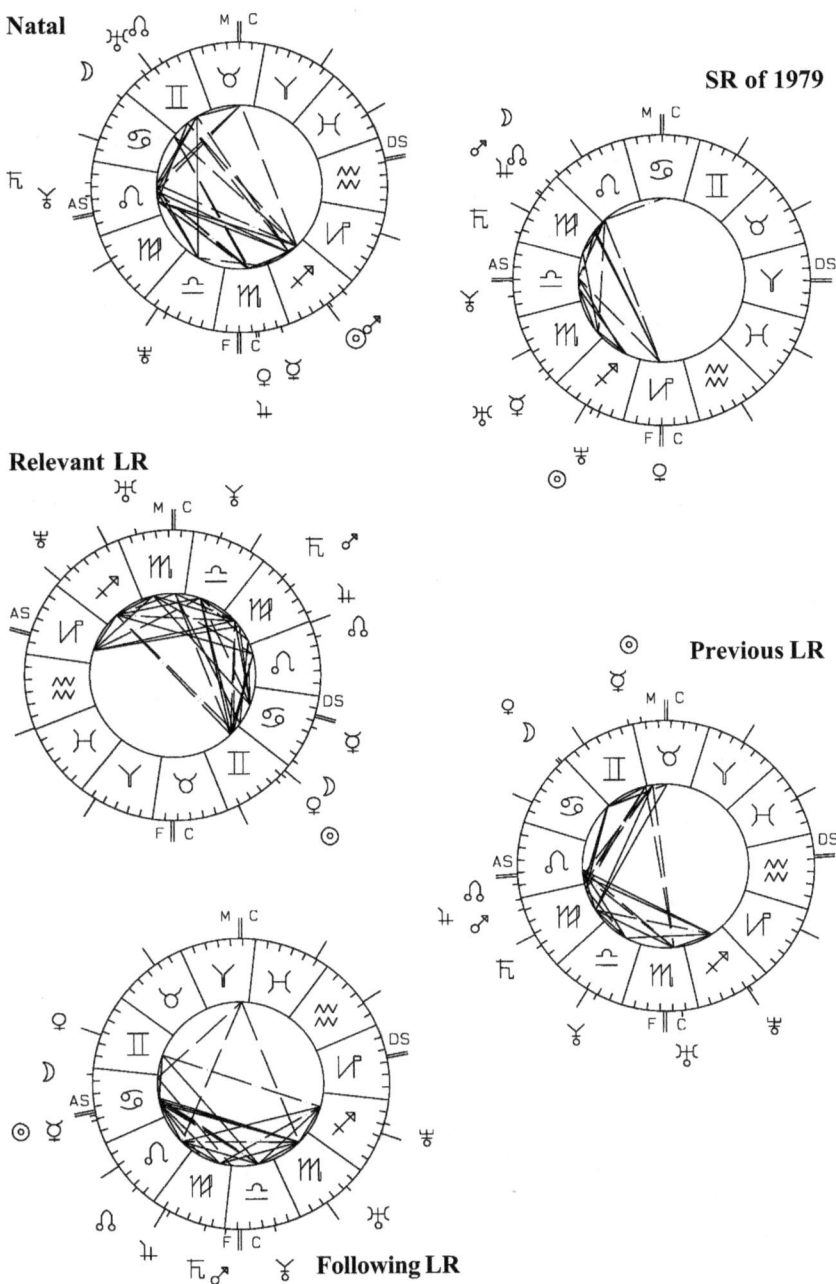

These are the transits for the death of her mother–in–law, Indira. Pluto trine the Moon (one degree of orb), **Pluto semisquare the Sun** (*one degree of orb*), **Neptune sesquisquare Pluto** (*one degree of orb*), Neptune semisquare Jupiter (two degrees of orb), Uranus trine Pluto (two degrees of orb), Uranus sextile Neptune (one degree of orb), Saturn conjunct Jupiter (one degree of orb), **Saturn square Ascendant** (three degrees of orb), **Saturn conjunct Venus** (*zero degrees of orb!*), **Saturn sesquisquare Moon** (*one degree of orb*), Jupiter square Neptune (two degrees of orb), Jupiter trine Medium Coeli (one degree of orb), Mars sextile Jupiter (two degrees of orb) and Venus (one degree of orb); Venus trine Pluto (zero degrees of orb), Venus sextile Neptune (three degrees of orb), Venus conjunct Sun (three degrees of orb), Mercury square Ascendant (zero degrees of orb), Mercury conjunct Venus (three degrees of orb), Mercury semisquare Moon (two degrees of orb), Moon sesquisquare Uranus (one degree of orb), Moon opposite Saturn (three degrees of orb), Sun square Saturn (one degree of orb), Sun opposite Medium Coeli (two degrees of orb), and Sun semisquare Mars (one degree of orb).

The Solar Return of 1983–1984 shows Mars in the first House, and a stellium in the first House.

The Lunar Return covering the time of the attack, on the other side, has a stellium in the eighth House, the close conjunction Sun–Saturn in the seventh House (which has also much to do with attacks), and Mars in the tenth House (the mother or mother–in–law).

As for the transits in the natal Houses, we see Uranus transiting the fourth House (the parents or parents–in–law) together with Saturn; the latter is closely conjunct to Venus radix.


**Comparative Aspects**
**Death transits of Indira /Sonia Maino**

**Sun:**
　Trine with Moon 125 Degrees
　**Semi-squ with Mars 46 Degrees**
　**Opposit with Mid Heaven 178 Degrees**
　Joined with Jupiter 8 Degrees
　**Square with Saturn 89 Degrees**

# THE ATROCIOUS SAGA OF DEATH IN GANDHI'S "FAMILY"

**Moon:**
 Square with Mid Heaven 94 Degrees
 **Opposit with Saturn 177 Degrees**
 **Sesquiquad with Uranus 134 Degrees**
 Trine with Node 126 Degrees
 Trine with Neptune 115 Degrees
 Opposit with Pluto 172 Degrees

**Mercury:**
 **Sesquiquad with Moon 137 Degrees**
 Joined with Mercury 5 Degrees
 **Joined with Venus 3 Degrees**
 **Square with Ascendant 90 Degrees**
 Joined with Jupiter 4 Degrees

**Venus:**
 **Joined with Sun 3 Degrees**
 Trine with Ascendant 113 Degrees
 Trine with Saturn 124 Degrees
 Opposit with Uranus 173 Degrees
 Opposit with Node 182 Degrees
 **Sexstile with Neptune 63 Degrees**
 **Trine with Pluto 120 Degrees**

**Mars:**
 Semi-sex with Sun 31 Degrees
 **Sexstile with Venus 61 Degrees**
 **Sexstile with Jupiter 62 Degrees**

**Ascendant:**
 Square with Mercury 88 Degrees
 Sexstile with Mars 60 Degrees
 Opposit with Ascendant 184 Degrees
 Trine with Uranus 115 Degrees
 Sesquiquad with Neptune 134 Degrees

**Mid Heaven:**
 Trine with Saturn 117 Degrees

Opposit with Node 175 Degrees
Trine with Pluto 113 Degrees

**Jupiter:**
Opposit with Moon 185 Degrees
**Trine with Mid Heaven 121 Degrees**
**Square with Neptune 88 Degrees**

**Saturn:**
Semi-sex with Sun 29 Degrees
**Sesquiquad with Moon 134 Degrees**
Joined with Mercury 8 Degrees
**Joined with Venus 0 Degrees**
**Square with Ascendant 87 Degrees**
Opposit with Mid Heaven 188 Degrees
**Joined with Jupiter 1 Degrees**
Square with Pluto 94 Degrees

**Uranus:**
Joined with Sun 5 Degrees
Trine with Saturn 123 Degrees
Opposit with Node 180 Degrees
**Sexstile with Neptune 61 Degrees**
**Trine with Pluto 118 Degrees**

**Node:**
Opposit with Mercury 178 Degrees

**Neptune:**
Opposit with Moon 176 Degrees
Semi-sex with Mercury 32 Degrees
Joined with Mars 5 Degrees
**Semi-squ with Jupiter 43 Degrees**
**Sesquiquad with Pluto 136 Degrees**

**Pluto:**
**Semi-squ with Sun 44 Degrees**
**Trine with Moon 119 Degrees**
Opposit with Mid Heaven 172 Degrees

# THE ATROCIOUS SAGA OF DEATH IN GANDHI'S "FAMILY" 223

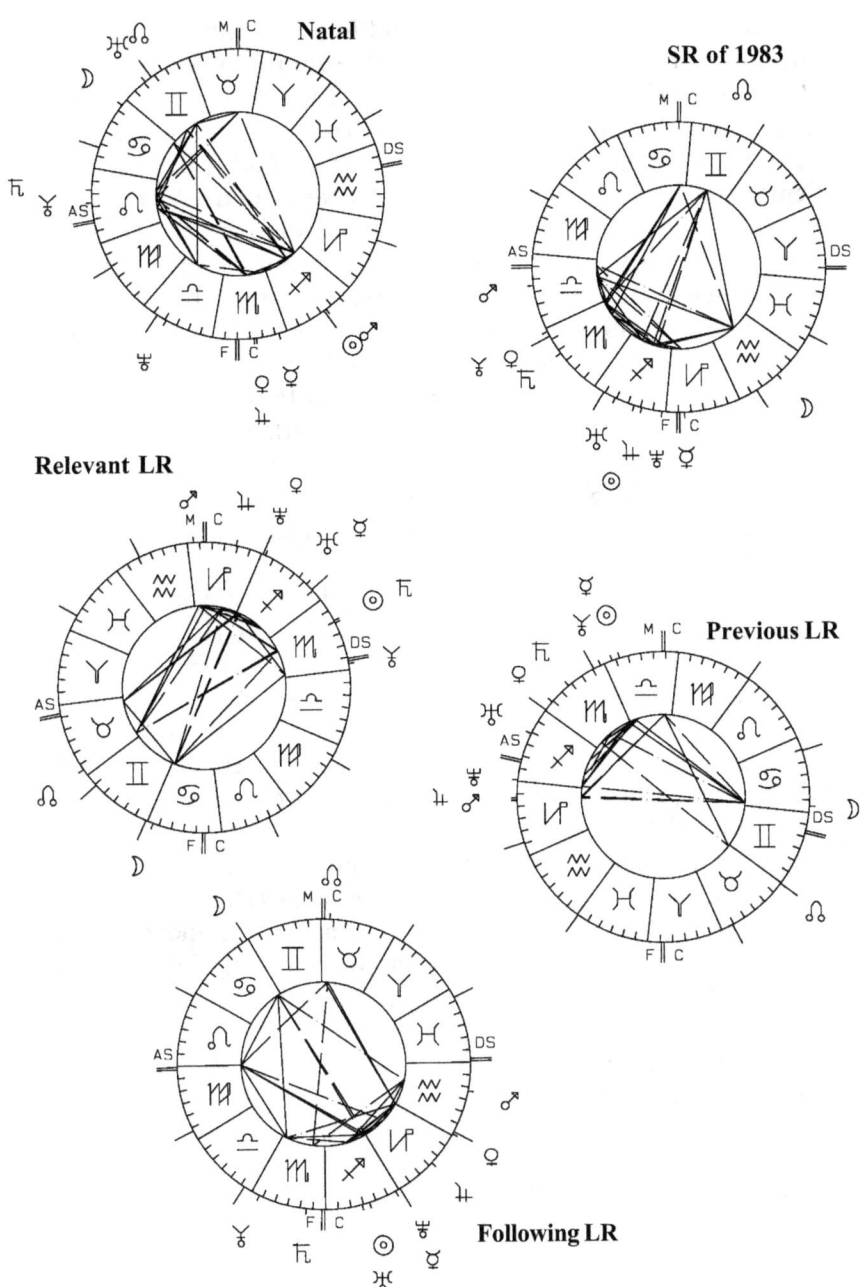

Finally, the transits of her husband Rajiv's death. Pluto conjunct with Jupiter (two degrees of orb), **Pluto square the Ascendant** (two degrees of orb), **Pluto conjunct Venus** (*one degree of orb*), **Pluto sesquisquare Moon** (*zero degrees of orb!*), Neptune sextile Jupiter (zero degrees of orb) and Venus (one degree of orb); **Uranus square Neptune** (two degrees of orb), **Uranus semisquare Mercury** (*one degree of orb*), **Saturn sesquisquare Uranus** (one degree of orb), **Saturn opposite Saturn** (two degrees of orb), **Saturn square Medium Coeli** (three degrees of orb), Jupiter sextile Neptune (three degrees of orb), **Jupiter semisquare Uranus** (two degrees of orb), **Jupiter conjunct Saturn** (one degree of orb), **Jupiter square Medium Coeli** (two degrees of orb), **Jupiter sesquisquare Mars** (one degree of orb), Mars trine Mercury (one degree of orb), Venus trine Jupiter (two degrees of orb) and Venus (three degrees of orb); Mercury semisquare Uranus (two degrees of orb), Mercury square Saturn (two degrees of orb), Mercury conjunct Medium Coeli (three degrees of orb), and Moon trine Medium Coeli (one degree of orb).

The Solar Revolution is really staggering for its extreme clearness and dramatic nature: the Ascendant falls in the eleventh House, the Sun of SR is in the sixth House of SR, Mars is in the twelfth House, there is a stellium in the seventh House, and Saturn is in the eighth House!

The Lunar Return has the Ascendant in the eighth natal House, Pluto of LR in the eighth House of LR, Saturn in the eleventh House, and the conjunction Uranus–Neptune in the tenth House (a sudden and painful change of social status).

As for the transits in the Houses, we can see the conjunction of Uranus and Neptune crossing the fifth House (this House, together with the seventh House, always talks about the native's partner or husband, boyfriend, girlfriend, lover etc...), Saturn was transiting through the sixth House, and Mars had just entered the twelfth House.

**Comparative Aspects**
**Death transits of Rajiv/Sonia Maino**

**Sun:**
Semi-sex with Moon 32 Degrees
Opposit with Mercury 176 Degrees

**Moon:**
   **Trine with Mid Heaven 121 Degrees**
   Semi-sex with Saturn 32 Degrees
   Square with Node 89 Degrees
   Semi-sex with Neptune 29 Degrees

**Mercury:**
   **Joined with Mid Heaven 3 Degrees**
   **Square with Saturn 92 Degrees**
   **Semi-squ with Uranus 43 Degrees**

**Venus:**
   **Trine with Venus 123 Degrees**
   **Trine with Jupiter 122 Degrees**
   Semi-sex with Node 32 Degrees
   Square with Neptune 86 Degrees
   Semi-sex with Pluto 29 Degrees

**Mars:**
   **Trine with Mercury 119 Degrees**
   Semi-squ with Node 45 Degrees

**Ascendant:**
   Sexstile with Mercury 57 Degrees
   Semi-sex with Mars 29 Degrees

**Mid Heaven:**
   Semi-squ with Sun 43 Degrees
   Trine with Moon 120 Degrees
   Opposit with Mid Heaven 173 Degrees
   Sesquiquad with Uranus 133 Degrees

**Jupiter:**
   **Sesquiquad with Mars 136 Degrees**
   **Square with Mid Heaven 88 Degrees**
   **Joined with Saturn 1 Degrees**
   **Semi-squ with Uranus 47 Degrees**
   **Sexstile with Neptune 63 Degrees**

Joined with Pluto 5 Degrees

**Saturn:**
   **Square with Mid Heaven 93 Degrees**
   **Opposit with Saturn 178 Degrees**
   **Sesquiquad with Uranus 134 Degrees**
   Trine with Node 125 Degrees
   Trine with Neptune 116 Degrees
   Opposit with Pluto 173 Degrees

**Uranus:**
   **Semi-squ with Mercury 46 Degrees**
   Trine with Mid Heaven 117 Degrees
   Sexstile with Jupiter 57 Degrees
   **Square with Neptune 92 Degrees**

**Node:**

**Neptune:**
   Semi-sex with Sun 29 Degrees
   **Sexstile with Venus 59 Degrees**
   Trine with Mid Heaven 113 Degrees
   **Sexstile with Jupiter 60 Degrees**

**Pluto:**
   Semi-sex with Sun 28 Degrees
   **Sesquiquad with Moon 135 Degrees**
   Joined with Mercury 7 Degrees
   **Joined with Venus 1 Degrees**
   **Square with Ascendant 88 Degrees**
   **Joined with Jupiter 2 Degrees**
   Square with Pluto 95 Degrees

# THE ATROCIOUS SAGA OF DEATH IN GANDHI'S "FAMILY"

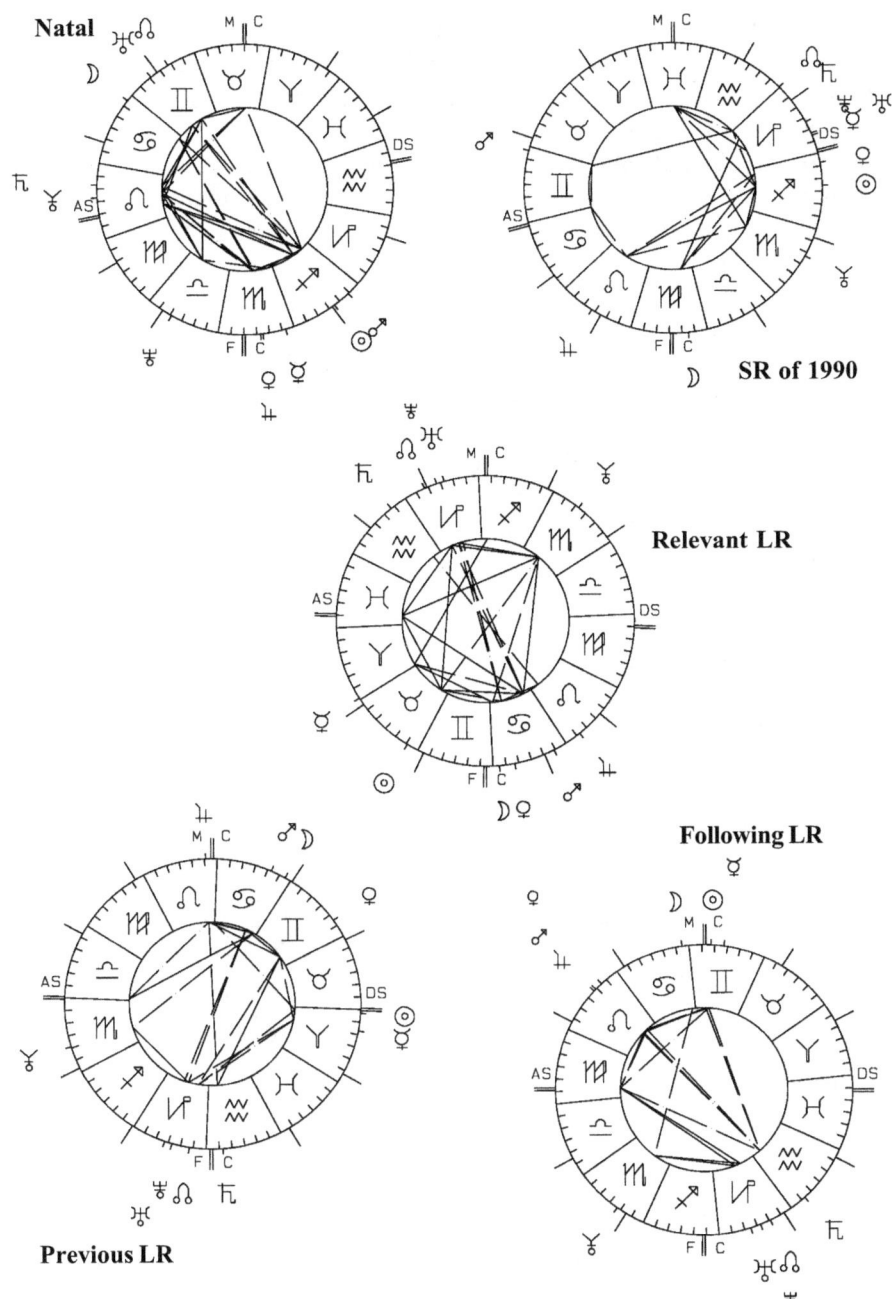

Natal

SR of 1990

Relevant LR

Previous LR

Following LR

Let me add only a few notes after this long analysis.

I find the proposed example very interesting, especially if considered from a particular angle. It has always been claimed that horoscopes work even after the death of an individual, and I think that no astrologer can still have doubts about this. What has probably never been said – or it has not been said enough – is that horoscopes work relatively well even for people who are not yet born. In our case the three young members of the 'family' in question (Sanjay, Rajiv, and Sonia) were already born when the Mahatma was killed, but I am completely convinced that – even if they were born after the events discussed in this chapter – their astral maps would have show the print foot of what would be: I mean their transits, their Solar Returns, and their Lunar returns.

Similarly, I find not only legitimate but even a duty, to examine the transits and SRs and LRs of Sonia Maino at the time in which the Grand Old Man of the 'Gandhi dynasty' was shot to death – even if Sonia would link herself to this man, indirectly, only several years after her own childhood.

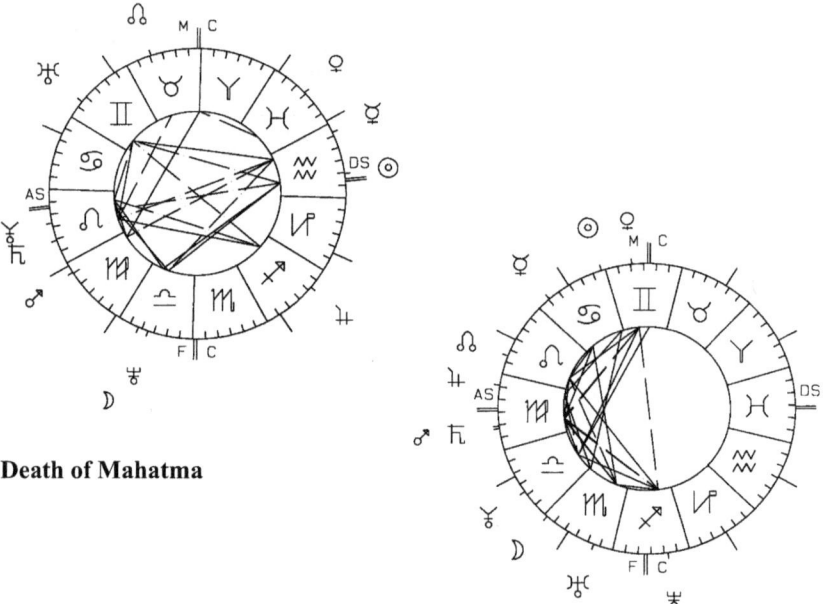

**Death of Mahatma**

**Death of Sanjay**

THE ATROCIOUS SAGA OF DEATH IN GANDHI'S "FAMILY"    229

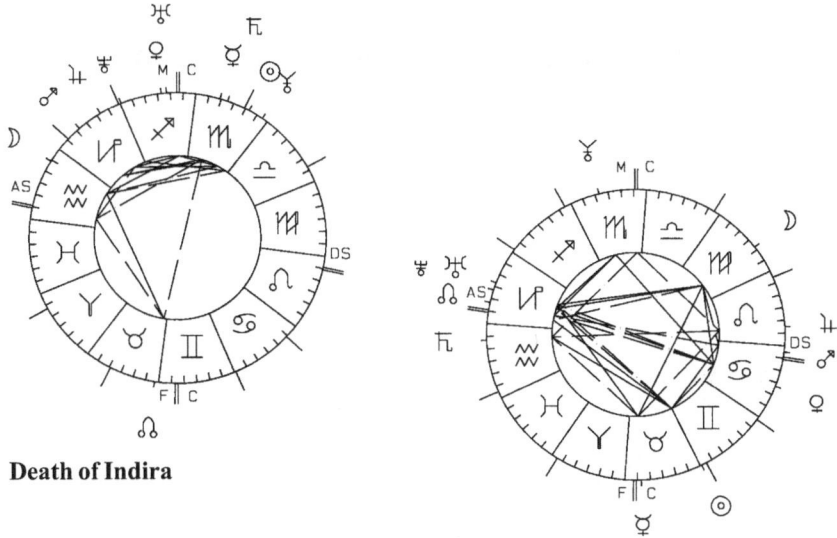

**Death of Indira**

**Death of Rajiv**

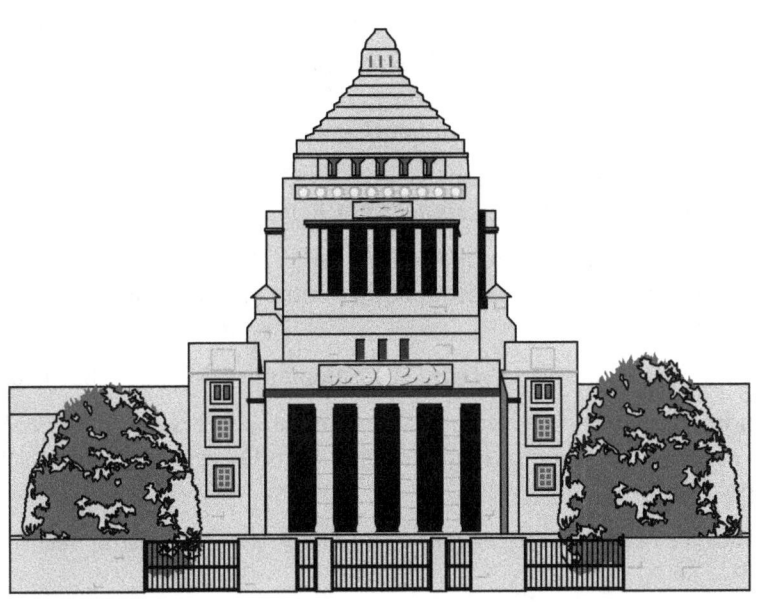

# 19.
# An essential astrological bibliography

- Various Authors: *Articles appeared on the quarterly* Ricerca '90 *from 1990 to 2008*, Edizioni Ricerca '90, 128 pp.

- Various Authors: *Special university issue (#45-46) of* l'astrologue, Éditions Traditionnelles, Paris

- John M. Addey: *Ritmi armonici in astrologia [Harmonic rhythms in astrology]*, Elefante ed., Catania, 1979, 352 pp.

- Antonino Anzaldi, Luigi Bazzoli: *Dizionario di Astrologia [Dictionary of astrology]*, BUR, Milan, 1988, 470 pp.

- Francesco Aulizio and Domenico Cafarello: *Considerazioni preliminari su un nuovo modo di studiare l'astrologia [Preliminary considerations about a new way of studying astrology]*, Cattedra di Storia della Medicina dell'Università di Bologna, Edizioni Capone, Turin

- André Barbault, H. Latou, B. Rossi, G. Simon: *Kepler*, Éditions Traditionnelles (l'astrologue *issue #52*), Paris

- André Barbault and Various Authors: *Soleil & Lune en Astrologie [Sun & Moon in Astrology]*, Publications du Centre International d'Astrologie, Paris, 1953, 280 pp.

- André Barbault: *Ariete [Aries]*, La Salamandra, Milan, 1985, 160 pp.

- André Barbault: *Astrologia e orientamento professionale [Astrology and professional orientation]*, Edizioni Ciro Discepolo, Naples, 1984, 93 pp.

- André Barbault: *Astrologia mondiale [World astrology]*, Armenia, Milan, 1980, 272 pp.

- André Barbault: *Dalla psicanalisi all'astrologia [From psychoanalysis to astrology]*, Morin, Siena, 1971, 224 pp.

- André Barbault: *Giove & Saturno [Jupiter & Saturn]*, Edizioni Ciro Discepolo, Naples, 1983, 214 pp.

- André Barbault: *Il pronostico sperimentale in astrologia [The experimental prediction in astrology]*, Mursia, Milan, 1979, 210 pp.

- André Barbault: *La Précession des Équinoxes et l'Astrologie [The precession of the equinoxes and Astrology]*, Centre International d'Astrologie, Paris, 1972, 32 pp.

- André Barbault, *La scienza dell'Astrologia [The science of Astrology]*, Nuovi Orizzonti, Milan, 1989, 186 pp.

- André Barbault: *L'astrologia e la previsione dell'avvenire [Astrology and the forecast of future]*, Armenia, Milan, 1993, 308 pp.

- André Barbault: *L'astrologia e l'avvenire del mondo [Astrology and the future of the world]*, Xenia, Milan, 1996, 212 pp.

- André Barbault: *Toro [Taurus]*, La Salamandra, Milan, 1985, 153 pp.

- André Barbault: *Trattato pratico di astrologia [A practical treatise of astrology]*, Morin, Siena, 1967, 317 pp.

- Armand Barbault: *Technique de l'interprétation [The technique of interpretation]*, Dervy Livres, Croissy-Beaubourg, 1991

- A. Barbault and others: *La luna nei miti e nello zodiaco [The Moon in the myths and in the Zodiac]*, Nuovi Orizzonti, Milan, 1989, 190 pp.

- Enzo Barillà and Ciro Discepolo: *Astrologia: sì e no [Astrology: yes and no]*, Edizioni Ricerca '90, Naples, 1994, 240 pp.

- Angelo Brunini: *L'avvenire non è un mistero [Future is not a mystery]*, published by the Author, Rome, 1964, 528 pp.

- Federico Capone: *Astronomia oroscopica [Horoscopic Astronomy]*, Edizioni Capone, Turin, 1977, 112 pp.

- Federico Capone: *Dizionario Astrologico [Astrological Dictionary]*, Edizioni Capone, Turin, 1978, 224 pp.

- Charles E.O. Carter: *An Introduction to Political Astrology*, Fowler,

London, 1951, 104 pp.

- Charles E.O. Carter: *The Astrological Aspects*, Fowler, London, 1930, 160 pp.

- Charles E.O. Carter: *The Astrology of Accidents*, The Theosophical Publishing House Ltd., London, Unknown date of publishing, 124 pp.

- Charles E.O. Carter: *The Principles of Astrology*, The Theosophical Publishing House Ltd., London, 1925, 190 pp.

- Marco Celada: *Articles appeared on the quarterly* Ricerca '90 *from 1990 to 2008*, Edizione Ricerca '90, 128 pp.

- Yves Christiaen: *La Domification [Domification]*, Dervy Livres, Paris, 1978, 40 pp.

- Nicholas De Vore,: *Encyclopedia of Astrology*, Littlefield Adams and Co., New Jersey, U.S.A., 1977

- Arato Di Soli: *I fenomeni ed i pronostici [Phenomena and predictions]*, Arktos, Turin, 1984, 120 pp.

- Ciro Discepolo and Andrea Rossetti: *Astro & Geografia [Astro & Geography]*, Blue Diamond Publisher, Milan, 1996, 102 pp.

- Ciro Discepolo and Various Authors: *Osservazioni politematiche sulle ricerche Discepolo/Miele [Polithematic remarks on the researches of Discepolo & Miele]*, Edizioni Ricerca '90, Naples, 1992, 196 pp.

- Ciro Discepolo and Various Authors: *Per una rifondazione dell'astrologia o per il suo rifiuto [For a refoundation of Astrology or for its refusal]*, Edizioni Ricerca '90, Naples, 1993, 200 pp.

- Ciro Discepolo and Francesco Maggiore: *Elementi di astrology professionale [Elements of professional astrology]*, Blue Diamond Publisher, Milan, 1996, 93 pp.

- Ciro Discepolo and Francesco Maggiore: *Introduzione alla sinastria [An introduction to synastry]*, Blue Diamond Publisher, Milan, 1996, 106 pp.

- Ciro Discepolo and Luigi Galli: *Supporto tecnico alla pratica delle Rivoluzioni solari mirate [Technical support to the practise of Aimed Solar Returns]*, Blue Diamond Publisher, Milan, 2000, 136 pp.*

- Ciro Discepolo: *Astrologia applicata [Applied astrology]*, Armenia, Milan, 1988, 294 pp.

- Ciro Discepolo: *La ricerca dell'ora di nascita [The quest for the time of birth]*, Edizioni Ricerca '90, Naples, 1994, 64 pp.*

- Ciro Discepolo: *Astrologia Attiva [Active Astrology]*, Edizioni Mediterranee, Rome, 1998, 144 pp.*

- Ciro Discepolo: *Come scoprire i segreti di un oroscopo [How to unveil the secrets of a horoscope]*, Albero ed., Milan, 1988, 253 pp.

- Ciro Discepolo: *Esercizi sulle Rivoluzioni solari mirate [Exercises of Aimed Solar Returns]*, Blue Diamond Publisher, Milan, 1996, 96 pp.*

- Ciro Discepolo: *Guida ai transiti* (prima e seconda edizione) *[A guide to transits – 1st and 2nd edition]*, Armenia, Milan, 1984, 510 pp.*

- Ciro Discepolo: *Il sale dell'astrologia [The salt of astrology]*, Edizioni Capone, Turin, 1991, 144 pp.

- Ciro Discepolo: *Nuova guida all'astrologia [A new guide to astrology]*, Armenia, Milan, 2000, 818 pp.*

- Ciro Discepolo: *Nuovo dizionario di astrologia [The new Dictionary of Astrology]*, Armenia, Milan, 1996, 394 pp.*

- Ciro Discepolo: *Nuovo trattato delle Rivoluzioni solari [The new treatise of Solar Returns]*, Armenia, Milan, 2003, 216 pp.*

- Ciro Discepolo: *Piccola guida all'astrologia [A concise guide to astrology]*, Armenia, Milan, 1998, 200 pp.

- Ciro Discepolo: *Suite of software modules ASTRAL*, developed by the Author and Luigi Miele, Naples, 1979-2003

- Ciro Discepolo: *Prontuario calcoli [Ready reckoner]*, Edizioni Capone, Turin, 1979, 72 pp.

- Ciro Discepolo: *Quattro cose sui compleanni mirati [A few facts on Aimed Birthdays]*, Blue Diamond Publisher, Milan, 2001, 104 pp.*

- Ciro Discepolo: *Traité complet d'interprétation des transits et des Révolutions solaires en astrologie*, Éditions Traditionnelles, Paris, 2001, 502 pp.*

- Ciro Discepolo: *Transiti e Rivoluzioni solari [Transits and Solar Returns]*, Armenia, Milan, 1997, 502 pp.*

- Ciro Discepolo: *Trattato pratico di Rivoluzioni solari [A practical treatise of Solar Returns]*, Edizioni Ricerca '90, Naples, 1993, 208 pp.*

- Ciro Discepolo: *Various volumes of ephemerides*, Various publishers

- Ciro Discepolo: *Various volumes of Tables of Houses*, Various publishers

- Ciro Discepolo: *Ci siamo con la datazione informatica degli avvenimenti? [How far have we gone with the computerized dating of events?]*, Edizioni Ricerca '90, 2007, 168 pp.*

- Ciro Discepolo: *365 nap alatt a Föld körül a szolárhoroszkóppal*, DFT-Húngaria, Budapest, May 2006, 190 pp. B5*

- Ciro Discepolo: *Temelji medicinske astrologije: osnove za razumevanje clovekove patologije s pomocjo nebesnih teles*, Zalozba Astroloskega instituta, 2007, pp. 262*

- Ciro Discepolo: *I fondamenti dell'Astrologia Medica [The fundaments of Medical Astrology]*, Armenia, Milan, end of January 2006, 246 pp.*

- Ciro Discepolo: *L'interpretazione del tema natale [Reading the natal chart]*, Armenia, Milan, September 2007, 336 pp.*

- Ciro Discepolo: *Transits and Solar Returns*, Naples, Ricerca '90 Publisher, September 2007, 560 pp.*

- Ciro Discepolo: Russian edition of the 'Nuovo Trattato delle Rivoluzioni solari', end of 2008*

- Ciro Discepolo: *Enquête sur l'hérédité astrale*, issue #67 of *l'astrologue*, Éditions Traditionnelles, Paris, 1984

- Ciro Discepolo: *Statistique sur 834 nominations ministérielles*, issue #67 of *l'astrologue*, Éditions Traditionnelles, Paris, 1986

- Ciro Discepolo: *Nouvelle recherche sur l'hérédité astrale*, issue #106 of *l'astrologue*, Éditions Traditionnelles, Paris, 1994

- Ciro Discepolo: *L'Hérédité astrale sur 50 000 naissances*, and *Astrologie activiste – Réflexions sur l'astrologie*, issue #125 of *l'astrologue*, Éditions Traditionnelles, Paris, 1999

- Reinhold Ebertin: *Cosmobiologia: la nuova astrologia [Cosmobiology: the new Astrology]*, Edizioni C.E.M., Naples, 1982, 208 pp.

- Michael Erlewine: *Manual of Computer Programming for Astrologers*, American Federation of Astrologers, Tempe (Arizona), 1980, 215 pp.

- Hans J. Eysenck, S. Mayo, O. White: *Un metodo empirico sul rapporto tra fattori astrologici e personalità [An empirical method on the relationship between astrological factors and peersonality]*, issue #42 of *Linguaggio astrale*, Turin, 1981

- Serena Foglia: *Prolusione al convegno di studi astrologici tenutosi a Napoli nel 1979 [Opening speech at the congress of astrological studies held in Naples in 1979]*, issue #37 of *Linguaggio Astrale*, Turin

- H. Freiherr Von Klöckler, *Corso di astrologia [Course on Astrology]*, ed. Mediterranee, Rome, 1979

- Luigi Galli and Ciro Discepolo: *Atlante geografico per le Rivoluzioni solari [Geographical Atlas for Solar Returns]*, Blue Diamond Publisher, Milan, 2001, 136 pp.*

- Luigi Galli: *Articles appeared on the quarterly* Ricerca '90 *from 1990 to 2008*, Edizioni Ricerca '90, Naples, 128 pp.

- Michel & Françoise Gauquelin: *Actors & politicians*, Laboratoire d'étude des relations entre rythmes cosmiques et psychophysiologiques, Paris, 1970

- Michel Gauquelin: *Il dossier delle influenze cosmiche [The file of cosmic influences]*, Astrolabio, Rome, 1975, 232 pp.

- Michel Gauquelin: *La Cosmopsychologie*, Retz, Paris, 1974, 256 pp.

- Michel Gauquelin: *L'astrologia di fronte alla scienza [Astrology face to science]*, Armenia, Milan, 1981, 312 pp.

- Michel & Françoise Gauquelin: *Méthodes pour étudier la répartition des astres dans le mouvement diurne,* Gauquelin ed., Paris, 1970

- Michel & Françoise Gauquelin: *Painters and musicians*, Laboratoire d'étude des relations entre rythmes cosmiques et psychophysiologiques, Paris, 1970

- Françoise Gauquelin: *Problèmes de l'heure risolus en astrologie,* Guy Trédaniel

- Michel Gauquelin: *Ritmi biologici e ritmi cosmici [Biological rhythms and cosmic rhythms]*, Faenza spa, Faenza, 1976, 226 pp.

- Luigi Gedda and Gianni Brenci: *Cronogenetica [Chronogenetics]*, Est-Mondadori, Milan, 1974

- Sergio Ghivarello: *La realtà al di là dell'astrologia [Reality beyond astrology]*, Edizioni Capone, Turin

- Sergio Ghivarello: *L'astrologia e la teoria dei cicli nel quadro dei fenomeni ondulatori [Astrology and the theory of cycles withing the frame of undulatory phenomena]*, C.I.D.A. ed., Turin, 1974

- Sergio Ghivarello: *Lo zodiaco siderale e le costellazioni boreali [Sidereal Zodiac and Boreal constellations]*, #43/44/45, C.I.D.A. ed., Turin, 1981

- Sergio Ghivarello: *Verso una scienza alternativa [Towards an alternative science]*, issue #37 of *Linguaggio Astrale*, Turin, 1979

- Henri J. Gouchon and Jean Reverchon: *Dictionnaire Astrologique – Supplément Technique*, H. Gouchon Éditeur, Paris, 1947, 40 pp.

- Henri J. Gouchon: *Dizionario di astrologia [Dictionary of astrology]*, Siad ed., Milan, 1980

- Henri J. Gouchon: *Les Directions Primaires Simplifiées*, Éditions Traditionnelles, Paris, 1970, ca. 150 pp.

- Henri J. Gouchon: *L'Horoscope Annuel Simplifié*, Dervy Livres, Paris, 1973, 214 pp.

- Hadès: *Guide pratique de l'interprétation en Astrologie*, Éditions Niclaus, Paris, 1969, 228 pp.

- Robert Hand: *I transiti [The transits]*, Armenia, Milan, 1982, 512 pp.

- Eugen Jonas: *Articles appeared on the quarterly* Ricerca '90 *from 1990 to 2008*, Edizioni Ricerca '90, Naples, 128 pp.

- Eugen Jonas: *Il controllo naturale del concepimento [The natural control of conception]*, Blue Diamond Publisher, Milan, 1995, 76 pp.

- Helene Kinauer Saltarini: *Bioritmo [Biorhythm]*, Siad ed., Milan, 1977

- George C. Noonan: *Spherical Astronomy for Astrologers*, American

Federation of Astrologers, Washington DC, 1974, 62 pp.

- Tommaso Palamidessi: *Astrologia mondiale [World astrology]*, Archeosofica P., Rome, 1941, 588 pp.

- Johanna Paungger and Thomas Poppe: *La Luna ci insegna a star bene [The Moon teaches us how to be fine]*, Frasnelli - Keitsch, Bolzano/ Bozen, 1995, 260 pp.

- Johanna Paungger and Thomas Poppe: *Servirsi della Luna [To use the Moon]*, Frasnelli - Keitsch, Bolzano/Bozen, 1995, 166 pp.

- Mariagrazia Pelaia: *Articles appeared on the quarterly* Ricerca '90 *from 1990 to 2008*, Edizione Ricerca '90, 128 pp.

- Andrea Rossetti: *Articles appeared on the quarterly* Ricerca '90 *from 1990 to 2008*, Edizioni Ricerca '90, Naples, 128 pp.

- Andrea Rossetti: *Breve trattato sui transiti [A concise treatise on transits]*, Blue Diamond Publisher, Milan, 1994, 125 pp.

- Andrea Rossetti: *Transiti, rivoluzioni solari e dasa indù [Transits, Solar Returns, and Hindu Dhasas]*, Blue Diamond Publisher, Milan, 1997, 188 pp.

- Alexander Ruperti: *I cicli del divenire [The cycles of becoming]*, Astrolabio, Rome, 1990, 301 pp.

- Frances Sakoian and Louis Acker: *Transits of Jupiter*, CSA Printing and Bindery Inc., USA, 1974, 72 pp.

- Frances Sakoian and Louis Acker: *Transits of Saturn*, CSA Printing and Bindery Inc., USA, 1973, 76 pp.

- Frances Sakoian and Louis Acker: *Transits of Uranus*, CSA Printing and Bindery Inc., USA, 1973, 78 pp.

- Vanda Sawtell: *Astrology & Biochemistry*, Rustington, Sussex, England, 86 pp.

- Françoise Secret: *Astrologie et alchimie au XVII siecle*, Studi francesi, new serie, vol. 60, issue #3

- Nicola Sementovsky-Kurilo: *Trattato completo di astrologia teorico e pratico [A complete theoretical-practical treatise of astrology]*, Hoepli ed., Milan, 1989

- Heber J. Smith: *Transits*, American Federation of Astrology, Tempe (Arizona), Unknown date of publishing, 42 pp.

- Kichinosuke Tatai: *I bioritmi [The biorhythms]*, ed. Mediterranee, Rome

- George S. Thommen: *Bioritmi [Biorhythms]*, Cesco Ciapanna ed.

- Claudius Ptolemy: *Descrizione della sfera celeste [Description of the Celestial Sphere]*, Arnaldo Forni, Bologna, 1990, 96 pp.

- Claudius Ptolemy: *Tetrabiblos, Le previsioni astrologiche [Tetrabiblos – the astrological predictions]*, Mondadori, Milan, 1985, 490 pp.

- Claudius Ptolemy: *Tetrabiblos*, Arktos, Carmagnola, 1980

- Claudius Ptolemy: *Tetrabiblos*, Arktos, Turin, 1979, 270 pp.

- Alexander Volguine: *Tecnica delle rivoluzioni solari [Technique of Solar Returns]*, Armenia, Milan, 1980, 226 pp.

- Herbert Von Klöckler, *Astrologia, scienza sperimentale [Astrology – an experimental science]*, Mediterranee, Rome, 1993, 183 pp.

- Ritchie R. Ward: *Gli orologi viventi [The living clocks]*, Bompiani, Milan, 1973

- Lyall Watson: *Supernatura [Supernature]*, Rizzoli ed, Milan, 1974

- David Williams: *Simplified Astronomy for Astrologers*, American Federation of Astrologers, Washington DC 1969, 90 pp.


**\* These are writings that deal – partly or extensively – with the subject 'Solar Returns' and 'Lunar Returns'.**

# Index

Preface to the English Second Edition ................................................ pag. 7
Preface to the English Edition ............................................................ pag. 8
Preface .................................................................................................. pag. 9
   1.   Some short considerations ......................................................... pag. 20
   2.   The unconscious roots ............................................................... pag. 27
   3.   Why and how do Solar Returns and Lunar Returns work ...... pag. 29
   4.   Lunar Returns ............................................................................ pag. 56
   5.   Twenty trustworthy rules .......................................................... pag. 67
   6.   The concept of modulation ....................................................... pag. 71
   7.   Do Aimed Lunar Returns work? ............................................... pag. 75
   8.   New fields of research for Lunar Returns ................................ pag. 78
   9.   A thrilling Lunar Return ........................................................... pag. 87
  10.   An Aimed Lunar Return for an intervention of rhinoplasty ... pag. 93
  11.   Lunar Return in San Severo di Foggia ..................................... pag. 97
  12.   How to choose an ALR for eye surgery ................................... pag. 102
  13.   A few practical exercises on the dating of events .................... pag. 110
  14.   SRs and LRs in the attack on Pearl Harbor ............................. pag. 120
  15.   Lunar Return on airliners ......................................................... pag. 127
  16.   Lunar Return in Flores ............................................................. pag. 133
  17.   Lunar Return in Peterhead ....................................................... pag. 138
  18.   The atrocious saga of death in Gandhi's "family" .................... pag. 141
  19.   An essential astrological bibliography ..................................... pag. 230

www.ingramcontent.com/pod-product-compliance
Lightning Source LLC
Chambersburg PA
CBHW060509100426
42743CB00009B/1268